This property belongs to:
          Rev. Stephen Kelley
Please return it to:
          P.O. Box 4006
          Worthing, West Sussex
          BN13 1AP, U.K.

A MOMENT
OF TRUTH

The Confession of
the Dutch Reformed Mission Church

edited by
G. D. CLOETE
and
D. J. SMIT

WILLIAM B. EERDMANS PUBLISHING COMPANY
GRAND RAPIDS, MICHIGAN

Copyright © 1984 by Wm. B. Eerdmans Publishing Co.
255 Jefferson Ave. SE, Grand Rapids, Mich. 49503

Translated from the Afrikaans edition, *'n Oomblik van waarheid,*
© 1984 Tafelberg-Uitgewers Beperk, Waalstraat 28, Kaapstad

Library of Congress Cataloging in Publication Data

Oomblik van waarheid. English
  A moment of truth.

  Translation of: 'n Oomblik van waarheid.
  1. Nederduitse Gereformeerde Sendingkerk in Suid-
Afrika — Doctrines — Addresses, essays, lectures.
2. Reformed Church — Doctrines — Addresses, essays,
lectures. 3. Race relations — Religious aspects —
Nederduitse Gereformeerde Sendingkerk in Suid-Afrika —
Addresses, essays, lectures. 4. South Africa — Race
relations — Addresses, essays, lectures. I. Cloete,
G. D. II. Smit, D. J. III. Nederduitse Gereformeerde
Sendingkerk in Suid-Afrika. IV. Title.
BX9623.Z506613   1984   238'.4268   84-13573

ISBN 0-8028-0011-4

Contents

Abbreviations

ABRECSA   Alliance of Black Reformed Christians in Southern Africa
CD   Church Dogmatics (Karl Barth; Edinburgh: T. & T. Clark, 1936–1969)
DRC   Dutch Reformed Church (South Africa; in Afrikaans, Nederduitsch Gereformeerde Kerk [NGK])
DR Church in Africa   Dutch Reformed Church in Africa (South Africa; in Afrikaans, Nederduitsch Gereformeerde Kerk in Afrika [NG Kerk in Afrika])
DR Mission Church   Dutch Reformed Mission Church (South Africa; in Afrikaans, Nederduitsch Gereformeerde Sendingkerk [NGSK])
EKD   Evangelische Kirche in Deutschland (West Germany)
EKL   Evangelische Kirchenlexicon
EKU   Evangelische Kirche der Union (West Germany)
GS   Gesammelte Schriften (Dietrich Bonhoeffer; 6 vols., 2nd ed., Munich: Christian Kaiser Verlag, 1965–1974)
LWF   Lutheran World Federation
RB   Reformierter Bund (West Germany)
RE   Realencyklopädie für protestantische Theologie und Kirche
RGG   Religion in Geschichte und Gegenwart
SACC   South African Council of Churches
TRE   Theologische Realenzyklopädie
VELKD   Vereinigte Evangelische-Lutherische Kirche Deutschlands (West Germany)
WARC   World Alliance of Reformed Churches
WCC   World Council of Churches

Preface

It is the firm conviction of many Christians in South Africa that the ideology of apartheid has its roots within the church itself, especially the Dutch Reformed Church. Several historical studies have demonstrated how this ideology gradually grew into a widespread and popular religious way of life after the famous synodical decision of 1857 to allow separate services of the Lord's Supper "because of the weaknesses of some." The DRC itself developed along racial lines into a "family of churches," largely consisting of the white DRC (1,231 congregations, 1,415,000 total membership), the "colored" Dutch Reformed Mission Church (258 congregations, 450,000 total membership), the black Dutch Reformed Church in Africa (475 congregations, 600,000 total membership), and the "Asian" Reformed Church in Africa (10 congregations, 2,300 total membership).

When the pseudoreligious ideology of apartheid was implemented as an economic and political policy during the forties, theologians and ministers from the ranks of the DRC developed and popularized a theological, scriptural, and moral justification. Through the years no serious challenge to the ideology of apartheid, its pseudoreligious character, or its theological and moral defense came from the so-called "daughter churches" in the Dutch Reformed "family," although some of its "practical implications" or "the concrete way in which it was implemented" was criticized from time to time. Several reasons for this silence can be advanced, among others the powerful influence of white ministers in church structures, ministerial training, and ecumenical relations.

Gradually, however, a new situation arose. The number of "colored" and black ministers increased rapidly and the authentic voice of the people was articulated more and more. Several of these ministers were trained overseas and made a new, independent, and important contribution. The social, economic, and political structures and aspirations of the members and congregations of the daughter churches were no longer exclusively rural as they had once been. These churches became increasingly involved in ecumenical relationships and received a great deal of support from people sensitive to racism and discrimination and critical of apartheid. An influential fraternity of Christians, the Broederkring, was established within the Dutch Reformed churches.

Especially during the last decade, the DR Mission Church and some of its members played a growing role in the opposition to apartheid in South Africa as well as in wider ecumenical circles. In August 1982 the World Alliance of Reformed Churches declared a *status confessionis* concerning apartheid, calling it a heresy, suspended the membership of two white South African churches (the DRC and the much smaller Nederduitsch Hervormde Kerk in Afrika), and elected Dr. Allan A. Boesak of the DR Mission Church as its president.

At the meeting of the synod of the DR Mission Church in Belhar during October of the same year, several very important steps were taken. The events surrounding this synod, including the declaration of a *status confessionis* and the resultant drafting of a confession, had various far-reaching implications. The draft confession addresses three issues, namely the unity of the church, reconciliation in Christ, and the justice of God (paragraphs 2, 3, and 4 of the draft confession). On all three points, the authors of the confession express some fundamental convictions, often illustrating them with allusions to familiar citations from the Old and New Testaments. In all three articles the positive statements are followed by a rejection of false doctrine. No explicit mention is made of apartheid, except in an explanatory footnote on the motivation for the drafting of the confession. The importance, however, of all three articles—both the positive declarations and the refutations—for church and society in South Africa is abundantly clear. Along with the confession, the synod adopted an official accompanying letter explaining the need to confess as well as the seriousness, spirit, and purpose of the confession.

These events created waves that continue to spread wider and wider. Matters will without doubt never be the same again in the ecumenical circles in which the DR Mission Church moves, as well as in the ecclesiastical community in South Africa, the family of Dutch Reformed churches, and undoubtedly in the DR Mission Church itself. That church undoubtedly feels the effect most strongly. The implications of the events of 1982 are being discussed at almost all levels: in all congregations and presbyteries, in the church magazine, and at a multitude of meetings. An already growing process of "awareness" has suddenly and forcibly been aroused—and quite rightly so, since it is imperative for the church to realize what the implications of her recognition of a *status confessionis* are for herself and for her own decisions, resolutions, and actions. If matters proceed as the 1982 synod unanimously envisioned, the draft confession will eventually become a formal confession of the DR Mission Church.

The Faculty of Theology of the University of the Western Cape, which also trains the ministers of the DR Mission Church, wanted to promote this growing awareness, this lively process of study, reflection, discussion, and identification of possible consequences for the church, by means of this collection of essays. The book is intended, first and foremost, to provide the interested members of the DR Mission Church, her church councils, and her ministers with material helpful for further reflection upon and growing insight into this process. Because of the variety of subjects touched upon, some contributions are of a more technical nature, while others are more generally interpretive and therefore more readily accessible to all readers. At the same time, however, the significance of the events discussed here touches more than the DR Mission Church alone—the ripples are indeed spreading wider and wider. The events at Belhar are still surrounded by misunderstandings and questions, not to mention open criticism. Although it is not our primary aim, still we hope that the publication of this volume will clear up at least some of these misunderstandings and questions, both in the DR Mission Church and in its wider ecumenical circle.

The title suggested itself. As the first chapter will show, the declaration of a *status confessionis* quite simply means that Christians, or a church, feels that a "moment of truth" has arrived, that a situation has developed in which the gospel itself is at stake. Since such a declaration does not automatically imply the drafting of a confession, the second contribution asks the question whether this surprising and much criticized step was really necessary, concluding that the confession was intended to express more precisely the truth that was at stake in the "hour."

In the next chapters, the draft confession is first scrutinized from a missionary viewpoint, and particularly close attention is given to the third article (dealing with God's righteousness), which has been the subject of especially severe criticism. The church historian's contribution makes it quite clear that the crisis which emerged at the synod regarding the position of (white) ministers in the DR Mission Church who had not become members of the church, placing both themselves and the church in a very personal "moment of truth," was in fact nothing new, but simply the culmination of a century-old protest. In chapter 6, the phenomenon of true and false prophecy is discussed, revealing the central role of the "hour" or concrete situation in rendering preaching "true" or "false." Prophetic "truth" is not merely a "timeless" truth, but a concrete one in a particular situation. This inseparable bond between "truth" and "hour or moment," or between "confession or articles of faith" and "situation or circumstances," is illustrated in the book of Hebrews and is analyzed in chapter 7. In Hebrews, the central and common confession of Christ had to be reinterpreted and made real in a "new" situation of beleaguered second generation Christians.

After these *kairoi* or "moments of truth" in the life of the church have been identified, however, its confession does not stop functioning. Spreading out from the liturgy of worship, which in fact becomes a weekly "hour of truth" in which the central truths of the faith of the church inspire the members anew, the congregation lives its daily life in the world as a confessing fellowship. The divergent ways in which this takes place are the subject of chapter 8. In closing, it is shown that the events at Belhar do indeed constitute a moment of truth, a "crisis" for the entire Dutch Reformed church family.

We wish to thank all those who helped us to prepare this translation at such very short notice, in particular Mrs. Ria Smit, our faithful typists, and especially William B. Eerdmans Publishing Company for their willingness to publish it.

A MOMENT
OF TRUTH

The Confession 1982*

1. We believe in the triune God, Father, Son, and Holy Spirit, who gathers, protects, and cares for his Church by his Word and his Spirit, as he has done since the beginning of the world and will do to the end.

2. We believe in one holy, universal Christian Church, the communion of saints called from the entire human family.

We believe

Eph. 2:11–22   that Christ's work of reconciliation is made manifest in the Church as the community of believers who have been reconciled with God and with one another;

Eph. 4:1–16   that unity is, therefore, both a gift and an obligation for the Church of Jesus Christ; that through the working of God's Spirit it is a binding force, yet simultaneously a reality which must be earnestly pursued and sought: one which the people of God must continually be built up to attain;

John 17:20, 23   that this unity must become visible so that the world may believe; that separation, enmity, and hatred between people and groups is sin which Christ has already conquered, and accordingly that anything which threatens this unity may have no place in the Church and must be resisted;

Phil. 2:1–5   that this unity of the people of God must be manifested and be
1 Cor. 12:4–31   active in a variety of ways: in that we experience, practice, and
John 13:1–17   pursue community with one another; that we are obligated to
1 Cor. 1:10–13   give ourselves willingly and joyfully to be of benefit and bless-

---

*This draft confession was officially adopted by the Synod of the Dutch Reformed Mission Church in session at Belhar, Cape Town, Republic of South Africa, 22 September–6 October 1982, following the declaration of a *status confessionis* in connection with the rejection of the defense of apartheid on moral and theological grounds.

1

Eph. 4:1–6
Eph. 3:14–20
Cor. 10:16–17
Cor. 11:17–34
Gal. 6:2
2 Cor. 1:3–4

ing to one another; that we share one faith, have one calling, are of one soul and one mind; have one God and Father, are filled with one Spirit, are baptized with one baptism, eat of one bread and drink of one cup, confess one name, are obedient to one Lord, work for one cause, and share one hope; together come to know the height and the breadth and the depth of the love of Christ; together are built up to the stature of Christ, to the new humanity; together know and bear one another's burdens, thereby fulfilling the law of Christ; that we need one another and upbuild one another, admonishing and comforting one another; that we suffer with one another for the sake of righteousness; pray together; together serve God in this world; and together fight against all which may threaten or hinder this unity;

Rom. 12:3–8
1 Cor. 12:1–11
Eph. 4:7–13
Gal. 3:27–28
James 2:1–13

that this unity can be established only in freedom and not under constraint; that the variety of spiritual gifts, opportunities, backgrounds, convictions, as well as the various languages and cultures, are by virtue of the reconciliation in Christ opportunities for mutual service and enrichment within the one visible people of God;

that true faith in Jesus Christ is the only condition for membership of this Church.

Therefore, we reject any doctrine

which absolutizes either natural diversity or the sinful separation of people in such a way that this absolutization hinders or breaks the visible and active unity of the Church, or even leads to the establishment of a separate church formation;

which professes that this spiritual unity is truly being maintained in the bond of peace while believers of the same confession are in effect alienated from one another for the sake of diversity and in despair of reconciliation;

which denies that a refusal earnestly to pursue this visible unity as a priceless gift is sin;

which explicitly or implicitly maintains that descent or any other human or social factor should be a consideration in determining membership of the Church.

2 Cor. 5:17–21
Matt. 5:13–16
Matt. 5:9

3. We believe that God has entrusted to his Church the message of reconciliation in and through Jesus Christ; that the Church is called to be the salt of the earth and the light of the

2 Pet. 3:13
Rev. 21–22

world; that the Church is called blessed because it is a peace-maker; that the Church is witness both by word and by deed to the new heaven and the new earth in which righteousness dwells;

Eph. 4:17–6:23
Rom. 6
Col. 1:9–14
Col. 2:13–19
Col. 3:1–4:6

that God by his lifegiving Word and Spirit has conquered the powers of sin and death, and therefore also of irreconciliation and hatred, bitterness and enmity; that God by his lifegiving Word and Spirit will enable his people to live in a new obedience which can open new possibilities of life for society and the world;

that the credibility of this message is seriously affected and its beneficial work obstructed when it is proclaimed in a land which professes to be Christian, but in which the enforced separation of people on a racial basis promotes and perpetuates alienation, hatred, and enmity;

that any teaching which attempts to legitimate such forced separation by appeal to the gospel and is not prepared to venture on the road of obedience and reconciliation, but rather, out of prejudice, fear, selfishness, and unbelief, denies in advance the reconciling power of the gospel, must be considered ideology and false doctrine.

Therefore, we reject any doctrine which, in such a situation, sanctions in the name of the gospel or of the will of God the forced separation of people on the grounds of race and color and thereby in advance obstructs and weakens the ministry and experience of reconciliation in Christ.

Deut. 32:4
Luke 2:14
John 14:27
Eph. 2:14
Isa. 1:16–17
James 1:27
James 5:1–6
Luke 1:46–55
Luke 6:20–26
Luke 7:22
Luke 16:19–31
Ps. 146
Luke 4:16–19
Rom. 6:13–18
Amos 5

4. We believe that God has revealed himself as the one who wishes to bring about justice and true peace among men; that in a world full of injustice and enmity he is in a special way the God of the destitute, the poor, and the wronged and that he calls his Church to follow him in this; that he brings justice to the oppressed and gives bread to the hungry; that he frees the prisoner and restores sight to the blind; that he supports the downtrodden, protects the stranger, helps orphans and widows, and blocks the path of the ungodly; that for him pure and undefiled religion is to visit the orphans and the widows in their suffering; that he wishes to teach his people to do what is good and to seek the right;

that the Church must therefore stand by people in any form of suffering and need, which implies, among other things, that the Church must witness against and strive against any form of injustice, so that justice may roll down like waters, and righteousness like an ever-flowing stream;

that the Church as the possession of God must stand where he stands, namely against injustice and with the wronged; that in following Christ the Church must witness against all the powerful and privileged who selfishly seek their own interests and thus control and harm others.

Therefore, we reject any ideology which would legitimate forms of injustice and any doctrine which is unwilling to resist such an ideology in the name of the gospel.

Eph. 4:15–16 5. We believe that, in obedience to Jesus Christ, its only
Acts 5:29–33 head, the Church is called to confess and to do all these things,
1 Pet. 2:18–25 even though the authorities and human laws might forbid them
1 Pet. 3:15–18 and punishment and suffering be the consequence.

Jesus is Lord.
To the one and only God, Father, Son, and Holy Spirit, be the honor and the glory for ever and ever.

ACCOMPANYING LETTER

1. We are deeply conscious that moments of such seriousness can arise in the life of the Church that it may feel the need to confess its faith anew in the light of a specific situation. We are aware that such an act of confession is not lightly undertaken, but only if it is considered that the heart of the gospel is so threatened as to be at stake. In our judgment, the present church and political situation in our country and particularly within the Dutch Reformed church family calls for such a decision. Accordingly, we make this confession not as a contribution to a theological debate nor as a new summary of our beliefs, but as a cry from the heart, as something we are obliged to do for the sake of the gospel in view of the times in which we stand. Along with many, we confess our guilt, in that we have not always witnessed clearly enough in our situation and so are jointly responsible for the way in which those things which were experienced as sin and confessed to be so or should have been experienced as and confessed to be sin have grown in time to seem self-evidently right and to be ideologies foreign to the Scriptures. As a result many have been given the impression that the gospel was not really at stake. We make this confession because we are convinced that all sorts of theological arguments have contributed to so disproportionate an emphasis on some aspects of the truth that it has in effect become a lie.

2. We are aware that the only authority for such a confession and the only grounds on which it may be made are the Holy Scriptures as the Word of God. Being fully aware of the risks involved in taking this step, we are nevertheless convinced that we have no alternative. Furthermore, we are aware that no other motives or convictions, however valid they may be, would give us the right to confess in this way. An act of confession may only be made by the Church for the sake of its purity and credibility and that of its message. As solemnly as we are able, we hereby declare before men that our only motive lies in our fear that the truth and power of the gospel itself is threatened in this situation. We do not wish to serve any group interests, advance the cause of any factions, promote any theologies, or achieve any ulterior purposes. Yet, having said this, we know that our deepest intentions may only be judged at their true value by him before whom all is revealed. We do not make this confession from his throne and from on high, but before his throne and before men. We plead, therefore, that this confession should not be misused by anyone with ulterior motives and also that it should not be resisted to serve such motives. Our earnest desire is to lay no false stumbling blocks in the way, but to point to the true stumbling block, Jesus Christ the rock.

3. This confession is not aimed at specific people or groups of people or a church or churches. We proclaim it against a false doctrine, against an ideological distortion which threatens the gospel itself in our church and our country. Our heartfelt longing is that no one will identify himself with this objectionable doctrine and that all who have been wholly cr partially blinded by it will turn themselves away from it. We are deeply aware of the deceiving nature of such a false doctrine and know that many who have been conditioned by it have to a greater or lesser extent learnt to take a half-truth for the whole. For this reason we do not doubt the Christian faith of many such people, their sincerity, honor, integrity, and good intentions and their in many ways estimable practice and conduct. However, it is precisely because we know the power of deception that we know we are not liberated by the seriousness, sincerity, or intensity of our certainties, but only by the truth in the Son. Our church and our land has an intense need of such liberation. Therefore it is that we speak pleadingly rather than accusingly. We plead for reconciliation, that true reconciliation which follows on conversion and change of attitudes and structures. And while we do so we are aware that an act of confession is a two-edged sword, that none of us can throw the first stone, and none is without a beam in his own eye. We know that the attitudes and conduct which work against the gospel are present in all of us and will continue to be so. Therefore this confession must be seen as a call to a continuous process of soul-searching together, a joint wrestling with the issues, and a readiness

to repent in the name of our Lord Jesus Christ in a broken world. It is certainly not intended as an act of self-justification and intolerance, for that would disqualify us in the very act of preaching to others.

4. Our prayer is that this act of confession will not place false stumbling blocks in the way and thereby cause and foster false divisions, but rather that it will be reconciling and uniting. We know that such an act of confession and process of reconciliation will necessarily involve much pain and sadness. It demands the pain of repentance, remorse, and confession; the pain of individual and collective renewal and a changed way of life. It places us on a road whose end we can neither foresee or manipulate to our own desire. On this road we shall unavoidably suffer intense growing pains while we struggle to conquer alienation, bitterness, irreconciliation, and fear. We shall have to come to know and encounter both ourselves and others in new ways. We are only too well aware that this confession calls for the dismantling of structures and thought, of church, and of society which have developed over many years. However, we confess that for the sake of the gospel, we have no other choice. We pray that our brothers and sisters throughout the Dutch Reformed church family, but also outside it, will want to make this new beginning with us, so that we can be free together and together may walk the road of reconciliation and justice. Accordingly, our prayer is that the pain and sadness we speak of will be pain and sadness that lead to salvation. We believe that this is possible in the power of our Lord and by his Spirit. We believe that the gospel of Jesus Christ offers hope, liberation, salvation, and true peace to our country.

D. J. SMIT

1
What Does
Status Confessionis Mean?

The sudden way in which the almost unknown expression "*status confessionis*" appeared in the churches in South Africa and became common property practically overnight, vigorously discussed in every forum from the daily press to church council meetings, is simply amazing. Anyone trying to determine the exact meaning of "*status confessionis*" from dictionaries, encyclopaedias, or textbooks in systematic theology would be disappointed.[1] It is clearly a strong expression applied to a very important issue and an extremely serious situation, but exactly what that issue is, or what the suppositions or implications may be, is less obvious.[2] The expression is in fact not a technical term with a fixed and definite content, but one which must be understood in the light of the few occasions in history when it was used or when similar expressions played a part.[3]

The issue was raised for the first time during the sixteenth century in discussions concerning the question whether certain situations in the Church were "neutral matters" or whether the gospel was at stake. The conviction gradually grew that something which may be neutral under "normal circumstances," in the sense that it could be done or not done without endangering the heart of the gospel itself, may not be neutral any longer in "a situation of confession" or "a time of confession." Under these circumstances it may suddenly attain such grave importance that it becomes a matter in which the gospel is indeed threatened.

In the twentieth century this conviction was applied again, especially in connection with three important conflicts in the Christian Church. The first was the so-called German church struggle (*Kirchenkampf*), when the Confessing Church in Germany came into existence in opposition to the so-called German Christians, who were loyal to Hitler and advocated the exclusion of Jews from the offices of the church. The important figures of that time included, among others, Karl Barth and Dietrich Bonhoeffer, and the most well-known document was the Barmen Declaration of 1934. Essentially, the Confessing Church argued that church structures and arrangements of church discipline, which are "neutral matters" under normal circumstances and may therefore be handled in

7

several ways, can become of such fundamental importance in a specific situation that the very essence of the Church and the credibility of the gospel itself are threatened. Therefore, they judged, the hour had come in which they were compelled to confess—because everything was indeed at stake.

The second church debate in which the expression *status confessionis* has featured was the ecumenical rejection of racism. In 1977 at Dar es Salaam the Lutheran World Federation announced a *status confessionis* concerning racism and apartheid and declared that, once again, the situation did not involve merely "neutral matters," but the essence of the Church itself. An appeal was made to member churches to express themselves on this matter. Since then a lively discussion has continued in the Lutheran world community. In 1982 the World Alliance of Reformed Churches adopted a similar resolution at its meeting in Ottawa.

The third debate is being carried on at present, particularly in Germany. The Reformierter Bund, a segment of the large German Protestant Church (the Evangelische Kirche Deutschlands [EKD], which also includes the Lutherans), announced a *status confessionis* on the possession of nuclear arms in 1982. However, that conviction radically differs from the Lutheran point of view, and a heated debate is raging at present.

For the sake of particularly interested readers and students, and on account of the very interesting parallels from history with our present situation, I have provided a detailed and technical summary of the historical data in the excursus that follows. This material, however, is not absolutely necessary in order to follow the rest of my argument, and the reader could pass it by. In the remainder of the chapter important viewpoints and resolutions from these debates will be used as illustrations.

During the so-called "first adiaphora conflict" around 1548, several Catholic customs and procedures were reintroduced into Lutheran Protestantism. Because they judged that these changes amounted to adiaphora, or neutral matters, several theologians, including Melanchthon, accepted these alterations. Others, especially Matthias Flacius, opposed them strongly; Flacius was of the opinion that in a situation of "confession and offense" there were not adiaphora or neutral matters (*nihil est adiaphoron in casu confessionis et scandali*).[4] Later Melanchthon also admitted that more than neutral or insignificant matters were at stake and that the issue indeed concerned sin.[5]

In the compilation of the Formula Concordiae in 1577[6] the same question arose in article 10, which dealt with "the church customs which people call adiaphora or mediocre matters." In a detailed argument, the authors made it clear that church arrangements were indeed adiaphora, meant to be practical and to serve the interest of good order; consequently, they could be amended freely so long as all changes were made responsibly.

In paragraph 10, however, it was added that "a time of confession" could develop in which "the pure doctrine of the gospel" was threatened by external or concealed moral constraint in the church. A so-called "plus" or "extra" was then forced upon the congregation. In such a time "the congregation of God, yes, every Christian, but especially the preachers of the Word" were called to public confession, not only with words, but also with deeds. Galatians 2 was referred to emphatically as an instance in which the gospel itself was at stake on account of matters that under normal circumstances would have been adiaphora. Though the specific words were not used, this point of view has since then been popularly summarized in the expression *in statu confessionis nil adiaphoron*.[7] In the Formula Concordiae itself, however, the phrase was not used as a technical term.

In the Calvinistic tradition, several distinctly *ethical* resolutions were adopted as bearing directly on confession. Church discipline was exercised on a variety of matters, including attending plays, dancing, smoking, etc. This tradition was strengthened among the English Puritans, the moralistic Calvinists in the Netherlands, and the ever-growing pietist movement. The so-called "second adiaphora conflict" hinged upon purely ethical resolutions when certain pietistic theologians in Hamburg rejected the opera in 1681 as anti-Christian, and two preachers refused absolution to operagoers. There is, however, no evidence that the term *status confessionis* played any significant role.

During the nineteenth century the expression "state of confession" (*Bekenntnisstand*) was in fact used in a very technical sense in issues of church law during the unpleasant conflict of German territorial churches and congregations to determine and describe accurately their "confessional integrity." The aftereffects of this history probably still play an important role in the discontent and confusion concerning the use of the term *status confessionis* among Germans even today.[8]

The expression was probably used for the first time in its technical sense (in the form *in statu confessionis*) in 1927 in Horst Stephan's article on "Confession" in *RGG*.[2] He wrote that in certain situations "matters which are in themselves insignificant obtain inner necessity."

In the German church struggle (*Kirchenkampf*), especially after 1933, the term suddenly became extremely relevant. In April 1933, Bonhoeffer foresaw in his article "Die Kirche vor den Judenfrage"[9] that a moment of decision can occur in which ongoing disputes in church and theology are suddenly ended and changed into a situation of confession, because the gospel itself is put at risk and everything becomes concentrated on one crucial issue. He was of the opinion that the Church, in such a moment, would have to confess an act over against a double threat, namely "too little order and justice" in that the rights of some citizens, that is, the Jews, were threatened, as well as "too much order and justice" in that the very life of the Church was threatened by the state, because its membership, formerly determined only by Christian baptism, was now determined by biological (racial) factors. In such a situation the Church would find herself in a *status confessionis*, while the state would have exceeded its own limits ("hier befänd sich der Staat im Akt der Selbstverneinung").[10] The Church then would have to express itself verbally-prophetically against this "too little" and "too much," would have to identify itself in solidarity and Christian stewardship with those who suffer under the "too little" and "too much," and would have to enter into political conflict with the state by deeds of disobedience whenever the essence of the Church was really threatened by a racist restriction on its membership.

In Barth's influential *Theologische Existenz heute!*, the first booklet of the famous series of publications under the same title, precisely the same question arose, though the expression *status confessionis* was not used. Barth wrote that in all probability there might occur a moment when the expected unevangelical (*evangeliumswidrigen*) doctrines, preaching, and arrangements of the German Christians would have to be opposed with all the consequences attached to such resistance, even if 99 percent of all the so-called "evangelical" Germans would side with the German Christians.[11] The matter came to a head when the so-called Aryan paragraph was introduced into the church. According to it, only Aryans—no Jews—were allowed to become preachers or officebearers in the German Evangelical Church. Miscellaneous forms of protest broke out, while German Christian theologians reminded people about adiaphora and explained that the paragraph concerned merely "neutral" matters like membership and church discipline, not the pure preaching of the gospel. In a private letter of 9 September 1933, Bonhoeffer reminded Barth of his declaration that whenever the Aryan paragraph was introduced into a church, that church would stop being a Christian church.[12] He asked on behalf of many friends, preachers, and students whether Barth considered it possible to remain in a church that had stopped being a Christian church and to stay on serving in a ministry that had become the exclusive right of Aryans only.[13] Barth answered by acknowledging that the *status confessionis* had undoubtedly dawned, but that it was not equally clear what exactly were the right steps to take immediately. Especially because the Jewish Christians were as yet not excluded as members, he pleaded for a "highly active, polemic period of waiting," so that the schism, which surely had to come, would come from the other side.[14]

Martin Niemöller formed the well-known Pastors' Emergency League (*Pfarrernotbund*) in 1933 and between six and seven thousand pastors signed the four propositions of confession, resistance, and solidarity. In 1934, the "synods of confession" of Barmen and Dahlem took place. On 2 December 1934, Barth wrote to Hans von Soden in connection with the oath of loyalty to Hitler that a personal situation of *status confessionis* had developed.[15] At the fourth "synod of confession" of Rheinland in April 1935 a resolution was adopted that a *status confessionis* was now applicable to everyone.[16] During that time the term became common property and was used more and more frequently in connection with article 10 of the Formula Concordiae. Also at that time a whole series of publications on confession and the forming of confessions was published.

The term *status confessionis* has also been frequently applied in the debate on nuclear armament. In 1958 Barth wrote, at first anonymously, a number of theses in which he objected to the godless character of nuclear arms. In conclusion he said that any other position, or even a neutral attitude with regard to this matter, was "impossible for a Christian, because it would mean a denial of all three articles of the Christian faith."[17] He later prepared a kind of draft for a church confession concerning nuclear armament for a meeting of the "Brotherhoods" in Frankfurt. This was accepted with certain additions and laid before the synod of the EKD. Serious differences of opinion prevailed during that time. A series of articles in the periodical *Politische Verantwortung* revived the confession dispute of the thirties.[18] Diem warned that the false doctrine in the church must be pointed out very clearly before it could be rejected, so that the danger of a "politicizing sect"—"with all the tragic features and accompanying phenomena of sectarianism"—could be avoided. E. Wolf presented a detailed study of the meaning of a *status confessionis* and even tried to give a definition of it. According to him, it implied first of all a moment in which the possibility of further neutrality or the possibility of remaining silent any longer had expired. At such a moment the Church was in fact called to take three important steps. The *status confessionis* must be acknowledged, precisely determined (stated in detail and confessed openly), and answered. However, in this debate on nuclear armament the different viewpoints were so diametrically opposed and the clear-cut evidence necessary for a situation of confession so profoundly lacking that the synod of the EKD finally rejected the draft by affirming, in a balanced and calculated point of view, the so-called Heidelberg Doctrines. The EKD said: "We stay together under the gospel."

Meanwhile, the Nederlandse Hervormde Kerk in the Netherlands, like many other churches, was continuously engaged over many years with the question of nuclear armament. A whole series of articles, study documents, pastoral letters, and reactions were published beginning in 1952.[19] Finally in a *Handreiking* (1979) and a *Herderlijke Brief* (1980) the church defended the position that not only the use but also the possession of nuclear arms ought to be rejected. Although the term *status confessionis* was not used, the documents stated that this viewpoint grew out of the conviction that the "obedience of faith of the church was put to the test."

In Germany two very dissimilar church documents on nuclear disarmament appeared in succession during 1981. The EKD, the large Protestant denomination that consists mainly of the VELKD (the Evangelical Lutheran Church), the EKU (a united church of Lutheran and Reformed members), and the Reformierter Bund (RB), largely repeated in their *Frieden wahren, fördern und erneuern* the calculated, balanced viewpoint of 1959. The executive church council of the RB (which makes up about 10 percent of the EKD), however, raised their voices in a totally different manner. Their declaration "Das Bekenntnis zu Jesus Christus und die Friedensverantwortung der Kirche" (adopted on 12 June 1982 and published in August 1982[20]) was very closely related to the documents of the Nederlandse Hervormde Kerk, but went even further and declared that a *status confessionis* had arisen. In the preface the authors rejected the "calculation, the equilibrium, ambiguity, and indecision" of the EKD and declared that they felt called to object against a "blasphemy destroying all life" with an act of confession of faith. They explicitly noted that the nuclear preparation of the universal "holocaust" was no adiaphoron, but was taking place in direct conflict with the basic articles of the Christian faith. In seven doctrines the authors repeatedly developed a threefold argument: first, they offered a basic thesis or ground (Christ as our peace; reconciliation; God as creator and supporter; God's justice; the lordship of Christ; the powerful presence of the Holy Spirit; the parousia); second, they demonstrated how this particular aspect of the Christian confession was in direct conflict with nuclear armament; and third, they declared what kind of conduct necessarily flows from their argument ("in confidence . . . ," "in obedience of faith . . . ," "in hope . . ."). In addition to these summarizing doctrines the document contained a large second part in which every thesis was discussed separately and in more detail, as well as an accompanying letter of explanation on behalf of the executive church council.

A stream of reactions followed.[21] The document was vehemently rejected in the official commentary of the other groups within the EKD as well as by many (especially Lutheran) theologians, church leaders, and members. The objections were lodged against such issues as: the fact that a political issue was converted into a matter of confession, a point made even by many who fully agreed with the political stance of the document; that the content was misleading, because other Christians also shared the political aim (peace) and only differed on a legitimate means or the best strategies needed in order to realize that common goal; that the other church groups involved were not sufficiently consulted; that some of the theological grounds were disputable and were taken to such extreme lengths that the document amounted to ''Utopianism'' and ''radical fanaticism.'' The RB laid the report before the meeting of the World Alliance of Reformed Churches (WARC) in Ottawa in August 1982. That body took a strong stance on the issue, but avoided the term *status confessionis*.

Meanwhile, the expression *''status confessionis''* became known worldwide in the ecclesiastical and theological rejection of racism. In South Africa the possibility or necessity of a confessing church had been mentioned on several occasions since 1960.[22] The *Message to the People* (1968) of the South African Council of Churches (SACC) was regarded by many as a possible base for a confessing church. After a visit to South Africa in 1973, Eberhard Bethge wrote an article in which he also suggested this possibility, saying: ''In many quarters (in South Africa) the view is that a *status confessionis* now exists.''[23] In February 1975 the Federation of Evangelical Lutheran Churches in South Africa (representative of mainly the black Lutherans in southern Africa) composed a declaration in Swakopmund as ''a call . . . to unity and confession.'' They pointed out the danger that foreign principles could undermine the *doctrine, confession, and practice* of the Lutheran church and could threaten her *faith*. The authors grounded these convictions in several carefully formulated arguments, especially concerning the present situation in church and theology. They expounded their point of view in terms of ''the justification by grace and its implications for the mutual acceptance of all people in church and society''; ''the Church'' (the admission to this body is not dependent on birth, race, or natural ties); ''the unity of the Church and the diversity of nations, races, cultures, and traditions'' (God enriches the Church by this diversity and it must not be the cause of divisions; the Church is not a fellowship of homogeneous people, but of those who ''in spite of and precisely on account of'' their diversity and strangeness belong together under the gospel; a separation in the Church based on this diversity may only occur to the degree in which it is helpful to bring the gospel nearer to people in their very special situation and as long as the confession concerning the unity of all believers does not lose its credibility before the world); ''the meaning of the church structures for the unity of the Church'' (these are not secondary questions, but concern the essence of the Church; those who separate Christians or who want to keep them separated on an organized or official basis on account of race and do not want Christian brothers and sisters of other races to have a free share and right of participation in the sacraments and the preaching of the gospel in fellowship with them exclude themselves from the community of believers; the evangelical ministry of the Word and the unity of the Church are disturbed where another preacher is refused on account of racial considerations); ''the worth of a human being''; and ''the responsibility of the Church for the world'' (the Church itself must be a truly reconciled community; the Church is the conscience of the people). Although the term *status confessionis* was not specifically used, it is evident that arguments from the content of the Christian confession played a major part in formulating the Swakopmund declaration.

At the Sixth Plenary Assembly of the Lutheran World Federation in Dar es Salaam (1977) almost the reverse took place. Under the assembly theme "In Christ—a New Community," Manas Buthelezi delivered an address on "In Christ—a Community in the Holy Spirit."[24] In the end the meeting adopted a concise threefold resolution with the title "Declaration on Confessional Integrity (*Status Confessionis* in Southern Africa)." The third point is especially important: "Under normal circumstances Christians may have differences of opinion on political issues. Political and social structures can, however, become so perverted and oppressive that it is in agreement with the confession to reject them and to work for change. We call especially upon our white member churches in Southern Africa to acknowledge that the situation constitutes a *status confessionis*. This means that the churches on the basis of their faith and in order to make the unity of the church visible will have to reject the apartheid system publicly and unambiguously." The statement clearly involves the question of what constitutes adiaphora ("under normal circumstances"), and it does not spell out what "in agreement with the confession" means. Some interpreters and translators understand "the confession" to be the Confessio Augustana (especially article 16), which is mentioned explicitly in the first point. Others see it rather as the active and visible confession of the Church, with which the second point is dealing. The only theological grounds that are mentioned are the (unqualified) reference to the "agreement with the confession" and the clear reference to the unity of the Church. (For that reason Bethge writes that everything in the statement was concentrated on the single little word *unum*.[25]) That the statement, however, concerns much more than theological arguments and the effect of apartheid in the Church is abundantly clear. At issue are divergent "political opinions" which under abnormal circumstances cease to be adiaphora, the "situation" in South Africa, and especially the apartheid "system" which must be rejected.

It is on account of this direct connection between confession (*status confessionis*) and politics that a vehement polemic exploded in the Lutheran world. While the majority of churches, groups, and individuals accepted the resolution with great appreciation[26] and even derived several far-reaching political and economic implications from it,[27] others were critical in differing degrees and some even rejected it sharply (although most of them agreed cordially with the rejection of apartheid on purely political and moral but not on confessional grounds[28]). Even a study commission of experts which was gathered to advise the LWF recommended that the term *status confessionis* should be abandoned, though the designation of an abnormal confessional situation could still be retained.

Totally independent of these developments, the 1978 synod of the DR Mission Church adopted a number of strong resolutions concerning the ideology of apartheid and rejected it as being in conflict with the teaching of the gospel on church unity and on reconciliation.

On 14 February 1980, the black delegates at a Consultation on Racism of the SACC at Hammanskraal appealed to white Christians to show their willingness to purify the Church of racism. They declared that, if after twelve months still no sign of repentance and concrete actions were perceived, the black Christians would have no other choice than to witness to the gospel of Jesus Christ by becoming a confessing church.[29] In August 1980 the Central Committee of the World Council of Churches in Geneva released a declaration on South Africa in which an appeal was made on the World Council and all its member churches together with all other Christians to witness that apartheid was a sin which was to be rejected as a travesty of the gospel, because it was in conflict with the fundamental truths of faith. This rejection could find expression in a solemn declaration of intent or in the proclamation of a *status confessionis*.[30]

In October 1981 The Alliance of Black Reformed Christians in Southern Africa (ABRECSA) held its first conference at Hammanskraal. In his opening address ''Black and Reformed: Burden or Challenge?'' Allan Boesak pleaded for a ''black'' rediscovery in the South African situation of the basic Reformed convictions, but went even further by declaring: ''I indeed believe black Christians should formulate a Reformed confession for our time and our situation in our own words.''[31] In the final ABRECSA charter something like this was implemented when a theological basis was composed, in which five matters were raised in the style of confession (the authority of the Word of God; the Lordship of Christ; the Christian responsibility for the world; the authority of the state; and the unity of the Church). This was immediately followed by a declaration which read: ''We . . . unequivocally declare that apartheid is a sin, and that the moral and theological justification of it is a travesty of the Gospel, a betrayal of the Reformed tradition, and a heresy.''[32] Though the term *status confessionis* was not used here, this point of view would play a significant role at the meeting of the WARC in Ottawa during August 1982.

In his speech at that assembly, Boesak argued that apartheid was not merely an evil ideology, but ''a pseudo-religious ideology which was born in and is still being justified out of the bosom of Reformed Churches.'' According to him the ''credibility of the Gospel of Jesus Christ'' itself is at stake here. He maintained with several arguments that racism is ''sinful,'' even ''a form of heresy,'' which ''has not only contaminated society,'' but ''also defiled the body of Christ.'' ''Christians and the Church,'' he added, ''have provided the moral and theological justification for racism and human degradation.'' What is especially unique to the South African situation, he continued, is the role of the (Reformed) churches in the establishing and implementing of this ''pseudo-gospel.'' Finally he requested the World Alliance to identify itself with the resolution of the 1978 synod that apartheid ''is irreconcilable with the Gospel of Jesus Christ'' and ''to declare apartheid a heresy.'' In his conclusion he explained once more that the decisive point was precisely that apartheid is not merely a political ideology. ''Its very existence as a political policy has depended and still depends on the theological justification of certain member Churches of the WARC. For Reformed Churches, this situation should constitute a *status confessionis*. This means that Churches should recognize that apartheid is a heresy, contrary to the Gospel and inconsistent with the Reformed tradition, and consequently reject it as such.''[33]

Finally, the World Alliance issued a detailed declaration on Racism and South Africa on 25 August which consisted of three sections. The actual argument was contained in the first part. (The second part dealt with the implications for the membership of the WARC of the white Reformed churches from South Africa, while the third part addressed the guilt of racism in the ranks of all the member churches of the World Alliance.) Paragraphs 1 and 2 expressed some basic truths of the gospel. Paragraph 3 read that racism was essentially a form of idolatry. Although the sin of racism occurred universally, according to paragraph 4, the situation in South Africa "at the present time" demanded "special attention," especially because of the role of the white Reformed churches. They had throughout the years developed both the policy and the theological and moral justification of that policy in detail. Apartheid (or "separate development") was therefore a pseudoreligious ideology as well as a political policy. It depended to a large extent on this theological and moral justification. The division of the Reformed churches in South Africa on the basis of race and color was being defended "as a faithful interpretation of the will of God and of the Reformed understanding of the Church in the world. This leads to the separation of Christians at the table of the Lord as a matter of practice and policy, which has been continually affirmed save for exceptional circumstances under special permission by the white Afrikaans Reformed churches."

Paragraphs 5–7 reminded the Alliance that it had already adopted several resolutions on this matter: "Therefore the exclusion of any person on grounds of race, colour or nationality from any congregation and part of the life of the Church contradicts the very nature of the Church. In such a case, the Gospel is actually obscured from the world and the witness of the Churches made ineffective" (Frankfurt, 1964); "The Church must recognize racism for the idolatry it is. . . . The Church that by doctrine and/or practice affirms segregation of peoples (e.g. racial segregation) as a law for its life cannot be regarded as an authentic member of the body of Christ" (Nairobi, 1970). With an appeal to the famous words of Calvin ("None of the brethren can be injured, despised, rejected, abused or in any way offended by us, without at the same time injuring, despising, and abusing Christ . . ."), paragraph 8 declared that the Alliance felt itself obliged by the gospel to raise its voice and to stand by the oppressed.

In the important paragraphs 9 and 10 the conviction was expressed that "in certain situations the confession of a Church needs to draw a clear line between truth and error," that the Alliance believes that "this is the situation in South Africa today," and that "the Churches which have accepted Reformed confessions of faith . . . contradict in doctrine and in action the promise which they profess to believe."

In paragraphs 11 and 12, the conclusion was stated: "Therefore the General Council declares that this situation constitutes a *status confessionis* for our Churches, which means that we regard this as an issue on which it is not possible to differ without seriously jeopardizing the integrity of our common confession as Reformed Churches. We declare with black Reformed Christians of South Africa that apartheid ('separate development') is a sin, and that the moral and theological justification of it is a travesty of the Gospel and, in its persistent disobedience to the Word of God, a theological heresy."[34]

When the synod of the DR Mission Church debated a resolution on this matter on 1 October 1982 in Belhar, the synod took note of the proposal by its delegates to Ottawa that the synod should accept the resolution of the WARC on racism.[35] After much discussion and the rejection of a number of amendments the DR Mission Church finally decided: "Because the secular gospel of apartheid most fundamentally *threatens the reconciliation in Jesus Christ and the very essence of the unity of the Church* of Jesus Christ, the DR Mission Church declares that it constitutes a *status confessionis* for the Church of Jesus Christ.'' After that followed the explication and the exact text of the second part of the WARC's resolution. Thus only in the first part of its own resolution did the DR Mission Church deem it necessary to state once again explicitly the theological grounds on which it judged that the Christian confession itself was threatened.[36]

The term has also been used on a few other occasions. It often came up in the conflict of orthodox and evangelical groups against so-called modernism.[37] When the synod of the Rheinland resolved not to donate money for the "special fund" of the WCC, some groups of the Brotherhoods reacted on 13 March 1982 with a declaration of a *status confessionis*.[38] In August 1980 Harry de Lange of the Netherlands requested the Central Committee of the WCC to declare a *status confessionis* in response to world poverty.[39] This haphazard use of the term caused it to lose much of its preciseness and power and therefore gradually to come into disfavor.

It is immediately clear that in the German church struggle the term gradually achieved some fixed and technical meaning, only again to disappear from the stage, except for incidental use. In the two ecumenical debates concerning racism and nuclear disarmament it became topical again. On account of numerous objections against its use[40]—moreover, its inflationistic use, which eventually made the expression so common that it actually became meaningless[41]—many theologians and church leaders today are inclined to abandon the term.[42]

Strictly speaking, one could say that the expression *status confessionis* means that a Christian, a group of Christians, a church, or a group of churches[43] are of the opinion that a situation has developed, a moment of truth has dawned, in which nothing less than the gospel itself, their most fundamental confession concerning the Christian gospel itself, is at stake, so that they feel compelled to witness and act over against this threat.

The implications of this description will become more obvious when a few of its aspects are scrutinized more closely.

First it supposes that Christians share the opinion that a *situation* has developed, a *moment of truth* has struck, in which the gospel itself is at stake. The role of the situation, the *kairos,* the moment that has ripened, cannot be overemphasized. In the foregoing historical survey it was evident again and again. *In statu confessionis nihil est adiaphoron.* Precisely the abnormal situation itself causes viewpoints and arrangements which are adiaphora or neutral matters under normal circumstances to lose their innocence and neutrality. The power of the confessional word emerging·from a *status confessionis* lies exactly in the fact that it is a word aimed at the concrete moment in the present.[44] In the German church struggle, Bethge said, there came an "acute present"[45] when "in a moment" several long-continued theological and church controversies "suddenly and unpreparedly" demanded decision making and resolution.[46] In the debate on nuclear disarmament this was again precisely the crucial point. In the balanced and fundamental Heidelberg Doctrines formulated by the EKD in 1959, the church had built in an hourglass, saying that "now" was not yet the moment to take a stronger point of view, although such an hour might come eventually. When the EKD showed practically the identical attitude in 1982, the RB judged that the sand had run out, that the "now" had dawned after nearly twenty-five years, and that therefore the same fundamental and well-balanced position, at this hour, was false.[47] They recognized the problematic element in the viewpoint of the EKD precisely in the "blindness to the *mene-tekel*-like signs of the times."[48] They themselves repeatedly described very explicitly the *kairos* which compelled them to acknowledge a *status confessionis*. Already in the preface to their declaration the authors stated that they as Germans lived "in the focal point of the tensions" and that they pleaded from out of "this threatened situation" against this "blasphemy and logic of insanity," when politicians "still" wanted to defend the nuclear armament which had fallen "long ago" under the ban of desperate fear. In their explanatory comment on the first statement, they defended their announcement of a *status confessionis* with a reference to the nature of the "situation." Precisely the fact that they were Germans, "who have already carried the burning torch of war into the world twice during this century" and thus were "partners in responsibility for the tensions that exist at present," played a very important role. "In view of the catastrophe that is possible any moment," "in view of the obvious willingness of the military and politically responsible people to use mass-destroying devices in a military conflict," and "in view of the way in which many people have become dulled and accustomed to live on the edge of a nuclear precipice," they proclaimed the issue of peace as a question of confession. The decisive role of the present *situation* was obvious. When the RB moderator, H. J. Kraus, answered the objection of Landesbischof E. Lohse, the chairman of the council of the EKD, that the RB decision was unilateral, Kraus frankly admitted it, but rejected once again the balanced position of the EKD by arguing that "the peace inside the church"[49] is not the "command of the hour" ("das Gebot der Stunde").

It is undoubtedly true that the analysis of the existing situation plays a decisive role in arguing for a *status confessionis*.[50] Hence the necessity of penetrating preliminary discussions, airing all different viewpoints and theological arguments. Under normal circumstances the Church has a variety of ways in which she can act and fulfil her task of constant confession (*confessio continua*). Only when all other avenues have been explored may she come to the conclusion that an abnormal situation has arisen.[51]

The recognition that a *status confessionis* exists may never be a premature and arbitrary attempt to cut the Gordian knot with force instead of unraveling it with fairness, wisdom, and responsibility. It may not be a unilateral standpoint in a discussion where a unilateral standpoint is not yet justified. It may not merely be an attempt to proclaim the point of view inherent in one's own group with the pretense of a last word, as a sort of "ethical protest, but with 'the volume tuned up.' "[52] In this connection Berkhof distinguishes a prophetic from a chokmatic (characterized by wisdom) mode of speech by the Church. For a long time, he says, the calculated and balanced voice of wisdom, the debate, the attempt at persuasion and at the critical broadening of insight remains the obvious way of speaking for the Church. There may, however, come "moments" in which the analysis of the here-and-now and the experience gained by the foregoing chokmatic speaking can convince Christians that the hour for a prophetic word has dawned.[53]

That the analysis of the situation plays an important part, does of course not mean that the confession is derived from the situation or that it originates in the situation. The situation does not speak, but the gospel. The confession does not receive its content from the situation and consequently does not lose its truth or validity outside the situation; at the most, it may lose some of its immediate relevance. This is the fate of all polemic confessional utterances, from some of the old ecumenical creeds to the Canons of Dort. The involvement with the concrete present is not a weakness; on the contrary, it is the very power of the confession. The gospel is being concentrated on the need of the hour—and in another hour and in another place the same truth may indeed suddenly become relevant and alive again.[54] Whoever wants to help an alcoholic does not explain the doctrine of the Trinity, and when someone struggles with the doctrine of the Trinity nobody would advise him on help for addicts. There comes an hour in which general truths and timeless principles, all neatly balanced with a "yes" and a "but," in their very balance fail to understand the demand of the hour; they then become false doctrine, an escape from the urgent need for prophecy. If a church council were to decide in a case of child abuse that parents have the biblical right—and responsibility—to discipline their children and that the fifth commandment remains an eternal principle which should carry much weight, precisely those "timeless truths" might be changed into a lie-for-the-moment.[55]

Of course the dangers are very great. The possibility always threatens that Christians can analyze the situation wrongly or—worse still—that the Word is projected into the situation by the desire or the interests of the group and that only the "echo" of this projection is heard and not the gospel, as is claimed. Several critics believe that precisely this has happened in the position which the Reformierter Bund took on disarmament. The presiding bishop of the general synod of the VELKD, K.-H. Stoll, declared on 27 October 1982:

We reject a theology of fear. . . . Fear does not have the quality of revelation! The gospel wants to free us from paralysing agony or blind zeal. With the death and resurrection of Jesus Christ the decisive word has been spoken on our life and death. We can only hold on to this assurance of salvation, if we do not make it dependent on our own measures of encouragement. Confession is not an expression of our present perceptions and insight, but an answer to God's word of revelation.[56]

There are no guarantees that the situation has been analyzed correctly and that the issues which are really at stake have been fathomed correctly. Of course the persons addressed and sometimes accused will usually judge the situation differently than those pronouncing the *status confessionis*.[57] Christians can at most appeal to the evidence and clarity of the gospel, perhaps to the consensus among Christians and churches, and finally to their own convictions and conscience in responsibility before God.

This immediately lends to any such action the character of venture or risk. It is indeed a bold step, taken without any formal or objective criteria by means of which it can be ascertained conclusively that a *status confessionis* does clearly exist.[58] No confession is in any way absolutely necessary, writes Polman, but only hypothetically necessary, in the light of the historical situation.[59] The confession inevitably carries "the stigma of historical involvement on its forehead."[60] The recognition of a *status confessionis* has therefore always the character of a subjective decision. It is experienced as a compulsion, as something undertaken for the sake of necessity. Barth says, "Confession will always cause head-shaking among serious people who do not know the particular seriousness of confession. Why? they will ask themselves and us, and the more seriously we confess, the less will they find an answer."[61]

Schloemann correctly points out that the recognition of a *status confessionis* must therefore by no means have the overtones of triumphalism, self-assurance, complacency, a show of strength, or any other ulterior motive. It does not have the heroic features, he says, nowadays often attributed to it, but should remind us rather of Luther's reports on his temptations. It occurs in a moment which is not at the disposal of the people, a moment in which the people do not settle and arrange matters, but rather one in which God disposes and in which God imposes an obligation on people, whose speech and action must be "cautious, often probing."[62] *Status confessionis* is no weapon in a private struggle, no handy "stick to hit with" (Noordmans), but the trembling acknowledgment that an hour has struck from on high in which something needs to be said. Such a word of confession is consequently never calculated or planned, but is born, it is "bestowed" (Barth); in one sense it surprises all those concerned. Whenever this happens, it is of no avail to object that it is not a suitable time or that it has come too soon. Nobody chooses the hour. In a *status confessionis,* says Bonhoeffer, all tactical considerations are abandoned. "The apparent certainties, based on loud expressions of one's own viewpoint," he continues, "have nothing to do with the assurance of repentance and of the gospel, so that those who have been brought to a new knowledge are standing guilty as well, substituting and interceding next to the misdirected and misled brothers, because they themselves do not live from the confidence of being know-all's or from the complacency of being correct (*Rechthaberei*), but only of the remission of the gospel."[63]

Both from the absolutely surprising—for everyone—course of events at the Belhar synod as well as from the wording and spirit of the accompanying letter it seems clear that the DR Mission Church was thoroughly aware of this element of risk and of the compulsion that made it necessary. In the preface to the official publication of the draft confession the executive church council consequently expresses the wish that the deliberations in the DR Mission Church will also take place in the spirit of that letter.

In the second place *status confessionis* means that Christians are of the opinion that a moment of truth has dawned in which *the gospel itself is at stake.* That which may be adiophora under normal circumstances is transformed on account of the gravity of the situation into a gravely decisive issue. When Cephas (Peter) drew back and started to separate himself because of his fear of the supporters of circumcision (Gal. 2:12), Paul judged that his conduct was clearly wrong (11)—even worse, that it was hypocrisy in which even Barnabas was swept along (13). Therefore he opposed Cephas in public (11) and accused him "before them all" that he was "not straightforward about the truth of the gospel" (14); in fact, Paul admonished Cephas and the congregation not to reject the grace of God, lest it mean that "Christ died to no purpose" (21). *In statu confessionis nihil est adiaphoron.* The essence of the church and the credibility of the gospel are at stake. Berkouwer says that a moment of "to be or not to be" dawns for the Church.[64] That which under normal circumstances belongs to the "well-being" (*welwese*) suddenly becomes part of the "being" (*wese*). That which in the normal course of affairs is a nonfundamental article or custom becomes the focal point of the decision itself. An innocent matter suddenly becomes an article with which the Church stands or falls. "Separate houses of worship and structures of administration may be neutral in themselves," says Buthelezi, "but when racism sets up its idolatrous shrines in them they lose their neutrality, they become confessional symbols of a counter-church within the church of Christ."[65]

This means that a *status confessionis* can hardly be announced in terms of a whole series of arguments. In this respect the declaration of the

Reformierter Bund probably lost some of its power.[66] It lacks the direct evidence, the immediate clarity and powers of persuasion of the gospel. A (new) theological compendium is not coming into being when a *status confessionis* is recognized; what is needed is a simple reminder of the heart of the matter. Often the announcement of a *status confessionis* is expressed in terms suggesting that it merely concerns the recognition and acknowledgment of some (already clear-cut) "boundaries."[67] There was therefore some potential for misunderstanding (at least according to some interpreters) when the LWF's declaration referred to the Confession of Augsburg and when the WARC referred emphatically to the Reformed confessions it saw being denied. In a *status confessionis* it is primarily not a specific confessional tradition or its articles that are at stake, but the heart of the gospel itself. Any argumentation should not be based on quotations from creeds or articles of faith, but with an appeal to the heart of the biblical message. Just like all other confessional statements, the recognition of a *status confessionis* derives its authority from the Word itself and not in a secondary way from already existing confessional documents.

The recommendation of the study committee of the LWF at Bossey that Christians and churches all over the world should examine their own situations in order to determine whether there might be a need to declare a *status confessionis* (they preferred the term "extraordinary situation of confession" or "exceptional confessional conduct") was therefore also liable to misunderstanding. Their intention was clear and praiseworthy, namely to warn against a too easy and superficial verdict concerning circumstances in remote situations without any personal risk or involvement, which could all too easily serve as "an alibi for selective, preferential confessing." The solution, however, surely is not to be found in searching for such situations. They themselves acknowledged that the danger existed that every ethical problem can in that way become a cause for confession.[68] The fact remains that such an announcement may only occur in extremely extraordinary cases, where the gospel itself is truly and evidently at stake, where the "boundaries" are already drawn and the church need only acknowledge it, where Christians take a stand simply because "they cannot do anything else."

When it is judged that the gospel itself is at stake, it also means that an attitude of neutrality or nonalignment is no longer possible, or rather, having such an attitude implies that a choice has already been made. When Ernst Wolf described the Reformed view of a *status confessionis*, he said that "the possibility of further neutrality falls way, as well as the possibility to remain silent."[69] The Reformierter Bund judged that a situation had occurred in which silence or evasion would lead to new guilt.[70] At Ottawa, a statement by Bonhoeffer played a major role: "Not to act and not to take a stand, simply for fear of making a mistake, when others have to make infinitely more difficult decisions every day, seems to me to be almost a contradiction of love."[71] In his influential article on the community of the Church (1936), Bonhoeffer had examined in detail the so-called "neutral" people or "figures in the middle," who were themselves not guilty of the standpoints which were rejected as heretical, but who also were not willing openly to oppose that sort of doctrine:

> First of all it must be said that indeed there are no neutral people. They rather belong to the other side. But subjectively they would prefer to be neutral. To take up a simple position towards them is consequently not possible, because their own position is not simple, because the boundaries they themselves draw over against the true church are unclear. Jesus Christ made the double declaration concerning the "neutral" people: "Anyone who is not for me is really against me" (Matt. 12:30); and "For whoever is not against us is for us" (Mark 9:40). Neither can the neutrals only make the second word applicable to themselves, nor can the church use only the first word against them. But it must be said again and again that the neutrals are exactly in this questioned situation described by these two words together. As soon as the neutrality is elevated to the level of a principle, the possibility becomes manifest only to use the second word. . . . The acknowledgement of a *status confessionis* is a reminder to the church leadership that a choice must be made in this hour.[72]

These convictions were evidently also operating in the decisions of the DR Mission Church. Witness to that is the fact that the two basic theological arguments of 1978 are purposefully included again in the official resolution, as well as the fact that the synod pressed on to an even more precise articulation in the final drafting of a confession and especially in the fact that the draft confession focuses on only three central issues, with a direct appeal on the evident message of the Bible alone.

In the third place, announcing a *status confessionis* means that the Christians who make the announcement judge that a situation has developed in which the *gospel* itself is at stake. It is necessary to emphasize the term "gospel" once again, on the one hand because it recalls the deepest *intention* of every declaration of a *status confessionis* and on the other hand because it describes the *spirit* or disposition with which it ought to happen.

Precisely because it does not concern merely the postulation of a personal opinion or the viewpoint of one group (in the way, for example, that a specific institution sees the issue or even in the peculiarities of a confessional tradition), but the truth of the gospel itself, such an announcement is *never calculated to result in a schism*. The intention is, on the contrary, always the purification or (re-)uniting of the "true church," the defense of and witness to "the credibility of the gospel." When heresy (in the form of an ideological travesty of the gospel or a schism which may divide the Church and violate the community—to use Calvin's definition[73]) threatens to blind believers in the name of the gospel itself, the moment of confession has dawned. In an interesting article, R. Bertram discusses the Augsburg Confession as a model or paradigm of the forming of a confession under the title "Confessing as Re-defining Authority."[74] At Augsburg, the issue centered on rejecting "strange" powers of influence and sources of authority in the doctrine and life of the Church next to the gospel and the Scriptures. In an almost identical way, this was also exactly the focal point of the German church struggle and of Barmen. In the rejection of the moral and theological justification of apartheid, with the consequences which follow from this for church unity and reconciliation, the question is again one of "the re-defining of authority." The current situation is in the grip of "ideologies foreign to the Scriptures" (to quote the accompanying letter), the weight of "*custom*" and "practice" and "that to which our people are used," the powerful role which "prejudice and weaknesses" are still playing in determining the lifestyle of the body of Christ, and the threats of "harmful effects," of "people who might leave the church," and of "financial implications." In opposition to such thinking, the confession witnesses that the Word of God must be the only authority in doctrine and life for the Church and that the hour has come in which matters "innocent" in themselves, so-called "neutral" or "practical" arrangements, threaten and harm the Church and the gospel, so that everybody has now to return to that which is pure and correct—as proof for the world to see that the Word is truly the final guide and standard of the Church. In every instance that a *status confessionis* has been acknowledged, it has been repeatedly stressed that no schism is intended, but rather the real uniting of the Church is sought. Such an announcement is therefore in itself not a schism[75] and "the people dissenting from the *status confessionis* are not viewed as opponents or enemies."[76]

Of course this does not mean that a mere formal or false unity is not a real danger. But the moment is distinguished precisely by the fact that an appeal is made on the truth in order to achieve better unity. The unity strived after is unity on the common basis of this truth. Of course, says the Reformierter Bund, the balanced standpoint of the formal unity becomes then threatened by the unilateral confessional testimony, but "the inner peace in the church is not the command of the hour."[77] Wolf has criticized the EKD because they did not want "the unity of the church" to be "threatened or queried" by a clear confession. He has pointed out repeatedly that the so-called unity based upon the consensus of an organized *volkskerk* was not identical to the "true unity of the church in faith and obedience."[78] In a session of the Beienroder Konvent these convictions were formulated in two theses in defense of the standpoint of the RB:

> 1) The impression must not be made that the church as *volkskerk* must in the first place function as mediator between different groups and opinions and may therefore, according to its calling, say nothing which has to do with the content of the issue under discussion. We rather expect of our church a clear and unambiguous testimony. . . .
> 2) In spite of all the endeavour to achieve community in the church, we consider it to be a very doubtful undertaking whenever the prophetic witness of groups or individuals is criticized because it "places a burden" on the unity of the church. We rather expect of our church to place the preaching of the will of God above the striving for unity in the church. People must also not abandon the search after the truth with the argument that in that way painful divisions and schisms may occur.[79]

When the point at issue truly constituted an emergency and the very final consequences were drawn, wrote Barth, one had to testify for the truth even when 99 percent of the Christians chose the other way.[80]

The announcement of an extraordinary situation of confession by Christians or a church inevitably creates a "tension" between "binding decisions and ongoing church community."[81] This is clearly illustrated in the ambivalent declarations of the RB. On the one hand the authors acknowledged that it was impossible that in an issue of confession, which after all was a matter of life or death, mutually exclusive positions could in the long run exist simultaneously. On the other hand they reminded the church that the necessary and unequivocal "no" against a *standpoint* did not do away with the "yes" toward the *person* and that the recognition of a *status confessionis* did not mean excommunication or a threatening schism, but in fact the invitation to faith.[82] This (inevitable) ambiguity was heavily criticized. It was often said that division and schism might not be what was desired, but would in any case be the unavoidable result if other churches did not share the same opinion.[83] The explanations of the RB did not succeed in relieving this tension. They said that their standpoint was rather meant to be "an urgent appeal," the expression of "the urgency of the resolution," and not at all intended to query the unity of the Church or to deny anyone's Christianity.[84] Simultaneously they admitted, however, that there can be no doubt that the resolution could have very serious implications.

The most important cause for this tension is probably situated in the fact that such a recognition always concerns the *gospel,* in the very fact that it is a plea, a brotherly appeal, a "call for salvation" (Bonhoeffer),[85] an invitation,[86] a call to unity and not to schism,[87] an appeal to the Church as a whole,[88] an appeal for unity.[89] The acknowledgment of a *status confessionis* is ultimately "the idiom of the gospel!"[90] The spirit in which it occurs must be the disposition and attitude of the gospel, the love for the neighbor, the desire that everyone will indeed hear and unite under the gospel and will stay together in true fellowship. This is, however, precisely the reason also for the seriousness and the awesome possibility that that invitation may be heard differently and may even be rejected. Whoever calls in the name of the gospel does not count on this possibility beforehand, but trusts and hopes, often against all human probabilities, in him who calls on things which do not exist as if they exist. When that invitation, that plea for real unity, reconciliation, and community is rejected or ignored, then a division does indeed occur—but then the dividing line is drawn from the other side by those who declare that they interpret the gospel differently. In such a case possibilities arise which no one even wishes to consider beforehand. The confessing Christians must then show that the matter was indeed serious to them, that they were not opportunistic, but that they really spoke and acted out of their deepest religious convictions. A moment finally comes of which Bonhoeffer spoke when he said that the withdrawing of fellowship was still the very last offer of fellowship and community.[91]

That the DR Mission Church has meant the *status confessionis* to be "the idiom of the gospel" is clear from the very fact of making their confession as well as from the content of the accompanying letter (especially the fourth paragraph). By formulating a confession, the church sought, among other things, to avoid being misunderstood and breaking off discussion as the result of misunderstandings and misrepresentations. By formulating her own position as exactly as possible, she wanted to make sure that the choice she requested, the boundaries she acknowledged, the decision she considered necessary for the sake of the gospel was as evident and clear as possible, precisely for the sake of community. In a tense church situation like the one in the Dutch Reformed church family, people all too easily react against caricatures and misrepresentations. In order to be heard correctly, the DR Mission Church wanted to speak understandably. In addition, the DR Mission Church declared emphatically:

> This confession is not aimed at specific people or groups of people or a church or churches . . . [but] against a false doctrine. . . . Our heartfelt longing is that no one will identify himself with this objectionable doctrine and that all who have been wholly or partially blinded by it will turn themselves away from it. . . . Therefore it is that we speak pleadingly rather than accusingly. . . . Our prayer is that this act of confession will not place false stumbling blocks in the way and thereby cause and foster false divisions, but rather that it will be reconciling and uniting. . . . We pray that our brothers and sisters throughout the Dutch Reformed Church family, but also outside it, will want to make

this new beginning with us, so that we can be free together and together may walk the road of reconciliation and justice.

In order to clarify the meaning of a *status confessionis* even more, it may be meaningful to answer two frequent questions. The first and important question is one that concerns the *relationship between confession and politics,* or to state it more precisely whether it is at all possible to declare a state of Christian confession with reference to a political policy or state of affairs. In all three of the important cases of *status confessionis* a heavy debate raged around this problem. Bethge tried to point out that the weakness of Barmen was finally precisely to be found in the fact that it—mistakenly, according to him—was not concerned with the political issues, but primarily with the inadmissible interference of the state in church affairs. This would, according to him, have been in conflict with at least Bonhoeffer's own original intentions and was furthermore one of the reasons why Bonhoeffer gradually felt himself personally obliged to take even further steps. Bethge spoke of "tragic shifts of priorities" which gradually occurred in the Confessing Church, so that the original intentions were never fully realized.[92] Other interpreters did not share his negative view of Barmen, but on the contrary judged that the clarity and evidence of the words of Barmen were situated precisely on its concentration on the fact that the essence of the Church and the power and credibility of the gospel itself were at stake.

In connection with the resolutions of the LWF this was again the point at which the differences of opinion occurred, as is obvious from the title of the book published after the meeting of the special study committee, *Politik als Glaubenssache?* The fact that an obviously political point of view was adopted and aimed against the "system" of apartheid without the theological arguments of, for example, the Swakopmund appeal sounded strange and unacceptable to many Lutheran theologians. Although many of them were completely willing to reject the system and its many facets by way of resolutions, especially in the light of the violation of basic human rights, they still judged it hardly possible to do this as a deed of confession, motivated by a threat to the gospel itself. Given the Lutheran understanding of the two kingdoms, which always ascribes a major role to the evidence of natural morality and consequently to the autonomy of civil, political, and economic ways of opinion forming and decision making, a direct route from confession to politics is hardly possible. The fact that a *status confessionis* is moreover experienced as compulsory for the conscience of all Christians is totally in conflict with a Lutheran interpretation of such matters. One gets the impression that many individuals, groups, and denominations which do support the resolution to reject apartheid as a system because of the confession do so with a false view of the system of apartheid. Often, the fact that the state prohibits common prayer and the sharing of Holy Communion plays a major role as the decisive argument, probably as a result of the circumstances during the German church struggle. This is, however, not the whole truth, and oversimplifies the complicated South African situation in an impermissible way.[93] This approach, as Bethge pointed out regarding Barmen, still attempts to define the issue as a church matter which argues only from the fact that the state exceeds its limits and enters the terrain of the church. Even the detailed attempt of the study committee to defend a political rejection of apartheid on the basis of the confession is not fully convincing.[94]

This conflict rages just as fiercely over the resolution of the Reformierter Bund.[95] For the Reformed way of thinking, based on the all-encompassing lordship of Christ over all aspects of life, it is always much easier to go from confession to politics—and often very tempting.[96] Not without reason it is often said that the Reformed way of thinking—with its always slumbering theocratic ideal—is the blood-brother of Anabaptist radicalism.[97] According to Lutheran thought this stance amounts to an intentional and flagrant disregard for the boundary between the two kingdoms. Rendtorff even goes so far as to say that the contrary is actually true and that the RB has denied the Christian confession![98] People generally agree with the Reformed position that peace is a matter of confession, but some add that that is not the actual point of difference. The distinction which Moltmann made at Ottawa between "peace churches" and "nuclear churches" was in many circles received with bitterness.[99] While all Christians indeed agree on peace, they differ about the proper political strategy to serve that common ideal in the best possible way, and—the complaint goes—it is impossible to declare a *status confessionis* concerning such a strategy. Several Lutheran ethicists who agreed with the (political and strategic) standpoint of the RB consequently felt that a much stronger case could have been presented by means of political arguments than by way of a confession. The RB in its turn reacted by saying that the possession of arms with such an enormous destructive potential that all life and indeed creation itself can be destroyed beyond recall is no political strategy any more, but has already become a matter of confession.

In this regard there is frequent mention today of "ethical heresy."[100] W. A. Visser't Hooft especially popularized the expression in 1968 when he declared in Uppsala before the WCC that members who in practice deny their responsibility for the needy in any part of the world are equally guilty of heresy as those who deny this or that article of faith. On account of criticism, especially from Protestant ranks, that the concept of "grace alone" may be lost in this way, as well as objections that the term "heresy" should not be used in ecumenical circles, the full assembly finally avoided using the term and referred only to Christians who through their actions refuse to grant their fellow human beings their human rights and therefore deny Jesus Christ, in spite of any confessions of faith they may pronounce.[101]

It is of course true that doctrinal convictions have a great influence on life and are actually to be seen only in life. Show me your faith by your works, James demands. The tree is indeed known by its fruit, and both fresh and bitter water cannot flow from a spring. Not everyone that says "Lord, Lord" may enter the kingdom, but only those who do the will of the Father. In the New Testament it is therefore not possible to make a distinction between doctrine and life; in fact, the distinction between dogmatics and ethics developed rather late. In addition to that it is indeed a fact that just as the congregation's confession takes on a variety of forms, of which the theoretical formulation and the written articles are but a small part, so heresy takes on a variety of forms. In the same way that the truth of the confession is ultimately to be seen in, among other things, deeds, so heresy is finally to be seen in deeds. Christian—and un-Christian—conduct surely discloses the presuppositions and convictions which are concealed behind it.

In spite of all this, however, it still remains a doubtful undertaking to speak of "ethical heresy." To let it refer to unethical or sinful deeds simply leads to endless misunderstanding and confusion of speech, so that the term finally loses all power of expression. The appeal that is often made in Lutheran circles to the Confessio Augustana, article 16, where it is said that the Christian is obliged to obedience to the state only in-asmuch as this is possible "without sin," is not proof enough that something like apartheid is "heretical." At the most it could lead one to oppose such a system and to engage in forms of civil disobedience in those respects where obedience to God is directly contradictory to the laws and the state. Rendtorff correctly points out that the term "ethical heresy" is only applicable to an ethical *doctrine* which is in conflict with the gospel and that it is "to no avail" to apply it to unethical deeds or sins.[102] Even that definition must, however, be qualified more closely. One can only talk of "ethical heresy" when that false doctrine is present-ed or defended in the name of the gospel or the Bible. The term "heresy" implies by definition the deformation or distortion of the gospel and cannot be applied to something which is not presented in the name of or with the sanction of the gospel. In such a case, in fact, it does not make much sense to talk any longer of "ethical" heresy, because it then in any case concerns a normal form of heresy, as false interpretation of the gospel, with unethical implications, like all forms of heresy. This, how-ever, is clearly something totally different from what Visser't Hooft had in mind. Án example may explain this. In the event that someone assaults his wife, it is sin, not heresy. In the event that he is an unbeliever who defends his act by arguing that that is the only way in which he can ensure order in his household, it is an unevangelical doctrine or conviction, but no heresy. However, in the event that he is a Christian and defends his conduct by saying that it is his interpretation of the biblical truth that men "have authority over their wives" and that in his opinion it is the will of God and the way in which Christian households are to be organized, it might be regarded as heresy. In an interesting exposition, Steck has shown that the label "heretic" was in practice given almost exclusively to priests and preachers and that in the last three or four generations it was seen as a "matter of standing or class," a matter involving theologians and preachers only. [103] Believers are very likely influenced by an ideological travesty of the gospel, but the charge of heresy is normally lodged against those who were responsible to prove, defend, and propagate it theologically.

In ethical matters, which include political and economic questions, the Church normally has other ways of making resolutions, of speaking, and of acting. To put it even more clearly: it is indeed true that Christians may have certain mutual political aims, but they can still differ about the most suitable political strategies in order to achieve those. Christians simply must bear this in mind, however strongly convinced they might be of the evangelical necessity and obviousness of their own points of view. Moreover: the Christian-ethical process of making decisions does not operate with a single principle (e.g., justice, or love, or a certain model of human rights), or a simple hierarchy of principles, by means of which concrete conduct can be prescribed evidently and directly for every possible situation which might occur, even for the obvious reason that the reality simply sets limitations to that which is possible and immediately attainable. With the substitution of one government for another it is often all too clear that the promised ideal solutions do not materialize and that many of the much-criticized measures and the slow changes still have to be continued. The formation of ethical and the corresponding socio-political opinions or judgments is and remains an extremely intricate process—and Christians and churches must continuously strive to be reasonable and just. Still more can be added: under normal circumstances it is a risky matter to reject a total socio-political "system" on the strength of a Christian point of view, especially when such a rejection is interpreted as the rejection of almost any legislation, measure, or arrangement of the government in question and becomes nearly a license for all sorts of civil disobedience. To talk too easily of a government that has denied and therefore lost its God-given right to rule may be confusing and dangerously misleading. It is obvious that all this does not in the very least mean that silence must be imposed upon the Church. It only implies a serious warning against an all too direct connection between confession and politics and the uttering of all too final words.

The DR Mission Church did not step into these pitfalls. Apartheid is much more than merely a political "system" or "policy" and the implementation of political arrangements. It is nothing else than a philosophy of life and a way of perceiving reality, a lifestyle motivated by religion, a way of thinking about humanity and human beings, the arrangement of society in all its smallest details according to an ideology which—and this is the crux of the matter—historically, whether consciously or unconsciously, and still today for many people has been founded, motivated, and popularized out of the Word of God. The Church confesses against this. It is on account of this "doctrine," this "theology," this interpretation of the message of the Bible as it was put into daily practice that the DR Mission Church is protesting and confessing. The announcement of a *status confessionis* is an appeal from the heart to call fellow Christians, brothers and sisters in the Lord, back from this tempting but wrong track, this "power of deception" which may lead to subjective assurance but not to the freedom of the truth (see the accompanying letter).

On this level the Christian confession has everything to do with this kind of politics. The same philosophy of life which has carried and directed the political "system" has over the years also infiltrated into the church and has influenced it decisively. Although there was also direct intervention of the state into church affairs and although the effects of political arrangements on church life are serious enough, the real difficulty lies much deeper, at the very base of both of these spheres. Whoever has understood this and has agreed with it will also realize that the implications for the political and economic system in South Africa are not to be found in the ease with which different arrangements of "apartheid governments" may now be rejected, but, much more important, in the exposure that has taken place of a racist and ideological way of thinking which will never again be covered up or condoned.

The *second* question which must be asked is *if and why* it was necessary for the DR Mission Church to follow the announcement of a *status confessionis* with a new (draft-) confession.

It already became obvious that a *status confessionis* (according to Wolf) demands several steps: the existence of such a situation must first be spotted and acknowledged; then its focal point must be determined or pinned down precisely; finally the demand of the hour must be answered with appropriate forms of conduct. Naturally the initial determination and the resulting conduct or action will differ according to the subject who acknowledges the *status confessionis*. An individual may experience it personally as being concentrated on a very specific matter or choice—like the compulsory oath of loyalty to Hitler—and see the necessary conduct as refusing to take the oath and accepting the consequences of that deed. A group of churches, like the WARC, can appeal to its member churches to draw their own conclusions and consider likely implications; it might also reconsider the membership of churches who do not agree with the decision and attempt to enter into discussions with them. Specific churches or denominations, however, may experience the necessity of still other forms of conduct.

It is clear that the decision of the DR Mission Church to draw up a confession was an attempt to determine as precisely as possible the ways in which the gospel is at stake, as well as an act of obedience which flowed from the *status confessionis*. That the DR Mission Church would have joined the ecumenical bodies in their acknowledgment of a *status confessionis* was to be expected and was even, to a certain extent, a natural and rather ''easy'' step in view of the preceding history of this church. That this decision was still disputed in the synod was probably due to the fact that many members of the synod were not completely sure what exactly was happening; many were also burdened by the possibility that the event might not be a step toward greater clarity in the theological discussion of a church which had already come a long way. The nearer a church stands to the center of such a debate, the more imperative it is for her to use precise formulations and to give a clear testimony. Although unspoken, the feeling was probably present among many that concise theological declarations and the acknowledgment of a state of confession were often molded in a ''style which leads to short-circuiting'' (Lohse, addressed to the Reformierter Bund[104]), liable to misunderstandings, and therefore irresponsible and unbrotherly. It is only natural that a church inside the South African context and, even more, inside the Dutch Reformed church family has to testify more emphatically and clearly than, for example, an ecumenical body.

It was to accept this irresponsibility—which she took on herself with the acknowledgment of a *status confessionis*—and by doing that to take a first but almost compulsory step of obedience that the DR Mission Church set out to draw up a confession. When Professor G. Bam delivered to the synod his plea that the church must realize the seriousness of her deed and must be prepared to accept responsibility in the appropriate spirit and to articulate her faith concerning the relevant aspects of the gospel for this ''hour,'' it seemed an expression of the heartfelt desire of the whole synod and a view which, maybe unconsciously, lived within everyone. The devotion of the subsequent moments, the humble prayer of dedication, and the unanimity of the resolutions testify to this. That spirit also dominated the proceedings in which the draft confession itself was accepted.

The acceptance of a draft confession was therefore simultaneously a deed of love and of obedience. For the sake of *love* and the invitation to everyone concerned, the DR Mission Church did not want to bring any confusion, preach any unilateralism, break down any potential conversation, cause "short-circuits" and "false divisions" (accompanying letter), or erect false "boundaries." For the sake of *obedience* and the integrity of the Church she could not evade the responsibilities which she took on herself. Whoever is convinced that the truth of the gospel itself is at stake must be prepared to act accordingly and bear the still unknown consequences. By doing so, the DR Mission Church simply proceeded on the way she had previously started to go.

Whether it was wise—in any of the issues in question—to use the term *status confessionis* can probably be disputed. In all probability it often diverted attention from the actual issue at stake (racism or nuclear armament) to questions of church law and terminology. In all probability it often led in many circles to adverse emotional reactions which were confusing and harmful to the cause. In all probability it unnecessarily estranged people who belonged together and who agreed on the actual question. In all probability there are closely related concepts which express the matter even better. In all probability many of those concerned will use the term less frequently in subsequent discussions or abandon it completely. However, the author of the report of the Reformierter Bund, R. Wischnath, said that the term nevertheless served this aim: that their point of view, which again and again, over a very long period, had been ignored or lightly and routinely put aside was suddenly taken note of.[105] The DR Mission Church also had the feeling—correctly or incorrectly— that she was never taken seriously as a discussion partner in this matter, which, according to her judgment, is the most decisive issue of our age. This indeed is the "black experience."[106] This is the climax of powerlessness and ultimate frustration. This is the life experience of voicelessness. The acknowledgment of a *status confessionis* was a final cry from the heart to be heard and to be taken seriously. But it was an evangelical cry, a cry full of love—and therefore the Church confesses explicitly, in order that the real unity, based on the truth, may be restored.

J. J. F. Durand

2

A Confession—
Was It Really Necessary?

Publishing a confession of faith is not a common event. It is, in fact, very uncommon. The reason for this is not hard to find: confessions have always been controversial documents in the history of the Church. The serious differences of opinion they elicited related not only to the confessions as such but also to their inception. Invariably, some questions arose regarding the necessity for the confession.

There was, admittedly, a short period in the history of the Church when a multiplicity of confessions seemed the order of the day. In the Reformation of the sixteenth century and the period immediately following numerous confessions emerged in western Europe. The controversy surrounding these events, as well as the spirit of intolerance in which confessions were issued, undoubtedly contributed to the fact that Protestantism never achieved the unity of spirit it desired. Martin Bucer, the reformer of Strasbourg and one of Calvin's teachers, was aware of this danger. His reaction in 1529 to the question whether Strasbourg should adopt a confession of faith drawn up by Luther may be paraphrased roughly as follows: faith is based on the sure and only Word of God; the human mind is unable to comprehend and express this Word adequately; the unity of faith should therefore be sought in divine Scripture rather than in human words. Whenever the early Church relied on human words, discord inevitably resulted. Bucer does not disapprove of the confession, but warns against the danger of human inconstancy and calls for a confession that is expressed clearly and concisely, with words from the Bible—for those who do not yield to the Word of God will certainly not yield to the word of man.

But any look at the Reformation period in the history of the Church makes it apparent that Bucer's deepest intentions were not understood. His contemporaries did not usually seek the solution to the problem of "human inconstancy" in the direction he proposed. Too often, in fact, they took the opposite direction. Man's words were too quickly and too categorically equated with God's Word and proclaimed with great intolerance. One of the eventual results was that confessions of faith were, unfairly, treated with less gravity and the forming of confessions fell into discredit among many churches and religious groups.

In our own century the ecumenical movement encouraged this antipathy toward creating confessions of faith. In the quest for ecclesiastical unity, confessions that divide are easily dismissed. Furthermore, as we hear repeatedly, the deciding factor is not the word that divides but the deed that unites. Orthopraxy takes the place of orthodoxy. The Christian faith is verified in its daily praxis, according to this view, and it is in this praxis that the churches can become dynamically involved with one another and with the world. It is dynamic because the human deed is not fixed. The human word, on the other hand, is fixed, which is why a Christian confession divides while Christian action unites in a spirit of tolerance. And without tolerance in a world of religious plurality life becomes unbearable.

This is not to say that the twentieth century ignores words. It is in fact accepted that things have to be discussed. But in Christianity this should take the form of a theological dialogue. In contrast to a confession, it is said, a theological dialogue is open, tolerant, and conducive to new possibilities for mutual understanding. A fixed confession, on the other hand, implies a fixed and final stand and a denunciation of the opponent.

It is significant that the skepticism greeting any attempt at a new confession comes not only from those quarters placing a high value on tolerance and openness but also from those who hold the opposite view of the role of the confession in the Church. Precisely because they rate the confession so highly, frequently equating it with the Word of God, it acquires such an inviolable character that the addition of a new confession to the existing body is seen as an almost sacrilegious act.

In light of the above, the 1982 Belhar Confession was a risk of the highest order. It need come as no surprise that the confession was received with disbelief in the most divergent quarters. Those who were not exactly sympathetic toward the plight of the DR Mission Church immediately asked the question: Was a *confession* really necessary? Even the more sympathetic felt compelled to ask: Was the declaration of a *status confessionis* on apartheid not adequate in the light of existing confessions? The declaration of a state of confession does not of itself, after all, require the publication of a new confession. These and other questions were asked and are still being asked against the background of twentieth-century attitudes toward publishing a confession. All the foregoing objections and reservations now come into play in varying degrees of importance.

The objections can be answered in various ways. A strong theological case can, for instance, be made for the fact that a confession in words should not be valued less than a confession in deeds. On the contrary: a true confession, one that raises the highest life, the most noble deed, or the deepest suffering to a confession in New Testament terms, is a confession of the mouth; and the faith of the church arises out of hearing a word proclaimed (Rom. 10:10ff.). This path is followed, say the words of the confession; not, indeed, without deeds, attitudes, and even suffering, but still *this* way. Whoever underestimates the power of the words of confession, according to Karl Barth, will have to tell us why Jesus Christ is called the *Word* and not the *Deed* in the New Testament. But such arguments remain in the realm of theoretical theology and really beg the question. The question why a written confession had to be published *right now* remains unanswered. The decisive issue in this question is the nature of the conflict in which the confession has to verify itself and justify its existence. It should, after all, be clear from everything that has been said that only the existence of formidable reasons can justify the publication of a new confession.

In the following pages I will examine the nature of the situation in which the confession of the DR Mission Church was conceived. I do not attempt a historical analysis or a history of the confession in the ordinary sense of the word; this has been done elsewhere. Rather, I direct some attention to the factors that make the historical situation a typical confessional situation; that is, the factors that, in theological terms, create the circumstances in which the declaration of a confession is rendered understandable and justifiable—if not inevitable. At the same time we shall be looking at other aspects which come to the fore in such a situation and which, beyond asking questions about the justifiability of confession as such, place the confession itself under the microscope. What is it that constitutes a true confession? This is the question that we finally arrive at—a question that is implicitly woven through this entire discussion.

In the first place, in interpreting the historical situation that gave birth to the 1982 Belhar Confession as a conflict situation with confessional implications, we have to stress that not every situation of conflict in which the Church finds itself need give rise to a confession. A confessional situation is normally a polemical situation in which the Church addresses itself against a false doctrine, against the heresy in its midst that is offered under the cloak of Christianity and scriptural authority. The great ecumenical symbols of the Church, such as the Confession of Nicea as well as the confessions formulated during and after the Reformation, all have this distinctive characteristic. A confession does not, for instance, emerge from a situation in which church and state are engaged in conflict. In such a situation the Church will indeed confess its faith, obedient even unto death, but it will not publish a confession against a government policy or political philosophy as such. A state may be anti-Christian in its actions, it may sin against God and man, but it cannot be heretical. To be guilty of heresy is the dubious prerogative of the Church. The danger of heresy, as opposed to an ordinary political policy or philosophy, lies in the fact that it is presented in the guise of scriptural authority. In the confession, the heretic and his false doctrine, which he would preach with an appeal to the Word of God, are unmasked.

The polemical nature of the situation out of which the Belhar Confession arose can be readily recognized. Apartheid in South Africa is much more than a political system imposed on South African society through many years of legislation. It is a comprehensive ideology and view of life involving the organization and control of man and society with the pretense of a pseudogospel: the solution of social problems through—in this instance—the legal separation of groups and individuals on the basis of race and color. I speak deliberately of a "pseudogospel" because the "solution" that is offered is given biblical sanction. Apartheid is more than a political attempt to surmount the problems of a complicated society: it is God's will for southern Africa, expressed in his creative order and opposed only at the risk of dire consequences. This theological foundation came from the Church, in particular from the Reformed churches of the white South Africans. The development of the concept of apartheid in the Church has had a long history dating back to the previous century. Initially it was given religious expression in the establishment of separate church structures, but since the 1930s it has been held up with increasing urgency by the Church as the divinely inspired political solution to South Africa's social problems. It is no secret that some of the laws which are the cornerstones of apartheid (the Mixed Marriages Act, Section 16 of the Immorality Act, and the Group Areas Act) were promulgated under strong DRC pressure. Nobody can have any doubt that these churches presented apartheid to a greater or lesser extent as a scriptural doctrine.

The Belhar Confession opposes this heresy and shows in its three articles why it is a heresy. In the first place it causes a rift in the Church on the grounds of race and color, grounds that advance something more than just faith in Jesus Christ as the basis of the Church's existence. In the second place, it violates the evangelical message of reconciliation between man and man, rendering that reconciliation impossible in everyday life. And finally, in opposition to the biblical message of divine justice, it opens the door to the exploitation of the powerless by the powerful.

It is significant that the term "apartheid" is mentioned nowhere in the confession. The authors of the confession wanted in this way to underline the fact that it concerns itself in the first place with the *heretical church doctrine* that underlies the entire apartheid system. The DR Mission Church has clearly identified the polemical situation in which it finds itself. The conflict basically centers around a heresy which was not forced upon the Church by the state, but which flourished in the rich soil of the Church itself.

Although the confession itself does not mention apartheid by name, its political implications are so clear that no further discussion of them is necessary. Yet it is necessary for us to have a brief look at the politics of apartheid, for only in this way shall we be able to answer the further question that inevitably arises: granted that a polemical situation has developed around a heretical doctrine, is this heresy of so serious a nature that it justifies formulating a confession?

The answer to this question may of course be that every heresy is a serious matter, especially where the unity of the Church, reconciliation, and justice are involved. But then we must also immediately concede that all these issues have been at issue formerly in the history of the Church without the sense that a confession of faith was necessary to deal explicitly with them. The seriousness of the polemical situation of Belhar reaches further, however. The heresy in question did, after all, give birth to a political dispensation which affects the daily life of millions of people in a systematic process of dehumanization: a dispensation in which 9 million South Africans have been robbed of their citizenship and the right to share in the proceeds of the most developed parts of the country; in which 3½ million people have so far been uprooted and resettled, sometimes under terrible conditions, in order to eliminate ''black spots''; in which the privileged white population could resort to laws such as the Group Areas Act to claim the best for themselves and move 834,400 people from their homes and properties; and in which the list of injustices grows. The point is that it is a church-inspired doctrine that has affected so many people in this way—on an unprecedented scale. It was pointed out above that, in the light of twentieth-century attitudes toward the confession of faith, there had to be formidable reasons before any church could form a confession. I do not think we have to go beyond the effects of the ideology of apartheid on the lives of the people to find such a reason.

Now that we have established that the Belhar Confession had its origin in a polemical situation of such a serious nature that it both justifies and explains the forming of a confession, we come to the next question: were the Church's existing confessions not adequate to deal with the situation? In reply to this we may readily admit that the 1982 confession did not come up with anything ''new.'' The unity of the Church, reconciliation between God and man, and man and man in Jesus Christ, and the beautifying righteousness of God—these are being confessed. And yet, the context in which Belhar spoke on these matters differed so deeply from the times in which the Church's existing confessions were written that what the synod wanted to say explicitly could only be deduced implicitly from the existing confessions. And this was not good enough. The situation called for more. This applies not only to the first two articles, but perhaps more particularly to the third article on the righteousness of God. Does not the DR Mission Church here confess something that the Church should have confessed long ago—that God is very specifically the God of the poor and the weak? And can there be a more relevant situation in which this should be confessed than the very situation dealt with by the synod?

But, even if the above is true, a confession of faith always implies that the end of the road has been reached. Would it not have been better for the DR Mission Church simply to have entered into a theological dialogue with the DRC and any other churches who would care to join? Would this not have been a more tolerant attitude? Would it not have created the possibility of mutual understanding between the DR Mission Church and the DRC? Questions such as these have a right to be asked; but we must realize that the Church's discussion of a heresy could not continue indefinitely as if it were not a heresy. In the history of the Church's confessions, the polemical discussion was always taken to a decisive point at which the testimony in the matter stepped up to a different level and a confession emerged. Eventually the lines had to be drawn, the truth had to be attested with as much authority as man could master—not only for the sake of those who confess but also particularly for the sake of those against whom they are confessing. Sooner or later finality had to be reached. And yet it is important to point out that the finality with which the DR Mission Church speaks of the apartheid ideology after the Belhar Synod was not reached overnight. The church did in fact speak about it for many years and with increasing intensity. By 1978 the DR Mission Church unambiguously declared apartheid to be in conflict with the gospel of Jesus Christ. It was almost self-evident, the church said, that the theological justification of apartheid was, by implication, no less than heresy. But the DRC, with unbelievable theological indifference, took no notice of this declaration. The DRC told the DR Mission Church in so many words that its declaration was not worthy of serious attention. When this happened the dialogue at that level had, in effect, ended. All that remained for the DR Mission Church was to confess its faith. Paradoxically this reopened the dialogue, albeit at a different level. The DR Mission Church now conducts its discussion from the position of the finality of its confession. Its tolerance henceforth extends only to the people, and the church, who have not yet renounced the heresy (which is why it continues to confess its faith) and no longer to the heresy itself. Confessional tolerance does not go that far.

From the above we may identify the following factors accompanying the confessional process: the polemical nature of the situation, its intense gravity, the inability of existing confessions to provide an answer, and the finality of speech that the situation leads to. Our analysis of these elements makes it abundantly clear that the Belhar Confession is like all other confessions in that it was decisively determined by a historical context. And both the immediate relevance of the confession and its contentiousness have to be explained by this context. Although everyone will agree that a confession has to be immediately relevant, this relevancy does not have the last word on the quality of the confession. Its true quality lies in its ability to transcend its historical situation and still be relevant when the wheel of history has been turned and new circumstances have been created. This requires that a confession of faith should concern itself only with matters pivoting around the divine revelation in Jesus Christ. A confession may not concern itself with peripheral trivialities. It is true that every real confession can ultimately only be an extension of the Church's original confession that Jesus is Lord. This guarantees the constant relevancy of the confession. Nobody, for instance, would consider scrapping the Canons of Dort for the churches of Reformed origin in South Africa just because there is no Remonstrant movement in our country.

It is therefore my conviction that the Belhar Confession will survive apartheid and the heresy that gave rise to it and retain its message. The three issues at its crux—unity, reconciliation, and justice—lie close to the heart of the gospel. The factors that threaten the unity of the Church, bedevil reconciliation between people, and offend the justice of God by the exploitation of the weak are constants in the sinful nature of man which he rationalizes with great facility, even in theological terms. The fact that the confession itself contains no direct reference to the ideology of apartheid, that the synod decided to indicate the historical circumstances behind the confession by way of a footnote only, is an indication that they realized that a true confession will transcend its own temporal circumstances. The DR Mission Church confesses not only with a view to the immediate danger that threatens the churches in South Africa in this particular historical situation but also with a view to the future. The danger of falling into error must constantly be brought to the attention of Christ's Church.

In acknowledging this, the DR Mission Church admits implicitly that the danger of heresy does not come from without alone, but also from within. A confession that arises out of a polemical situation always involves the confessing church as well. In a confession the one does not judge the other (cf. Matt. 7:1); it is the church that judges itself. This implicit recognition accompanying every formation of a confession is explicitly acknowledged by the DR Mission Church in its accompanying letter to the Belhar Confession. The result of all this cannot—and dare not—be anything else than that the DR Mission Church will continually place itself under scrutiny. In conclusion, the credibility of the Belhar Confession will depend on the DR Mission Church's willingness, in its religious life, to reflect the spirit of that confession.

Out of the ability of a confession to transcend its own origins there arises a further issue that requires attention. The confession owes its existence to the negativity of a conflict situation, but it does not remain a negative document. The negative pronouncements in the 1982 Belhar Confession on various heretical findings are the other side to a positive confession with regard to the unity of the Church, the wonder of reconciliation in Christ, and the consolation of God's justice to the poor and the oppressed. The final aim of the confession is therefore not to create a division in Dutch Reformed circles, but to create the positive possibility of a true unity.

With its confession of faith the DR Mission Church presents itself as a church and requests fellowship with other churches on the basis of the truth as interpreted in this confession. By confessing the truth of the particular issues in question in this very way, the DR Mission Church eliminates the danger that the family of Dutch Reformed churches may continue to coexist in an apparent unity that is no real unity.

The reproach that the DR Mission Church is endangering its unity with the DRC could only be valid if there were, in the first place, a true unity in the biblical sense. But it is no secret that it was precisely such a visible unity, one which would transcend all ethnic and cultural differences, that was turned down by the DRC: it refused to hear the plea for a larger and more visible embodiment of the highly acclaimed spiritual unity between the Dutch Reformed churches. The Belhar Confession risks the apparent unity for the sake of the truth, for the sake of clearing the way for true unity.

Every confession of faith creates a division of spirits, but this does not detract from the fact that the confession is a document essentially intended to unite. This recognition relates closely to the ecumenical dimension of every confession. It is not for a church to interpret the particular opinions of a particular group in its confession of faith, but rather to be able to claim that it speaks the truth *on behalf of the universal Church,* even if it is for a specific and particular situation. For this reason any church wishing to confess in such a specific situation will think twice before confessing if its understanding of Scripture is so particular that it apparently receives no echo elsewhere in the universal Church. The Belhar Confession passes this test as well. It can be stated without fear of serious contradiction that this confession's rejection of a heresy with a racist origin interprets the general consensus of the Church worldwide, in its general essence and impact if not in its specific formulation. If there is one issue that has enjoyed growing unanimity among churches of all denominations since the Second World War, it is the general aversion to all forms of racism. It should surprise no one that this general aversion should have taken the form of a confession of faith in South Africa. Where else is racism currently not only constitutionalized but also backed by a heretical doctrine that has permeated an entire society?

The ecumenical dimension of the Belhar Confession could create the impression that its formulation was after all an easy and popular matter. Yet anyone familiar with South African religious life and society will know that this could not be the case. South Africa has alienated itself so much from world opinion—in religion as well—that it is in a position to exercise increasing internal pressure on its dissidents. The effects of this upon the DR Mission Church, if this church is prepared to accept the full consequences of its confession of faith, cannot yet be foreseen. The confession still has to work its way through the congregations, not only for approbation but also before its practical effect on individual congregations may be seen. This aspect will be given further consideration elsewhere. There can be little doubt of one thing, however: the road ahead will not always be easy. There is every indication of its being stormy at times, in spite of the sympathetic voices that are being heard not only inside but also outside the DR Mission Church. In the end, however, it is not for the church to care about the sympathies it may gain or lose, or about the happy or unhappy results that its confession may have upon its external existence. All these cares are irrelevant: according to Matthew 10, a confessing church will *always* stand in the shadow of the cross— albeit with the reassurance that the gates of hell will never close on it. And no one who flees from the cross will ever have the comfort of this promise.

P. J. ROBINSON

3

The 1982 Belhar Confession in Missionary Perspective

In reflecting on the Belhar Confession of the DR Mission Church, the question as to its missionary meaning and implications naturally arises. When a church feels driven to react in this way to the circumstances in which it finds itself, it becomes important to evaluate such a response for its missionary significance. The question is not whether or in what way the confession deals with the missionary task, but whether the document, which bears witness to heartfelt beliefs, actually assumes a missionary imperative in its specific situation. Could it be described as a "missionary document"?

If the confession can be so described, then the underlying concept of the witnessing and missionary role of the Church also becomes relevant. Will this confession succeed in safeguarding the Church against those crippling unilateralisms which had prejudiced so many of its efforts in the past? And further, what does it imply on a basic congregational level? Does the confession offer adequate guidelines to a congregation called to bear witness in a society fraught with complexities? Does not the way it addresses an extremely nuanced reality lack subtlety? Does the confession take adequate account of the vital need in the rest of Africa for arriving at an African confession? Many other questions remain, but more important are the possible answers and, we hope, the encouragement toward further reflection these questions offer.

In the light of the above, I want to consider first the confession as a significant development in the DR Mission Church itself; second, the confession as a document; and third, the confession in the light of the latest views in the field of ecumenical missionary theology.

FROM "OBJECT OF MISSIONARY ACTIVITY" TO "WITNESSING CHURCH"

It is commonly accepted that a congregation or church from its very inception should be regarded as a full-fledged witnessing body. No congregation or church can or should be seen as "an object for missionary work" by any other. Although this important principle in missionary philosophy is also professed by the DRC, the strange situation exists that the DR Mission Church, which to a large degree grew from the witnessing activity of the DRC, still figures as a "missionary object" in the thought and attitude of the DRC.

While the DR Mission Church is recognized in the synodal agenda of the DRC as a "sister"—previously "daughter"—church from whom formal greetings are accepted, it is also listed in the DRC's report on mission work. A regular feature on the DR Mission Church appears in *Die Sendingblad,* the official organ of the mission committee of the general synod of the DRC, and news about the DR Mission Church is habitually treated as "mission news." Members of the DRC who assist in some capacity or another in congregations of the DR Mission Church are considered to be engaged in "mission" work.

The increasingly sharp resistance and objection to this attitude and approach which resulted in the DR Mission Church is understandable. What the DRC saw as sincere missionary zeal was viewed in the DR Mission Church as the fruit of a twisted concept of the role of the Church and as materialism in disguise. So deep did feelings in the DR Mission Church run against so-called "mission work" that at its synod in 1978 the word "mission" was dropped from use in favor of "witness." However, two motions which called for the word to be removed from the name of the church itself failed.

As a result of its special relationship with the DRC, the DR Mission Church for years refrained from certain liaisons which the parent church regarded as harmful to their interchurch ties. It entered the ecumenical debate in an independent capacity only relatively late.

Through much of its history the DR Mission Church has been similarly inhibited from expressing its own convictions on a number of issues and reduced to echoing the DRC. But in recent years, especially since the 1970s, a decided change has occurred. The DR Mission Church, as a necessary and inevitable development, gradually distanced itself from the viewpoints of the DRC, often to the dismay of the latter. With a responsibility, after all, to interpret the gospel within the context of its own situation, this need was reflected pertinently in several synodical resolutions and in the stand taken by its delegates to ecumenical meetings during the 1970s.

Against this background, the Belhar Confession represents a definite turning point. With it the DR Mission Church broke through the traditional role of "receiver" and the "mentality of poverty" that held it captive for so long. Never again will the DR Mission Church be on the receiving end only with the DRC the sole "giver." The confession brought a radical change and liberated the DR Mission Church to assume the role of donor. The accompanying letter to the confession sees it as a hand of friendship to the DRC in the task of articulating the gospel message as clearly as possible in the complex reality of South African society.

While the fellowship of believers has sunk to a nearly invisible level among the various Dutch Reformed churches, with corresponding damage to the missionary credibility of the DRC, especially in Africa, the confession sets out to encourage a communion of the faithful and open the door to dynamic witness. In this sense the Belhar Confession and the accompanying declaration of a *status confessionis* represent, not the end of missionary activity in southern Africa, but in fact its continuation on a wider front and with more impact.

THE CONFESSION AS A MISSIONARY DOCUMENT

The question which flows from the above is whether it is technically correct to describe the confession as a meaningful missionary document. At first glance, the confession itself suggests that it is not. After all, the document does not use traditional missionary terminology, and the word "mission" does not occur once. Neither does it reflect a concern for the unconverted multitude. Nowhere is there a call to church members to become involved in proselytizing or in the founding of congregations. And no mention is made of the necessity of personal conversion. On the other hand, one is justified in wondering whether such criteria provide a valid yardstick by which to judge the missionary significance of the confession. The preoccupation with stereotyped missionary terminology ignores the real challenge to the witnessing church. It is thus important to appraise the actual content of the document for its missio-theological meaning.

The most striking characteristic of the document lies in the fact that it is not a normal church statement or viewpoint but a confession of faith. The introduction, the three articles, and the conclusion all commence with the words, "We believe." It thus deals with sincere sentiments and can rightly be described as "a cry from the heart," as the accompanying letter puts it. The most powerful witness available to a church lies in the act of confessing its most deeply held convictions. A confession does not pass judgment on external affairs, but declares those articles of faith which determine the very nature of the Church's existence and without which it cannot continue to be a church. For the purposes of the DR Mission Church and because of the situation in which it finds itself, the confession centers specifically on the message of reconciliation and everything which flows from it. If a church should renounce this in particular, it surely ceases to be the Church of Jesus Christ.

A second noteworthy characteristic of the confession is that it judges the situation of the DR Mission Church in the light of the gospel of Christ and thus concerns itself with the calling of the Church to relate its witness to a concrete situation. The presence of various powers and ideologies like secularism, materialism, nationalism, racism, and Marxism have forced the Church, including the DR Mission Church, into what Schleiermacher called "a frontline situation."[1]

This really means that the old distinction between "mission field" and "homefront" has fallen away. All around the world the Church finds itself in a missionary situation.[2] The confession articulates this by emphasizing the Church's responsibility to be the salt of the earth and a light to the world and its calling to bear witness in word and deed to a new heaven and a new earth where justice will reign (3, para. 1). This missionary situation requires that the church give substance to its message by its own total commitment. On the one hand it is called on to oppose those powers and ideologies which threaten the free working of the gospel, and on the other to lend verity to its viewpoint by placing its very existence on the line. The credibility of its witness is indissolubly tied to what it does and is.[3]

What has been said here stresses a third characteristic of the confession, one which is of determining significance for the Church's missionary role: whatever the Church is or does occurs in full view of the world. Early in the introduction to the confession, the authors profess their belief that the Church is the creation of a triune God who is present in the history of the world from beginning to end. The world should thus be able to discern the work of the Father, the Son, and the Holy Spirit in the life and actions of the Church. The Church's existence is integral to its message. Nothing should be tolerated in the life of the Church which imperils its credibility as the people of God. The moment that the Church loses its credibility, it ceases to be the salt of the earth and a light to the world.

By its very being the Church is therefore called to view the world with utmost earnestness. Its duty is to bring the world the gospel of God's present and coming kingdom. Involvement in and concern with the world is a basic attribute of the missionary church.[4] Alienation from the world and escapism is a denial of the triune God who chose to gather, protect, and care for his people, that is the Church, *in the world* (1). Reflection on the nature and function of the Church can thus not be separated from its missionary calling, and indeed has everything to do with it.

Seen against this background it is clear why the confession accords a central place to church unity. This unity, as the visible expression of reconciliation with God and between people, is of the greatest significance to the missionary witness of the Church. Discord and disunity vitally affect the Church as the body of Christ and seriously blunt its missionary witness and the impact of the gospel of Jesus Christ.[5] Church unity, however, remains a blessing of Christ and does not flow from human effort or church decisions. Wherever people submit to the working of his Spirit and his Word, there unity will spontaneously result. To persist in disunity and fragmentation, that is, with irreconcilability in the Church, is nothing less than disobedience to Christ and amounts to a blatant rejection of what he offers. It goes without saying that such a church cannot be taken seriously.

The Church in fact has been charged to maintain a given unity (Eph. 4:3), a unity which must be given visible substance in a world which bleeds helplessly from the wounds of dissension, strife, hate, suspicion, and divisive attitudes and relationships. This unity must be demonstrated as a "working unity" (2, paras. 4 and 7). The world cannot observe a spiritual unity,[6] and therefore the Church cannot content itself with confessing a spiritual unity alone. It should concentrate on making unity visible and practicable. The authors of the confession glean from Scripture various ways in which a fellowship of believers can grow into a harmonious community (2, para. 4). A church which sets out to do this provides the world with an opportunity to acknowledge the credibility of its claims. Church unity and mission work cannot be separated. A visible and working unity increases the missionary impact of the church in a tense and divided world. The lack of such unity not only subverts a church's witness but exposes it to a charge of willful sin (2, para. 9).

By taking its stand on this point, the DR Mission Church has pronounced itself unequivocally on an issue with a long and eventful history in missionary theology. It grapples with the question whether *separate churches* are scripturally justified and practically desirable on the grounds of natural diversity in language, culture, spiritual gifts, opportunities, background, and convictions. The view of the DRC in this matter is well-known. The separate existence of the DR Mission Church and of the various black ethnic churches is in fact its visible consequence. In a sense, DRC thinking here coincided with a specific line of thought in German missionary science. According to G. Warneck, B. Gutmann, and C. Keysser, national identity was regarded as essential for church formation.[7]

The danger in this way of thinking, however, lies in the ease with which cultural and ethnic categories can be elevated to theological principles.[8] Ethnicity becomes normative for church membership and as a result also for the establishment of separate churches. A loss of church unity inevitably results. In practice the different "ethnic" Dutch Reformed churches gradually became closed off in their own separate worlds. At the congregational level, little could be seen of Scripture's fellowship of believers across the barriers of language and national identity. Sporadic meetings between small groups from the various "ethnic" churches, mostly only on special occasions, cannot compensate for a lack of fellowship on a broad congregational level. The present system allows no opportunity for mutual closeness and exhortation in Christian love. To fall back on a "spiritual" unity which is supposed to provide some mystical bond between believers vitiates the doctrine of reconciliation and questions the use of preaching it.

On the issue of national diversity and the Church, the DR Mission Church thus assumes in its confession a position diametrically opposed to that of the DRC. In the light of Holy Scripture no other witness is possible for this church but that "the variety of spiritual gifts, opportunities, backgrounds, convictions, as well as the various languages and cultures, are by virtue of the reconciliation in Christ opportunities for mutual service and enrichment within the one visible people of God" (2, para. 5). Similarly any doctrine which, either openly or by implication, claims that birth or any other human or social factor codetermines membership of a church, is rejected (2, para. 10). The only condition for membership of the one holy, catholic, Christian Church is "the true faith in Jesus Christ" (2, para. 6).

This does not mean that race and national differences are erased or ignored within the family of God. Indeed, the act of reconciliation makes it possible to incorporate these differences in a diversity which glorifies the kingdom of God. The confession rightly rejects those doctrines which absolutize national identity or natural diversity or wants to use this diversity as an excuse to dull the power of reconciliation and reduce it to a superficial and artificial bond (2, para. 7). Christian reconciliation treats the reality of diversity and distinctiveness seriously, but only with an eye to eventual unity, the one new person in Jesus Christ, and not for the sake of separateness or self-esteem. Preoccupation with a single culture is only justified as a way by which a particular congregation can grow closer to Christ and more effective in their witness.[9] National ties should never keep Christians apart.[10] The new family of God is not constituted according to blood relationship but by virtue of the covenant, the sole and comprehensive category for establishing communion.[11] Only insofar as the Church faithfully articulates this truth does it become a bearer of a message of hope to a painfully divided humanity.

A fourth characteristic of the confession, of particular significance to the Church's witness in the world, is its clear outlining of the social implications of reconciliation. The gospel entrusted to the Church addresses man in his totality, life in its entirety, and the whole world. Acceptance of Christ, says J. H. Bavinck, affects not only one's personal life but all relationships. Society in its entirety becomes reborn.[12] Reconciliation has wide social implications. If the Church should neglect to sound the demands of the kingdom farther than just the heart of the individual, it forsakes its calling as witness and community to the kingdom. A church which concerns itself only with individual salvation while society in general denies and opposes Christ's kingship is in reality not enhancing the gospel message but impeding it. This was precisely why Protestantism in Latin America lost its chance to become a true liberation movement. According to Rubem Alves, it placed Christians in a dualistic instead of a dialectical relationship to society.[13] The DR Mission Church, however, finds itself in a situation where it critically experiences the social implications of such a stunted gospel. Significantly, therefore, the DR Mission Church in its confession has remained consistent on this score. When the people of God in obedience and through the act of reconciliation dwell in a new communion, this also opens up fresh possibilities for society and the world (3, para. 2). This spreading renewal of secular society is in fact what the metaphorical description of the Church as salt of the earth and a light to the world is all about. Thus every doctrine which aims at limiting Christian reconciliation to the walls of a church building is rejected as "ideology and heresy." The act of reconciliation which creates and maintains a new community inside the Church can also do this in society. The Church views the forced separation of people on the basis of race as a betrayal of the message of reconciliation. And the Church cannot acquiesce in such a policy without destroying the credibility of this, its own, message.

The fifth characteristic of the confession, the Church's striving for social justice (4), closely follows from the above. The confession states that "the Church as the possession of God must stand where he stands, namely against injustice and with the wronged" (4, para. 2). In a world full of injustice and enmity, God reveals himself as the one who in a special way becomes God of the needy, the poor, and those who are discriminated against (4, para. 1). He wants to bring justice and true peace to man. He therefore teaches his people to pursue what is good and just. The Church is called upon to witness against and combat every form of injustice and to sustain those in need.

The missionary church does not concern itself only with personal conversion and with the development of the Church as the body of Christ. As a living community of the kingdom, the Church also has a calling—within the horizon of the messianic realm—to participate in the battle against every form of human evil and need.[14] The message of the kingdom is one which wants to make the Church aware of those forces and powers responsible for evil, and also of the various forms wickedness assumes. J. Verkuyl remarks rightly that the extent and dimensions of a liberating messianic vision can only be grasped where there is a realization of the range of human wickedness and enslavement.[15] Once this is appreciated, a person feels obliged—in the name of the Spirit—to join the fight against evil wherever it may be. This realization is very much present in the Belhar Confession as well as in the accompanying letter. The document summons the Church to heed this call in obedience to Jesus Christ, its only leader (4, para. 4).

THE CONFESSION AND CONTEMPORARY MISSION THEOLOGY

The struggle of the DR Mission Church to be a credible witness for the kingdom of God within its particular context is not an isolated one. The question of what should be understood by "mission work" in today's world is one which occupies churches in many countries. The Belhar Confession should therefore not be seen in isolation but understood within this wider framework. Belhar has on occasion been compared with the Barmen Statement of the Lutheran Church in Nazi Germany.[16] Our main concern, however, is to define the missionary perspective of the confession, and therefore it should be read against the agonized reflection within the broader ecumenical community.

In Protestant ranks the past two decades have seen two distinct approaches: that of many member churches of the World Council of Churches and that predominant among the so-called "evangelical" churches. While all the relevant meetings of these two groups on mission strategies during this period are significant to this discussion, it is not necessary to review all those documents here. Instead, we will consider the main accents of two recent "mission conferences," namely that of the WCC's Commission for World Mission and Evangelism in Melbourne in May 1980 (entitled "Thy Kingdom Come") and the Lausanne Alliance's Consultation on World Evangelization in Pattaya, Thailand, in June 1980.

In an instructive article, D. J. Bosch has outlined the different emphases as follows:

MELBOURNE	PATTAYA
Shows a preference for the "Jesus language" of the Gospels	Shows a preference for the language of Paul's epistles.
Emphasises the present.	Emphasises the past and the future.
Begins with "man's disorder".	Begins with "God's design".
Stresses unity (at the expense of truth?).	Stresses truth (at the expense of unity?).
Believes that God also reveals Himself through contemporary experience.	Believes that God reveals Himself only through Jesus Christ (and in Scripture/the Church).

(*continued*)

MELBOURNE	PATTAYA
Emphasises the deed (orthopraxis).	Emphasises the word (orthodoxy).
Social involvement is part and parcel (or all?) of the Christian mission.	Social involvement is separate from mission, or a result of conversion.
Societal ethics of prime importance.	Personal ethics of prime importance.
Sin is also corporate.	Sin is exclusively individual.
Mission = humanisation = social change.	Mission = a call to repentance = a gathering into congregations.
The kerygma *renders support* to the koinonia and the diakonia.	The kerygma is primary; it *gives birth* to the koinonia and the diakonia.
Emphasises liberation.	Emphasises justification and redemption.
Hears the cry of the poor and the oppressed.	Hears the cry of the lost.
Considers man from the perspective of creation.	Considers man from the perspective of the Fall.
Judges the world positively.	Judges the world negatively.
There are no clear boundaries between the Church and the world.	The boundaries between the Church and the world are clearly defined.
Regards the world as the main arena of God's activity.	Regards the Church as the main arena of God's activity.
Underscores the Church's credibility.	Underscores the Church's opportunities.
Is concerned about witnessing where the Church *is*.	Is concerned about witnessing where the Church is *not*.
Divides the world into rich and poor, oppressor and oppressed.	Divides the world into "people groups".

(*continued*)

MELBOURNE	PATTAYA
Reveals a proclivity towards Socialism.	Reveals a proclivity towards Capitalism.
Highlights Jesus' human nature.	Highlights Jesus' divine nature.
Focusses attention on the universality of Christ.	Focusses attention on the uniqueness of Christ.[17]

Although the above admits of a certain oversimplification, it serves to identify the main emphases and the tendency on either side to one-sidedness.

Comparing the Melbourne and Pattaya positions to the Belhar Confession makes it clear that the confession does not fall into one or the other camp, but rather assumes a position in the center. It does agree with the Melbourne view that the kingdom of God is not a future promise but through Christ has become a present reality. Because of this, the Church has the right to call on people to realize the principles of the kingdom in their lives. The prayers "Let thy kingdom come . . ." and "Let thy will be done . . ." have tremendous missionary implications. Within this framework the Church's witness at the same time becomes a missionary appeal. It summons Christians to see their entire lives in a missionary perspective and to let something of the new order shine through. Salvation is not just spiritual, but encompasses man in his totality.[18] For this reason a dualistic view of the individual's relationship to society conflicts with the gospel and should not be tolerated. Christians are called upon to become socially involved and to strive for God's justice in all aspects of life. It thus goes without saying that any violation of human dignity by restrictive structures and systems will receive top priority in the Church's protest. The Church is vitally concerned with the honor of God and the restoration of his creation.

Therefore the Belhar Confession expresses itself clearly on the Church's responsibility to work for social justice. In this the DR Mission Church is fully in accord with the ecumenical community. As *the* community of people who claim to submit to the guidance of God's Word and Spirit, the Church has no choice but to be a disciple of and a collaborator with God in everything it is and does. A sensitivity to the distress of others and an unyielding opposition to all injustice is a necessary consequence of sharing a new commitment to God. In the suggestion that the Church as a fellowship of believers should be clearly differentiated from the world, the Belhar Confession is closer to the Pattaya view. With Pattaya, the DR Mission Church is also aware that it is God, and not human effort, who realizes his kingdom in this world. But the confession goes further than Pattaya in the view that this can also not happen *without* people. God in fact uses his new community of people to create, by a life of obedience, new opportunities for society and world (3, para. 2). The confession quite rightly avoids the one-sidedness of microethics (Pattaya) and of macroethics (Melbourne), by which the scope of either sin or salvation is distorted in turn. God is concerned with the whole person and the whole world.

The confession has not provided all the answers in the present missiological debate. Neither does it make that claim. But by according reconciliation a central position, the confession has presented a testimony which no church or institution in South Africa can ignore.

D. J. Smit

4

"In a Special Way
the God of the Destitute,
the Poor, and the Wronged"

The draft confession deals consecutively with three issues, namely the unity of the Church, reconciliation in Christ, and the justice of God. The first two issues have been widely discussed for many years by the churches and theologians in South Africa. The way in which the ideology of apartheid and its moral and theological justification handicapped the experience of unity and reconciliation has been pointed out repeatedly. At the synod of the DR Mission Church in 1978 it was consequently precisely these two basic objections which led to the rejection of apartheid. In the discussion within the Dutch Reformed church family, however, there was hardly any talk of an appeal to the *justice* of God and its implications for the Church in the South African context. The DR Mission Church has thus in a sense introduced a new element into the debate among the Dutch Reformed churches by bringing "the justice of God" into the discussion.

There must be no doubt or misunderstanding about the importance of this confession of "the one who wishes to bring about justice and true peace among men . . . and calls his Church to follow him in this." The opinion has steadily grown that the ideology of apartheid did not merely legitimate and stabilize irreconcilability and racial prejudice, but it also approved of and stabilized relations and structures in society which were unjust, humiliating, degrading of humanity, and often oppressive. Even more, it helped to design and implement such structures. From the point of view of the "black experience," the moral and theological justification of the ideology of separation is nothing more than the attempt to defend an unrighteous society on Christian or biblical grounds. In many concrete ways the daily black experience within the system differs radically from what supporters of apartheid—with their "good intentions" and "Christian motivations"—even suspect. The reasons are obvious. Supporters of the ideology of separation have gradually become estranged from both the process by which apartheid came about, when the

53

establishment of racist institutions was actually advocated in and by the church, as well as from the experience of the daily effects of this ideology on "the other side." Both these forms of isolation led to a misplaced feeling of confidence and a credulous assumption that everything was in good order. The psychological and social factors and processes which have made this gradual isolation-in-innocence possible and which still help to maintain it intact cannot be examined here. The result, however, is that many supporters (that is, beneficiaries) of apartheid even today view it predominantly in an ahistorical manner. In their opinion it is simply an ideal practical political solution, a righteous philosophy of life which affords everyone identical treatment, but does so (for the sake of peace and the identity of peoples) for everyone in his or her own place. This is the reason why even church and theological apologists can still claim that apartheid need not in theory be un-Christian under all circumstances and at any given historical moment.

Such talk about apartheid is clearly irrelevant and dangerously misleading, because something so abstract and unhistorical simply does not exist. In South Africa only one type of racist society exists—one which legally establishes and promotes inequality, unrighteousness, and discrimination in many ways. Apartheid is viewed from the black experience as totally unjust and oppressive. Though the emphasis on injustice and oppression may sound strange and even surprising, especially to the white Afrikaans churches, it must be said that the heart of the matter probably throbs here. In order to understand the deepest intentions behind the act of confession by the DR Mission Church, it is therefore of the utmost importance not to fail to see the connections within the draft confession and not to take seriously only the unity of the Church and the reconciliation in Christ while ignoring the appeal to the justice of God.

The lack of a visible and an active unity inside the Dutch Reformed church family is a direct obstruction in the way of combating injustice. The separation between congregations of the DRC, the DR Mission Church, the DR Church in Africa, and the Reformed Church in Africa does more than merely maintain the division of races—and, of course, not less of peoples! In reality it largely accomplishes the total separation within the Church of groups with differing economic standards, unequal degrees of privilege, and radical differences in education, training, and skills as well as in the degree of participation, influence, and power in society. These divisions are not based merely on innocent theological convictions about a church of the people (*volk*) and for the people, but also clearly involve sinful class prejudice and a refusal to become involved personally, yes, brotherly with the less privileged neighbor. It can easily be demonstrated historically that these factors did play a part in forming separate "churches" or "denominations" within the Dutch Reformed church family. The theological justifications were formulated only subsequently, to rationalize a practice which had been initially regarded as directly in conflict with the infallible Word of God.

Because the theological justifications were accepted so easily, the true nature of and the deepest motivations for the separations in the church are today not generally realized and acknowledged. The facts of the matter are, however, that the one body of Jesus Christ in a specific locale is torn along false dividing lines and that rich and poor, privileged and wronged, influential and voiceless, powerful and powerless, trained and untrained, are to a great extent estranged from each other in separate congregations. In this way Christians are deprived of opportunities to know each other and to learn to love and serve each other. In this way it gradually becomes more difficult—and most of the time almost impossible—really to understand and carry each other's burdens. In this way the mutual showing of love, which ought to be manifested as diaconal fellowship within a local congregation, is handled impersonally by means of anonymous contributions and the sporadic contact of "mission committees." In this way the Church finally tolerates and sanctions the unrighteousness in society, because the pain of social poverty, with all its devastating effects, its humiliations, and the concern it raises about the education, way of life, and future of the children of the covenant, can be unburdened before God, but hardly before the brothers.

Clearly, "church unity" is not simply a well-sounding slogan that can be easily bandied about. On the way to effective unity the pain of unrighteousness will be exposed in a thousand ways. This will not be easy for anyone. When a false peace thanks to segregation gives way to the true peace of knowing one another and still loving one another, we will indeed "suffer intense growing pains while we struggle to conquer alienation, bitterness, irreconciliation, and fear" (accompanying letter). The factors of "prejudice and weakness" which historically led to separate worship have only been aggravated throughout the years. Those who oppose church unity for fear of what it might imply in practice have possibly understood the tight connection between unity and justice in an intuitive way better than those who romantically advocate it.

The same observations apply to the connection between reconciliation and justice. True reconciliation is not possible without justice. A spirit of reconciliation does not simply mean to ignore, to overlook, or even to shut our eyes to injustice and guilt. The reconciliation with God in Christ did not come about in such a way either; the justice of God led to the death of his own Son on the cross. Paul wrote that it is consequently absolutely outrageous even to think that free grace implies that those who are reconciled with God can continue a life of unrighteousness. On a simple, personal level we all understand very well this close connection between reconciliation and justice. Suppose a quarrel develops between two brothers about a bowl of fruit their parents have given them. The older and stronger one takes almost everything and the smaller chap gets next to nothing. No parent would try to settle this quarrel by telling the children to show a spirit of reconciliation—they still are brothers!—and to be content with the amount of fruit they each had in the end. Any normal parent would first restore justice and only then expect of both to forgive and become reconciled. Or suppose a man commits adultery over many years. His wife knows of this, suffers because of it, talks about it frequently, begs, threatens, but without any repentance or change on his part. He does not take any notice of her pleas and even refuses to discuss the matter with her. One day everything reaches a climax. She threatens to leave him, says that now it is everything or nothing, and declares that she will go and shout her complaints up the street for the whole neighborhood to hear unless he undertakes to end the relationship unconditionally. Could he then phone the minister and summon him to talk to her about her irreconcilable attitude? Could he with a clear conscience expect her to make all sorts of concessions and be content with his promise to see the other woman less frequently in the future? Could he accuse her of irreconcilability when she rightly demands that he immediately and completely give up the rleationship and treat his wife justly?

The simple truth in these examples, which can be multiplied indefinitely, is clear indeed: everyone knows that reconciliation does not exist without justice—and for that matter, an all too easy appeal for reconciliation, without an honest willingness to listen to the cry for justice can indeed be audacious. It is therefore alarming to observe how easily an appeal for an "attitude of reconciliation" is presently used as a slogan by many white theologians (and even more by politicians). Obviously it means to many people that the black community has to endure the abundant injustice and pain of racial prejudice and discrimination still longer with patience and tolerance, helped by the promises that the white community will consider (essentially on its own) how much injustice it is willing to abandon. Such thinking is supported by a variety of warnings against "false" feelings of guilt. The most dangerous aspect of all this is that most of these appeals are made in the name of Christianity and Christian reconciliation. Those in the black community and churches who keep witnessing against injustice and who prophetically and critically keep on holding the norms of justice as a mirror in front of the South African community are dismissed as reactionaries and "irreconcilables." For understandable reasons many black Christians are at present suspicious of appeals for reconciliation, and in black circles people prefer rather to talk about justice.

The DR Mission Church, too, which is at present accused of "irreconcilability" for a variety of reasons, naturally desires reconciliation. The entire second part of the draft confession deals explicitly with the subject. One of the basic objections against apartheid is that the alienation which it promotes actually makes reconciliation more and more impossible. The confession asks, however, for a reconciliation which cannot be disconnected from justice. The accompanying letter explicitly says:

> Therefore it is that we speak pleadingly rather than accusingly. We plead for reconciliation, that true reconciliation which follows on conversion and change of attitudes and structures. And while we do so we are aware that an act of confession is a two-edged sword, that none of us can throw the first stone, and none is without a beam in his own eye. We know that the attitudes and conduct which work against the gospel are present in all of us and will continue to be so. Therefore this confession must be seen as a call to a continuous process of soul-searching together, a joint wrestling with the issues, and a readiness to repent. . . . It is certainly not intended as an act of self-justification and intolerance, for that would disqualify us in the very act of preaching to others.

The Christian attitude of reconciliation, which means among other things honest soul-searching and self-criticism, repentance and confession of guilt, a willingness to forgive and to be converted, tolerance, understanding, patience, and love, surely is present, but this attitude must not be confused with the willingness to be lightly satisfied with that which is viewed as sinful and unjust.

In view of the key role which the reference to justice plays in the confession, it is all the more striking that this is precisely the issue around which rather detailed discussions took place at the synod. Several objections were raised, explanations were given, and the formulations were discussed before the confession was finally accepted unanimously. In order to understand the unanimity of the synod, it is necessary to try to understand what exactly is confessed here; in other words, what is said and what is not said.

The logic of paragraph 4 is clear. Like the complete draft confession, it is first a confession concerning God: "We believe that God has revealed himself as the one who wishes to bring about justice and true peace among men." In the confession that God "revealed" himself in this way lies an unspoken reference to Christ and the Scriptures and consequently a denial that the statement appealed to natural theology, group projections, or an ideological and arbitrarily constructed image of God. With some well-known citations from the Old and the New Testaments this God is praised in a virtually doxological tone.

The second important logical step in the article is that several expressions are used to confess the conviction that "he calls his Church to follow him in this." Again a variety of biblical associations help to strengthen the impression that this God calls the Church to strive after the same justice and true peace. Such a faith in God has ethical implications—which does not at all mean that the Church operates as an activist on behalf of God or that the Church can fully realize the goal or that it is of importance for salvation. The confession explicitly states that the Church's task in this regard lies on the level of discipleship. This is made somewhat more concrete by asserting that the Church must consequently stand up against injustice and stand by the wronged, as well as witness against all the powerful and privileged who seek their own interest and dispose of others and do them harm. Finally any ideology which legitimates forms of injustice is rejected, as well as any doctrine which is not willing to oppose such an ideology on the basis of the gospel.

The discussion at the Belhar synod centered primarily on the statement that God is "in a special way" the God of the destitute, the poor, and the wronged. Several speakers implied that they had reservations about the idea that God is "the God of the poor" or that he would be "on the side of the poor." The commission responsible for the formulation explained that those expressions were avoided precisely in order not to create the impression of a class struggle in which God would as it were choose sides for a certain group and against another group. That which is expressed in the draft confession is simply the basic, historic biblical and Christian conviction that God is the help of the helpless. This has always been obvious for the Christian Church—although it has been frequently ignored in practice or spiritualized for the sake of convenience. Nevertheless the conviction is supported by a variety of central biblical data:* the Old Testament legislation, which protected in diverse ways the interests of the poor and wronged or powerless (the sabbatical and jubilee years, the donation of tithes, the prohibition of interest, etc.);[1] the repeated saving actions by God throughout the history of salvation to deliver individuals as well as his people from distress and misery;[2] the numerous ways in which the rights of the orphan, the widow, the foreigner, and the squatter were defended;[3] the doxological descriptions of God in the Psalms as the help of the helpless;[4] the protection of the poor in the wisdom literature;[5] the meaning of the "justice" of God as an active intervention to save and to restore justice;[6] the cutting prophetical criticism of social injustice, exploitation, and the gaping fissure between rich and poor;[7] the fact of the incarnation and humiliating self-surrender of Christ; the special role of the poor, especially in the Gospel of Luke (frequently called "the Gospel of the poor"), but also in the other Gospels;[8] the (for his contemporaries inconceivable!) solidarity of Jesus with social outcasts, the destitute, and the forsaken; the messianic meaning of his miracles, including the multiplication of the bread and his healings;[9] the moving doctrine of Matthew 25:31–46 that he who has done good to

*For a full discussion of contemporary interpretations of this biblical data, see Appendix, p. 127. The note numbers in this paragraph refer to the Appendix.

one of the least of the brethren did it to Jesus himself;[10] the charity and the striving for "equality" in the congregations according to Acts,[11] Corinthians,[12] and the Pastoral Epistles; the role of wealth and poverty in James;[13] and the warning call for an active showing of love in 1 John.[14]

The confession therefore does not operate with a number of subjectively chosen and ideologically inspired references which could be either refuted with an opposite set of quotations or ignored without harm. It deals with nothing less than the heart of the Christian faith in and confession of God himself. On the *issue* there can and must be no difference of opinion. God revealed himself as the one who wants to bring justice and true peace among people, and he calls his Church to follow him in this. There must also be no difference of opinion concerning the fact that it is a serious question which ought to help determine the actions and lifestyle, associations and loyalties, even the structure and priorities of the Church. God's justice does not in the least mean that he is neutral, unconcerned, and uninvolved with regard to human misery, distress, and suffering or with regard to relationships and structures of injustice, exploitation, and oppression. He is the God of justice precisely because he defends and protects those without any rights or those to whom justice is not being done. His righteousness is an active, helping righteousness which saves and liberates and restores justice.

Though there should be no difference of opinion on this issue, it is nevertheless clear that the way in which the statement was formulated can cause misunderstanding and create distrust. The problem does not lie in the words themselves, because the Bible as well as theologians and preachers through all ages and in all traditions uses much stronger formulations! More likely, the objections frequently come from the supposition that this confession was inspired by a so-called political theology: the theology of revolution, liberation theology, or black theology. On the one hand these fears are unfounded. What is expressed here is simply a biblical and general Christian conviction which may not be denied or neglected by any segment of the Christian Church. The DR Mission Church, including the supporters of black theology within her ranks, is in every possible way seeking to be part of the ecumenical and specifically the Protestant, yes, the Reformed, tradition. The fact of the confession itself, as well as its wording, differs in several fundamental ways from the ideological frame and the presuppositions of authentic liberation theology. Besides, these descriptions denote in an extremely inaccurate way such a wide spectrum of standpoints, frequently with radical differences among themselves, that it is not very helpful or clarifying to use such labels. In the already complicated ecclesiastical and theological discussions inside the DR Mission Church and the Dutch Reformed church family as a whole, any imprecise reproaches and insinuations, as well as misleading war cries and slogans, must be avoided as far as possible and be replaced by accurate formulations and completely openhearted expressions of viewpoints. The DR Mission Church tried by means of the draft confession to profess her convictions accurately and to declare her own position clearly, and she demonstrated that she was not content with the declaration of a *status confessionis*, because the latter could be susceptible to misunderstanding.

On the other hand, the fears we have just described are for obvious reasons not totally unfounded. It is simply a fact that the black experience plays a vital role in the life of the DR Mission Church and therefore also in the way she hears the biblical message and confesses the Christian faith. Terms like "liberation theology" and "black theology" have a positive resonance for many DR Mission Church members and officebearers. Everywhere within the Church, people are pleading for more "relevant" and "contextual" theology. Obviously the draft confession will be interpreted and implemented by many in terms of this experience and viewpoint. The confession is indeed now the common property of the Church and will obviously have its own course of operation and effect. It will gradually be appropriated, interpreted, and utilized. There is no authoritative commentary or explanation attached to it. Even the original historical intentions of the 1982 synod will not escape this process of understanding and interpreting. The confession will in a certain sense lead its own life. In this process care will surely have to be taken—once again for the sake of the general Christian confession and for the church's Reformed and ecumenical ties—that slogans and war cries, technical terms that are already ideologically tinted and could eventually create more misunderstanding than clarification, will not be used in a naive and popular way. Members of the DR Mission Church will have to pray and seek for brotherliness and understanding, sensitivity and patience, mutual trust and loyalty, accurate formulations, openhearted discussions, and a sincere desire to be one of heart and one of mind.

It is of decisive importance that the genre or mode or nature of this speaking be continually kept in mind. It is a *confession of faith,* an attempt to put into words some of the most fundamental Christian beliefs, about which there actually ought to have been no doubt, but which nevertheless (according to the opinion of the DR Mission Church) have become of vital importance in the present concrete situation. The statement is therefore formulated in confessional language. It deals with God and his saving revelation in Jesus Christ. It recalls by means of certain biblical associations, in a sort of doxological tone, central aspects of the calling of the Church in the world. In a sense it creates a new vision, an ideal, a dream of that to which God's people are called.

There must be absolute clarity about how this vision or dream can and must function in practice. That function is fourfold. This confessional vision surely provides a *view* on the eventual reign of God and on the calling to which he bids his "new creation," the Church, in the meantime. By doing this, it also shows the direction or *route* for the Church's lifestyle, alliances, priorities, and conduct in the present. In this way it provides a *test of criticism* by means of which the broken world, "full of injustice and hostility," as well as the involvement of the Church in this world can continuously be measured anew. Finally it serves as *inspiration* or reinforcement for the Church to pursue this dream with perseverance and hope, prepared for self-denial and generosity. Eschatology inspires ethics. Precisely because the congregation is expecting the new heaven and the new earth upon which justice dwells, she must strive to be found blameless and irreproachable in peace.

The document therefore speaks the language of confession, the language of faith, prophecy-inspiring language, the language of witness. This has serious implications for the way in which it can applied to political and economic affairs. Apartheid is nowhere explicitly mentioned (except in the note which explains the circumstances which led to the adoption of the confession). It is not confessed that the DR Mission Church believes in the democratic form of government, or in a system of one man, one vote. No choice is made between a free-enterprise economy or a form of socialism. No theological verdicts are pronounced about the ideal relationship between church and state. No political or economic "alternative" is presented—although, as a biblical ideal, the confession will serve as a critique held before any new policy and administration, and it will therefore remain relevant as a confession concerning the permanent calling of the Church. As a Christian confession of faith it is thus a minimum document. Only the obvious, that which ought to speak for itself, is avowed. Only the biblical dream is called to memory. Precisely because of this the DR Mission Church is confident that other Christians will be able to identify with this dream. Because of this the DR Mission Church says boldly that this is a "final" word, meant "not as a contribution to a theological debate . . . but as a cry from the heart, as something we are obliged to do for the sake of the gospel in view of the times in which we stand" (accompanying letter). This much cannot be altered. There must be no difference of opinion about these minimum truths. If someone is not willing to go along with this foundation of confession, not willing to accept these truths as a starting point for a discussion—which is of course something totally different from adopting the confession officially—but differs from it, it is clear that true unity and community, which exist only on the basis of the truth, are already seriously threatened. That which brought the DR Mission Church to the conviction that a situation of confession, a *status confessionis,* has developed, is precisely the awesome possibility that those obvious truths have become obscured, that there might be those who have to be called back to this common confession and perhaps even those against whom it has to be expressed.

On the one hand, the DR Mission Church will have to be on the alert for a superficial and opportunistic misuse of the confession. There is no easy shortcut from the biblical dream to complicated social, political, and economic realities. It is neither wise nor just to judge and reject almost any political conduct or economic arrangements outright on the grounds of the *status confessionis* or the draft confession itself. Politics remains "the art of the possible," and economics remains an intricate interplay of numerous factors and forces. Reality frequently places its limitations on both policymakers and citizens, so that nobody is really capable of realizing ideal solutions. It is therefore also possible for Christians to dream the biblical dream together but to differ (radically) on the best methods and the most appropriate strategies needed in order to realize this dream as fully as possible—and in any case never perfectly. We must leave sufficient room for these differences of opinion and display great patience—including within the DR Mission Church itself. The confession must not become a handy sledgehammer to strike mortal political and economic blows in an opportunistic way. The DR Mission Church in fact embraces many people who feel so strongly about the issues involved that they would have preferred to use much stronger formulations. And the DR Mission Church does indeed reject many concrete aspects of the South African political situation; the rest of the church's resolutions furnish abundant proof of that. These rejections, however, lie on another, secondary or derived, level. Usually they are not so clear and indisputable as the truths of the general Christian confession. For the church they indeed follow from its convictions of faith, but it is still possible that others who share these convictions can differ on the best way to put them into practice. The Christian confession is not always so directly and unambiguously at stake that those who differ from its application can lightly be accused of heresy. These resolutions must rather be seen as consequences or implications of the confession, as the conclusions that the church draws from it after analyzing and judging the situation.

On the other hand the church will have to beware of a superficial underestimation of the intention, power, and scope of the confession. Precisely because it is a confession and not merely a resolution or judgment which can easily be changed or withdrawn or whose seriousness diminishes when the situation changes it carries special weight. As confession and as biblical dream it will stay valid and will be held as a critical ideal before every new adjustment in politics or economics. The direct, concrete relevance of these issues for our time must not for a single moment be lost from sight. The DR Mission Church experiences the present political and church dispensation as a *status confessionis,* as a situation which brings the essence and the confession of the Christian Church itself at stake. In these circumstances the Church declares, with "a cry from the heart," the justice of God. There must therefore be no doubt that from the viewpoint of the DR Mission Church, this third article has everything to do with the circumstances of life in our country. Here and now the Church is summoned to stand by people in any form of suffering and distress. This requires among other things that the Church will witness and struggle against every form of injustice. Here and now the Church must stand against injustice and stand with the wronged. Here and now the Church must witness against all the powerful and privileged who selfishly seek their own interest while they disregard the interests of others and harm them. Here and now the Church must confront ideologies which legitimate forms of injustice and doctrines which are not willing to oppose these ideologies from out of the gospel. The Church witnesses in the *kairos,* in an hour of truth. A situation of confession is not a matter of timeless theological abstractions but a matter of deadly earnest.

Once a church has spotted the root of an ideology, the deepest philosophy of life behind it, and has rejected it as sinful, selfish, or discriminatory, no one can expect such a church to be satisfied with mere pragmatic adjustments and concessions, with ad hoc improvements and relaxations, or even with fairly drastic changes, which leave those ideological grounds virtually untouched. If such a church was easily satisfied with such pragmatic political conduct, it would be a clear indication that its actions had been opportunistic and politically inspired and not really theological and grounded in the confession itself. At present this issue is subject to many misunderstandings. For the DR Mission Church, apartheid is not merely an innocent political system which unfortunately did not work well and which therefore has to be adjusted and reformed. As apartheid is applied in South Africa, the DR Mission Church says, it is sinful, and its moral and theological defense from the Word of God is heresy. Whoever has realized this and agreed to it cannot be content with a disguised form of the same apartheid. For the sake of the biblical dream and for theological rather than—as is frequently asserted—political motives, all new variations and forms of the same racist attitude toward life will have to be consistently rejected. For this truth also—the fact that the confession has direct political consequences—needs to be comprehended. The irony of the present situation is precisely that people, even within the Church itself—especially among whites, the only ones entitled to vote—who think primarily as politicians in terms of *Realpolitik* and "practical realities" and who therefore ask only what "can be achieved" at present, or what is "practical," "feasible," "workable," "marketable"—these very people accuse the churches who reject apartheid as a sinful attitude toward life of "political motives"!

The third article, however, cuts even deeper than merely putting in the dock once again the traditionally accused, namely the apologists for apartheid in the white Afrikaans churches. Though the articles on the unity of the Church and the reconciliation in Christ contain some sharp criticism directed against the Lutheran and the traditionally English churches, the third article contains without doubt drastic implications for the English Christian community in South Africa. Increasingly, the assertion is being made that the deepest root of the problems in South Africa must not be sought in racism, but in class and economic differences. The Church has scarcely joined this complicated, but vitally important debate—but that it will soon have to is becoming more and more obvious. Along the way, totally new lines of division might (surprisingly) become apparent in the Church. When it is confessed that the Church must stand by people in poverty, suffering, and distress and that it must oppose injustice, the problem of how best to do so in practice has not yet been addressed. Whoever expresses this confession will have to search for ways to make at least some of it true in practice. This cannot be done by means of idealistic and eventually meaningless slogans, but only by means of a sensible and honest wrestling with realities, natural laws, and possibilities.

The draft confession should probably be seen from a double perspective. On the one hand it is the final result of a development in the life of the DR Mission Church in which the role of the church's own sons can hardly be overestimated. The time of voicelessness is past. The DR Church has gradually taken the initiative, in the Dutch Reformed church family as well as in ecumenical circles, to bear a clear and authentic witness. A historical moment in the process has now dawned. On the other hand, however, the events are only a starting point, a first small step on an unknown but decisive road. As articles of faith, the draft confession will surely also play a role in unlocking the Scriptures; it will function as "dogma between text and sermon"; it will serve as a horizon of interpretation in the preaching, catechesis, pastoral care, diaconal service, discussions, and witness inside and outside the DR Mission Church. A process of "growing awareness" ("making conscious") has already started in an unprecedented way. On nearly every level these issues are discussed and popularized. There should be no doubt about the fact that it can bring about a gradually growing unanimity in the Church. Around the fixed formulations of a confession frustrations and impatience can be restrained, while mistrust and fear of "new" and "strange" doctrines can also be silenced. The tensions which are frequently experienced between an alarmed and often unsure older generation and a disappointed and searching younger generation can also to a great extent be calmed.

One can only speculate about the role this article concerning God's justice is going to play in the immediate future. It is nevertheless a safe guess that it is going to fulfil a very important role in integrating the draft confession into the congregational and institutional life of the church. Christians do have a "catechism of the heart" (Rahner) next to the "catechism of the book." The catechism of the heart is those truths of faith which are integrated in the whole of life, which really matter and make sense and help the faithful to live their everyday lives. The catechism of the book is the truths of faith which are intellectually acknowledged as true, but whose daily relevance is difficult to demonstrate and which therefore do not really function at all. In all probability this article will become part of the catechism of the heart of the DR Mission Church.

The danger even exists that this can happen too easily. When in history the biblical message sounded too much like the slogans of the marketplace and the stage, and the gospel lost its surprising and strange element and was adapted all too obviously to the ideologies of the day, the Church often lost its own unique role and character—without any sense of betrayal or any feeling of repentance. A confession is not merely or even primarily addressed to others; it is always first of all a confession concerning the one who expresses it, concerning that person's own deepest convictions and intentions. The third article of this confession is surely not addressed to others as an imperative or call while it is intended to those who utter it only as a reassuring promise and consolation. That this article demands a heartfelt willingness to self-denial is certain. If God "wishes to teach his people to do what is good and to seek the right," it most definitely applies to the people who confess this themselves. A confession is always a two-edged sword. Words without actions are empty and despicable. It is better not to promise to go and work in the vineyard than to promise without going. Triumphalism and self-satisfaction do not belong here—"God is therefore on our side"—but rather honest self-examination and a willingness to discipleship—"are we really on God's side?" To spot the "destitute, the poor, and the wronged" in the South African situation and stand by them will demand Bonhoeffer's "cost of discipleship." There can be no doubt about that. Those who want to express their unanimity from outside the DR Mission Church "because apartheid is rejected once again" must calculate the cost of that position. And the DR Mission Church will have to know that she has spoken a bold word which will now have to be realized with acts of obedience.

5

Belhar—
A Century-old Protest

The 1982 Synod of Belhar must without doubt be acknowledged to be a turning point in the South African church history. This is common knowledge. But few people are aware of the difficulty the synod encountered in constituting the meeting. Not that it is a very difficult matter to constitute a synod of the DR Mission Church; the procedure is prescribed very clearly in that body's church order. Each congregation selects an elder to accompany its ordained minister to the synod, and the names of the representatives of each congregation must be supplied to the secretary of synod in an official letter of credence; this should reach the secretary not later than three weeks prior to the start of synod. A committee checks the credentials, and the synod is constituted with the delegates whose letters of credence meet the necessary requirements; after this, the business of the synod can proceed. One of the first tasks of the synod is to pay attention to those delegates whose credentials do not comply with all the requirements laid down by the church order. [1]

While the delegates were in the process of constituting the Belhar synod an objection was raised against the validity of certain white missionaries whose credentials were in order, but who were not official members of the DR Mission Church—a situation that clearly went against the request of the previous synod. The whole issue was referred to a temporary committee (not yet officially appointed by the synod) which could not act on the matter until the following day. The resigning moderator announced that he was not able to declare the meeting open, because the temporary committee on legal matters would have to advise synod before it could be officially constituted the next day. Synod would adjourn for the day, and the customary opening address was delivered to an unconstituted meeting.

The synod was officially constituted the following day, but only after the chairman had ruled from the chair that the recommendations of the legal committee be approved without any discussion. The recommendation was that all the delegates whose credentials met the formal requirements be given official standing at the synod—including those white missionaries against whom the objection had been made. Eight members asked their names to be recorded as opposed to this ruling.

The synod of Belhar thus started with a protest. But the protest can only be fully comprehended if its historical background is taken into account. The historical account reveals that this protest was the real driving power behind the confession approved by the synod, and it was a continuation of a protest that is more than a century old.

The controversy has its origin in the events of 1880 when the Commission for Inland Missions of the DRC recommended to the DRC synod that the colored members of the church be organized into a separate denomination, after consultation with the missionaries. The commission had not consulted the church committees of the colored members involved. The DRC synod decided on 11 November 1880 "in favour of a leisurely organising of the mission congregations of our church into a separate body, and approved the scheme proposed by the Commission for Inland Missions."[2]

This scheme, which, with minor alterations, became the origin of the DR Mission Church, did not in my judgment comply with the basic principles of Reformed church polity. It consisted of six articles, three of which can only be deplored, especially in the light of Kriel's statement that "it indicated the direction in which the young daughter church would develop and be guided."[3] Article 221 (2.b) stipulates that only those congregations who had paid one third of the missionary's salary out of their own pockets had the right to be represented at synod. Article 221 (c) required that all immovable property of such a congregation be transferred into the name of members of the Commission for Inland Missions on behalf of the congregation. Article 226 stipulated explicitly that no decision or decree of the leaders of the mission church would have the status of law, nor could it be implemented as such, before it had been approved by the Commission for Inland Missions, who had to take into account existing church polity.[4]

Here we find a clear case of domination—against the principles of Reformed church polity—in which a committee of one synod could veto the decisions of another. The Church Order of Dort, the doyen of Reformed church polity, states the principle very clearly: "No church will dominate other churches, no minister other ministers, no elder or deacon other elders or deacons."[5]

The first protest was in the form of a boycott. The authorities expected that twelve congregations would be represented when the young church was to be founded on 5 October 1881 in the "historical Mission Church, in Church Street, Wellington."[6] But only six delegates, four missionaries, and two elders, representing four congregations, took part in the event. (This historical building was later purchased by the Dutch Reformed church of Wellington and demolished to create parking space.[7])

The second protest was made somewhat late in the 1881 synod. The two delegates of the Beaufort-West Mission church took their seats after noon. After they were welcomed, the missionary, Rev. Teske, inquired whether the meeting had abided by the submitted constitution. When he had been answered in the affirmative, he made an objection and requested permission to make a proposal on the matter the following day. I quote his proposal because it contains the embryo of the protest that has been living in the hearts of the DR Mission Church for more than a century, the protest that led to the confession of Belhar:

> Moved that this gathering is of the opinion that article 226 of the decision of the synod of 1880 is not in compliance with the principles of a church—which should be able to develop and to decide freely. This article is or could be instrumental in increasing the distrust that is so deeply seated in the minds of the colored community. This article will estrange other congregations and bodies that might be willing to join the ranks of the new church. On these grounds this meeting requests the Committee on Missions to ask the next synod of the DRC to cancel article 226. If the Committee should not feel themselves free to do this, this meeting should send a point for discussion to synod in the full expectation that synod will remove the article. This meeting adjourns until after the next meeting of synod.[8]

All eight members of synod took part in the debate. Rev. Teske's motion was seconded by his own elder, P. Titus. During the discussion Rev. Teske even threatened that "if the meeting did not approve his proposal, he would not be able to go along with them any longer."[9] In spite of this, his proposal was rejected by six votes to two. Rev. Teske gave notice that he would leave the meeting and could not continue to be a member of this Mission Church, but that he and his congregation would remain under the jurisdiction of the Missionary Committee of synod, the status quo.[10]

Teske's protest did not bring about any change. It was cleverly nullified by the Rev. Pauw, who proposed that Rev. Teske should not leave the meeting but be invited to stay with them in an advisory capacity. This proposal was adopted by a unanimous vote, and both delegates accepted the invitation gladly.[11] At the DR Mission Church synod of 1891 Rev. Teske was elected vice-chairman. This, however, did not deter him from continuing his protest—now from within the DR Mission Church.

At the synod of 1891 he proposed that a committee be appointed to draft a specific church polity for the DR Mission Church.[12] Unfortunately this committee did not execute their commission because they felt that the time was not ripe for such a step. Kriel quite correctly remarks that they not only disobeyed a commission of their own synod, but also erred in their judgment. There were other factors which contributed to the realization in the DR Mission Church that the "constitution" was outdated. One of these factors was the position of the missionaries: Who had jurisdiction over missionaries of the DRC who served in the DR Mission Church? Was it the DRC or the DR Mission Church in which they served?[13]

The result of all this was that the Committee on Inland Missions drafted a church polity that delineated the authority of the DR Mission Church. The DRC synod of 1915 approved it, and the synod of the DR Mission Church followed suit in 1916. The document served as a basis for the church polity of the DR Mission Church, published in 1917. In view of the issues discussed at Belhar, article 6 is especially significant because it determined that the classes of the DR Mission Church would have supervision over the congregations in their respective areas, with the exception of the ministers, who were under the supervision of the "Mother Church," according to their own church polity. This stipulation should be read in conjunction with article 13, which asserts that the constitution "may only be changed, be improved, or be annulled with the approval of the synod of the DRC." In spite of these strictures, the DR Mission Church accepted the new constitution gratefully, since it was at least a step in the right direction, toward autonomy.

The next significant protest resulted in a painful schism in the DR Mission Church. Rev. I. D. Morkel, one of the first colored members to become a minister, having had a few degrading experiences before being ordained as the pastor of the Rondebosch congregation, quickly demonstrated leadership potential. But the election of 1948 drew him into the political arena. When the National Party came into power with their apartheid program, Rev. Morkel protested in no uncertain manner. He founded his objections against apartheid on the fact that it removed the spontaneous relationship between brown and white people. He could not accept the policy that equated black and brown, because he believed that the coloreds had strong cultural bonds with the whites. The fact that most of the members of the DRC were supporters of the National Party caused Rev. Morkel to become more and more alienated from the DRC.

He invited all members of the DR Mission Church to meet at Crawford on 3 September 1948 to reflect on ways to resist apartheid. Although there were only 116 members from 28 congregations, this gathering should not be regarded as a total failure. It elected a committee to discuss with the executive of synod ways to persuade the government to abandon the policy of apartheid. The classis of Wynberg adopted a resolution which must have had Mr. Morkel's full support and vote. The classis declared that it could find no scriptural grounds for color separation; consequently the policy of apartheid policy could not be supported on Christian principles. The classis requested synod to voice its rejection of apartheid.

Rev. Morkel was not alone in his efforts. He received strong support from the colored community. All the English-speaking churches opposed apartheid. The local newspaper, the *Cape Times,* opened its columns to Rev. Morkel to air his views. Even the DRC classis of Wynberg passed a motion in September 1949 in which it denounced the unbiblical and un-Christian enforcement of the policy of compulsory apartheid, which led to discrimination against the colored and consequently destroyed the disposition of Christ among them.

Morkel also had setbacks. He tried in vain to procure the support of the Committee for Inland Missions of the DRC. The committee members told him that they were not prepared to voice an opinion on political apartheid, but pointed out that ecclesiastical apartheid was an old custom in the DRC. In desperation he requested an interview with the prime minister, Dr. Malan, but to no avail. He was furthermore disappointed with certain actions taken by the DR Mission Church which seemed to support apartheid. He rejected the move for a separate hymnbook for the DR Mission Church, because it was "apartheid in principle" and contained words which were offensive to the coloreds. He preferred the hymnbook of the DRC, because he grew up with it and loved it. Even the name of the DR Mission Church dissatisfied him, because it implied a quality of inferiority. Why, he wondered, should the DR Mission Church have a separate book of instruction for new members? On 16 December 1949, the day the great Voortrekker monument was inaugurated and the Afrikaners held a massive gathering in Pretoria, he organized a prayer meeting, petitioning God for redemption from the affliction of apartheid. The following day a convention in the Town Hall of Cape Town "emphatically rejected apartheid, whether vertically or horizontally applied."

In 1950 the DR Mission Church appointed a committee to evaluate apartheid. This committee decided that "a discussion of this delicate issue would lead the Mission Church into the dark labyrinth of argumentation which has obscured the light of so many churches." This was a stunning blow to Morkel. On 30 September 1950 he and twenty-six members of his church council announced that they were leaving the DR Mission Church. They gave two reasons for their decision: they sought sound race relations and found that the guardianship of the DRC "is no longer acceptable to us, because we have become of age and feel capable of taking care of our own affairs." His protest resulted in the founding of a separate church, the Calvin Protestant Church.[14]

Morkel's protests, however, brought a little progress. In 1950 a very important addition was made to article 16 of the constitution: "In view of the mutual information as well as the advancement of sound relationships between mother and mission church, the Subcommittee for Inland Missions and the Moderamen of the DR Mission Church will form a liaison committee which will conduct meetings every six months to attend to problems arising from the situation under discussion."[15] In 1961 the constitution was drastically changed, and some of the rules that impeded the autonomy of the daughter churches were removed. Two points of discussion received careful attention: the authority to change the constitution, and the power of the representatives of the mother church in the meetings of the daughter churches. It became increasingly clear that the DRC realized that the DR Mission Church would not bear with the authoritative constitution any longer.[16]

It was on this point that the next protest came, in the form of a booklet written by Dr. W. D. Jonker from the Transvaal.[17] His protest was mainly directed at the situation in Transvaal, but he touched on issues that were relevant to all the DR Mission churches. He objected to the constitution because it gave the DRC controlling power in its relationship with the DR Mission Church. Only the DRC could alter any of the prescriptions of the constitution, some of them instructions which had to be obeyed. These powers concerned very important matters, such as confessions, church polity, and the structure of synodical meetings. Jonker argued that this constitution deprived the DR Mission Church of its autonomy.[18] He proved his case with six points:

1. The mother church retained its control over the DR Mission Church by way of the constitution in which the relationship between mother and mission church was arranged.

2. The mother church controlled the DR Mission Church through its representatives who had a deciding vote in the classes and synodical meetings of the DR Mission Church.

3. This guardianship of the DR Mission Church was reflected in the position of the white missionaries in the DR Mission Church. (This issue was vitally important at Belhar in 1982.) Jonker described that position as ambiguous. On the one side the white missionaries were regarded as full-fledged ministers of the DR Mission Church on absolute parity with their nonwhite colleagues. They could be called to a congregation of the DR Mission Church using the very same documents as those for a colored minister who was called as a shepherd of the flock, documents which were replicas of the documents used for calling ministers in the DRC. The only addition was a single sentence: "He must pay attention to the heathens living within the boundaries of his congregation."

The missionaries thus took part in the judicature of the DR Mission Church, and yet they were not regarded as members of the DR Mission Church, but fell under the jurisdiction of the DRC. Why? Because they were considered missionaries of the DRC? No, because then they could not serve as ministers of the DR Mission Church. A minister is expected to be a member of the congregation he serves. Professor J. du Plessis, in his book *Wie sal gaan?*, observes, "It is undesirable that native elders and ministers should have jurisdiction over white missionaries.'' But is that a biblical principle? The issue at stake in church government is not the race of the functionaries but whether Christ is using them as instruments to govern his Church. From a canonical viewpoint it is very wrong for the DR Mission Church to have no jurisdiction over persons serving as ministers in that church. It proves the fact that the DRC does not acknowledge the DR Mission Church as autonomous and able to handle its own affairs.

4. This paternalism was also visible in the stipulations regarding missionary fieldwork.

5. Even the prescriptions for local congregations betrayed this mistrust.

6. The dependent state of the DR Mission Church was linked to its financial position.[19]

Jonker suggested that the white minister should become a member of the church he served. In doing so, he would fall under the jurisdiction of that church.[20]

Again, some progress resulted. In 1965 the DRC decided to conduct an in-depth inquiry into the DR Mission Church's progress toward becoming self-supporting.[21]

The 1966 synod of the DR Mission Church was served with a report on the legal position of the white missionaries. This report was accepted by that synod and referred to the next meeting of the Federal Council of Dutch Reformed Churches. The report approached the problem from a Reformed church polity point of view, in which every congregation is seen as an autonomous church and its officebearers as the organs through which Christ governs the Church. The officebearers should come from within the congregation, not be imposed on it from without. A church is autonomous when it takes responsibility for its ministers and can supply their needs, legitimizes and ordains them, pays their salary, and has jurisdiction over them. A young church normally takes time to reach this self-supporting stage. During this development the older church usually supports the young church in different ways, but this support is temporary and differs from case to case. According to the report there should be no disparity between the missionaries and the local ministers. Because no minister can have two church affiliations, a minister ought to be a member of the congregation he serves. A missionary is a member of the congregation which sent him as long as he is gathering a flock, but the moment a congregation has been established, he has to make a choice: either stay as the minister of the new congregation, or move elsewhere to continue his missionary work.

The report analyzed the situation in the DR Mission Church as follows: The DR Mission Church in South Africa is not a spontaneous result of missionary work, although missionary work is the cause for the existence of many of its congregations. The DR Mission Church was founded because it was thought to be an ecclesiastical solution for the social issue of the South African community in the previous century, one which still exists today. Many congregations were part of congregations in which white and colored members shared their faith for more than a century. This means that this church never had a transition from the missionary to the congregation period. It was a church from the very beginning, a well-organized body with its offices actively at work. The DR Mission Church never did missionary work, because the DRC assumed that responsibility and simply added the fruits of their missionary work to the DR Mission Church.

The DR Mission Church operated under the church polity of the DRC until 1916. This was one of the reasons for the confusion on the issue of the legal position of the missionaries. That issue evoked many questions in the minds of the missionaries and in the DR Mission Church itself, as evidenced by a decision of the sixth synod of the DR Mission Church in 1912: "This meeting requests the synod of the DRC to change article 252 to allow the DR Mission Church the power to discipline ministers and other members of the church councils." This request, as well as the fact that the missionaries usually had their children baptized and confirmed in the DR Mission Church, demonstrates that the first generation of missionaries regarded themselves as full-fledged ministers of the DR Mission Church and, due to their calling and ordination, de facto members of the DR Mission Church.[22]

From this historical view the report concludes:

1. Legally there exists no reason why the DR Mission Church should be described in its constitution as inferior to the DRC, if the views of Calvin and Voetius be taken into account. Neither is there any missiological justification for this inferior position. The only possible explanation for this subordination may be the socio-economic position of the coloreds in relation to the whites.

2. It is in accordance with church polity that a minister should be a member of the congregation in which he is serving. He has been called legally to fill a post that developed in the congregation. His office grew out of the congregation. He was ordained after having received the approbation of the authorities of the DR Mission Church. He cannot be a member of two churches at the same time, and since he is not a missionary of the DRC but an ordained minister of the DR Mission Church, he cannot be a member of the DRC while he is serving as a minister in the DR Mission Church.

3. It would be very irresponsible and dangerous for the DR Mission Church to attempt to turn the clock back by changing the position of the

"missionaries" from an ordained minister in the DR Mission Church to a missionary of the DRC with no official status in the DR Mission Church. This would furthermore be a flagrant violation of Reformed church polity.[23]

As a result of this report the DRC of South Africa (the synod of the Cape Province) approved in principle the revoking of the constitution as soon as an act of agreement could be drafted and approved by both the churches. This was of great importance to the DR Mission Church, for it was busy drafting its own church order. When the issue of such a church order was raised at the DR Mission Church synod in 1970, the following decision was made: "The synod refers the drafting of a church order as well as the Act of Agreement with the DRC to its temporary committee on legal matters, for later submission to this synod."[24] This proves the significance and the contiguity of these two issues for the DR Mission Church.

The committee on legal matters submitted its report:

Our committee took cognizance of the fact that the DRC synod of 1969 instructed the liaison committee to submit a draft agreement that could replace the constitution and present it at the synod of the DRC. We took note of the fact that our own moderamen serve on this liaison committee as representatives of our church, and proposed that our synod should compose a draft agreement which could serve as basis for the negotiations and that the Federal Council of Reformed Churches should also pay attention to matters such as the position of the missionaries and joint actions of the two churches, all of which could contribute toward a meaningful agreement.[25]

The committee acknowledged that this work of the Federal Council was the guideline for their draft agreement. They also took into account Reformed church polity and the progress which had been made toward an acceptable agreement. Small wonder that the DR Mission Church was satisfied with what was proposed and decided that it would serve as the foundation on which the moderamen would have to negotiate. Synod referred the whole issue to the interim committee of synod with power to finalize the agreement—a proof of the urgency with which they regarded the matter.

From this draft agreement I cite three points which I judge to be the essence of the whole matter:

1. Both churches ground their creed and church order upon Holy Scripture and the three formulas of unity. Both churches undertake not to change their creeds or liturgical formulas without mutual consultation.

2. On the matter of white ministers doing duty in the DR Mission Church, the proposal is that they ought to become members of the con-

gregation where they had been ordained and where they served. Their membership would be terminated at their demission from service.

But due to the fact that the white ministers, when they accepted calls to DR Mission Church congregations, believed they would stay members of the DRC and fall under the jurisdiction of the DRC, they could not be compelled to change their membership; on this point they were safe-guarded by the legal principle of estoppel. This position had to be main-tained in the new constitution.

3. It is a fact that the white ministers and their families are, from a socio-economic point of view, members of the white society, and their standard of living would have to be determined accordingly.

Therefore the proposed agreement determined:

1. Any white minister in the DR Mission Church will be a member of the church in which he was called to serve, with all the privileges and obligations attached to that status.

2. He will remain eligible to be called in the DRC.

3. He will be allowed to be a member of the DRC if he prefers to have it that way.

4. On retiring, he will become a member of any DRC congregation where he chooses to live.

5. Even while in the service of the DR Mission Church, he will be allowed to be a member of the DRC congregation where he resides.

6. His minimum salary would not be less than the minimum scale fixed by the DRC for its members.

7. The DR Mission Church will supervise his ministry. If he should be accused of misdemeanor, the classis of the DR Mission Church will investigate the matter. If they find any substance in the accusation, he will have the choice of standing trial in either the DR Mission Church or the DRC.[26]

The authors also proposed that the agreement could only be changed with the consent of both churches.[27]

The moderamen of the DR Mission Church based their negotiations on this document, which had been approved by their synod.[28] They pro-posed it at the first meeting of the liaison committee, and with slight alterations it was approved and sent to the synodical committee of the DRC for consideration at the next synod. Suddenly there was resistance. This committee was not prepared to accept the proposals, because it was contrary to articles 25 and 26 of the general regulations for missionary work, the basis for all missionary work in the DRC. I quote the two articles:

Article 25(a) The DRC could provide ministers to the DR Mission Church. These ministers may be called and ordained in the DRC for the DR Mission Church if so agreed, or they may be called by the DR Mission Church, and they will be regarded as officials of the DRC seconded to the DR Mission Church, thereby retaining their membership in the DRC.

Article 26 Missionaries in service in the DR Mission Church will remain under the jurisdiction of the DRC, although the DR Mission Church will supervise their services. In the event of misfeasance, the DR Mission Church will supply the necessary evidence for the trial in the DRC.[29]

The delegates of the DR Mission Church were caught in a dilemma, because the draft agreement was clearly contrary to these articles from which the DRC felt it could not diverge. They argued that this attitude of the DRC excluded any agreement and that these articles de facto replaced the old constitution that had been abolished.

The deadlock was referred to a subcommittee of the liaison committee to see if there was any solution, but after intensive discussion the subcommittee failed to reach a compromise. The matter was then referred to Rev. Sieberhagen, the Secretary for Inland Missions of the DRC, and two members of the DR Mission Church delegation, Revs. Botha and Malherbe, to consult with Dr. J. D. Vorster, a DRC leader and authority on legal matters. Dr. Vorster reiterated that the two articles were binding for the delegates of the DRC. The only solution seemed to be that the agreement had to comply with the prescriptions of the quoted articles. The delegates of the DR Mission Church reported back to their synod in 1974 that they were unhappy about the turn of events, but had had no choice but to abide by the conclusion.[30]

The DRC did not discuss the issue in 1974 because that year's meeting was postponed until 1975. The DR Mission Church referred the matter to their temporary committee on legal matters. They came forward with a newly formulated draft agreement,[31] arguing according to very sound Reformed legal principles that the DR Mission Church is an independent church which strives to reach autonomy as soon as possible, not only in its doctrine but also in its church government and its discipline. That implies that every minister of the church falls under the jurisdiction of the DR Mission Church who will accredit and ordain him and supervise his ministry. The DR Mission Church has its own training for the ministry and accredits its candidates for service, but it also acknowledges the training of churches with the same creed. Nevertheless, accrediting candidates for office has been the exclusive right of the DR Mission Church, and whenever a minister is ordained in a congregation he becomes a member of the DR Mission Church and falls under its jurisdiction. In spite of this view, the committee was not in a position to propose a draft agreement, for the following reasons:

1. The relationship of the DRC and the DR Mission Church had never been approached from a sound Reformed legal perspective and had never been, until recently, queried by anyone. In due time the DR Mission Church came to recognize the correct legal point of view, but owing to their powerlessness to implement it, they called upon the "missionaries" involved to apply the principle themselves and accept the new situation in faith and courage and to have comprehension for the honest desire of the "sons of the church" to keep their church unadulterated.

On the other hand the DR Mission Church requested its ministers to be patient with a deep-rooted way of thinking in the DRC from which there is no easy deviation. They must take into account the immense contribution of the so-called "missionaries" toward the establishment of the DR Mission Church and guard against giving them the impression that they are not wanted in the DR Mission Church. The DR Mission Church cannot and does not want to do without their services.

2. The constitution, which is controlled by the DRC, is an obstacle on the road to independence. Any change in the legal status of the church can only be given by the DRC. The only logical solution seems to be a contractual agreement between the two churches—but for this the general regulation for missionary work is an impediment. The temporary committee on legal matters proposed that the Act of Agreement should read as follows:

(i) The Mission Church acknowledges the training and accreditation of ministers by the DRC for service in the DR Mission Church.

(ii) Ministers trained by the DRC may be called to serve in the DR Mission Church.

(iii) Ministers trained by the DRC but doing service in the DR Mission Church may be called to the DRC.

(iv) The calling, ordination, and demission of a minister who has been accredited by the DRC will be done according to the requirements of the church laws of the DR Mission Church.

(v) He will serve in accordance with the requirements of the church laws of the DR Mission Church.

(vi) Being an ordained minister of the DR Mission Church makes him a member of the DR Mission Church. After completing his ministry, he automatically becomes a member of the DRC congregation where he chooses to reside.

(vii) He will be under the supervision of the DR Mission Church according to the requirements of its church laws, but his accreditation can only be cancelled by the DRC.

(a) The classis of the DR Mission Church will investigate any complaint against him, give a verdict, and take punitive measures. He will have the right of appeal to the synod of the DR Mission Church.

(b) If the punishment is severance from his congregation, his membership in the DR Mission Church expires, and he automatically falls under the jurisdiction of the classis of the DRC where he chooses to settle. This classis can restore him to the ministry in accordance with the prescriptions laid down by the DRC.

(c) If the punishment is of such a nature that his credentials ought to be cancelled, the authorities of the DR Mission Church notify the DRC and provide all the relevant documents.

When this draft agreement was put forward, synod received it with appreciation[32] and accepted (i) to (v), but added the following to (vi) and (vii) after a lengthy discussion: "The white ministers who served in the DR Mission Church before the Act of Agreement was signed are given a free choice regarding church membership, in view of the exceptional circumstances under which they entered their ministry in the DR Mission Church."[33]

The synod then instructed its permanent committee on legal matters to make a thorough study of the following and report back to the next synod:

1. The principle of double membership with regard to the concepts "church" and "church affiliation."

2. Membership of a minister with special reference to the broad approach of church affiliation.[34]

The mere fact that synod endeavored to acquire jurisdiction over all its officebearers, proves how strongly it felt about the matter. But the entire issue of the autonomy of the DR Mission Church revolved around this problem. It was important that the DRC had to be sensitive on this point.

The moderators of the DR Mission Church reported back to synod in 1978 that they had submitted the decisions of 1974 to the liaison committee.[35] The recommendations were passed through all the required channels and were duly signed by the two moderators on 27 November 1975. But then a new difficulty arose. The DRC of South Africa was merely a regional synod of the DRC, and only an agreement with the general synod of the DRC would be valid throughout South Africa. Accordingly, the moderators gave their assistance in proposing a draft agreement to be approved by the general synod of the DRC. They used this opportunity to adapt the agreement so that it might be in conformity with the official attitude of the DR Mission Church.

This new agreement stated in article 2.1 that both churches undertake not to make any changes in their creeds or liturgical formulas without consulting one another. On the sensitive issue of the church membership of ministers it stipulated:

3.1.6 On the ground of his ordination in the DR Mission Church, [the minister] becomes a member of that particular congregation.

3.1.7 In case of church discipline the prescriptions and laws of the DR Mission Church will be applied. If he is severed from his congregation or suspended from the ministry, the actuarius of the DRC will be notified about the matter.

3.1.8 Those ministers who were ordained prior to the finalization of this agreement will be free to choose where they prefer to exert their membership. Any member in good standing of the Mission Church may lay an official complaint against such a minister at an authorized meeting of the DR Mission Church, which will investigate the complaint. If the investigators agree that there are sufficient grounds for further inquiry, the issue will be referred to the DRC.[36]

Apparently the delegates to the synod of the DR Mission Church lost patience at this stage. Synod decided to reject 3.1.8 and to replace it with the following: "All the members of the DRC serving in the DR Mission Church are members of the DR Mission Church after having presented their credentials."[37] Another proposal was rejected: "Synod decides to investigate the legal principle of estoppel and how it affects 3.1.8." Synod approved the amended agreement.[38]

I have described the course of the debate on the membership of the white ministers at length, because it became the focal point of the struggle of the DR Mission Church to procure its autonomy. The spark that kindled the fire at the 1982 synod of Belhar was a motion forwarded to synod: "Synod decides that white ministers who were requested by letter, after legal advice had been obtained, to exert their choice of membership and who had opted, either by letter or by silence, not to do so and had thus indicated that they preferred to remain members of the DRC be accepted as such without curtailing their rights and privileges."[39] This motion was rejected by synod and an amendment was adopted:

Synod

(a) expresses its concern about the way in which the permanent committee on legal matters handled the decision of synod 1978 on the act of agreement.

(b) decides as one of the contracting parties in the agreement to withdraw its participation and commissions the permanent committee on legal matters to negotiate the termination of the contract.

(c) decides that this committee, after this has been attained,

(i) reports back to the synodical committee;

(ii) notifies the ministers of the DRC serving in the DR Mission Church of the development and gives them the option of continuing their service under the new dispensation;

(iii) advises church councils and classes about the implications of the choice made by these ministers. [40]

No fewer than forty-eight members of synod requested that their dissenting vote be recorded. Thus the protest that had lasted a century terminated in the severing of ties between the two churches, a decision with profound consequences.

In the meantime, a faint ray of hope has appeared in the form of certain recent decisions of the DRC which evidence a remarkable insight into the expectations and aspirations of the DR Mission Church. Whether anything positive will accrue from these decisions, it is still too soon to tell.

P. J. J. S. ELS

6

The Role of the "Hour" in True and False Prophecy

Truth, especially the truth about God, is never as vital as in the hour of crisis. A time of crisis in the life of an individual or community is therefore also a time to make a choice. It is the occasion when both preacher and listener are called upon to ascertain whether the proclaimed message is indeed a true or a false Word of God.

In order correctly to evaluate for ourselves the truthfulness of the Belhar confession as it functions within the South African context, it may be illuminating and useful to observe a few of the most important characteristics of the nature and function of true and false prophecy in the Old Testament.

A study of the Old Testament reveals that a distinction between true and false prophecy is usually not easily drawn. Scripture itself mentions a few characteristics or criteria in the light of which such a distinction may be attempted, as for example whether so-called divine revelations have been received by means of dreams or not (in the case of both true and false prophets, e.g. Jer. 23:25); whether or not the prophecy is actually fulfilled (Deut. 18:21–22); proclamation of salvation or of divine judgment (Mic. 3:5; Jer. 28:8); cultic association or not (cf. inter alia Amos 7:12–13); an awareness or lack of awareness of a prophetic vocation (Mic. 3:5); correspondence of new prophecies with the proclamation of earlier prophets (Jer. 28:8; 26:17–20). But none of these criteria seems to be adequate to evaluate and explain the whole phenomenon of false prophecy. There exists therefore no a priori criterion by which the proclaimed message can be verified to ascertain whether it really expresses the will of God or not.[1]

A. S. van der Woude describes the phenomenon and functioning of true and false prophecy correctly when he says: ''The difference between true and false prophecy is not simply a difference between objectively verifiable truth or falsehood, between proclamation of salvation or of judgment, between religious-political establishment or personal independence, between immoral or irreproachable conduct. The problem is much more complicated and the distinction often more subtle.''[2]

The true proclamation of the biblical message does not only entail the communication of abstract truths but also the relevant application thereof with respect to the situation of the preacher and his hearers. It is precisely on account of this fact that the fine distinction between a true proclaimer of the divine Word and will and a false preacher, representing a one-sided and tendentious picture of the same, can only be drawn by that individual or church which is truly guided and illuminated by the Spirit of God in a sincere effort to seek and implement the will of God (John 7:17; 1 John 4:1).

The matter is even more complicated, since according to 1 Kings 13 even a true prophet may experience moments of insensitivity and disobedience with regard to the will of Yahweh as a result of his being misled by a so-called colleague. Under such circumstances such a true but misguided prophet falls, just as a false prophet, under the wrath and judgment of God.

According to Gerhard von Rad just such a confusing state of affairs, in which prophets who made similar claims of acting on behalf of Yahweh (Jer. 27:4; 28:2) radically contradicted each other in their theological and political analyses of the people's situation, existed especially during the final and critical period of the Judaean monarchy, that is, during the last century before the Babylonian exile.[3] It is therefore quite understandable that it is precisely the Deuteronomistic theology of this period, especially in conjunction with Jeremiah and Ezekiel, that earnestly seeks an infallible criterion for distinguishing between true and false prophecy (cf. Deut. 18:21).

Significantly, the false prophets who misled the people of God and who were challenged by the true spokesmen of Yahweh were not themselves originally pagans. On the contrary, precisely the fact that they were also from Israel and shared the same historical and theological traditions as the true prophets complicated even more the people's task of recognizing and choosing between the true and false divine Word.

Various texts in the Old Testament make it clear that the false message of the pseudoprophets resulted from its faulty origin. In contrast to the true prophet who receives his message directly from God, the false prophet, according to Jeremiah and Ezekiel, produces his message from the depths of his own mind and soul. Jeremiah puts it as follows: "Then the Lord said to me, 'The prophets are prophesying lies in my name. I have not sent them or appointed them or spoken to them. They are prophesying to you false visions, divinations, idolatries and the delusions of their own minds' " (Jer. 14:14). Yahweh's instruction to Ezekiel was: "Son of man, prophesy against the prophets of Israel who are now prophesying. Say to those who prophesy out of their own imagination:

'Hear the word of the Lord! This is what the Sovereign Lord says: Woe to the foolish prophets who follow their own spirit and have seen nothing! Your prophets, O Israel, are like jackals among ruins' " (Ezek. 13:2–4; cf. also Jer. 23:26). Their own reasoning and desires make them prophesy a message which is futile ("empty visions," Ezek. 13:7) and misleading to themselves and their hearers (Ezek. 13:6, 7). Ezekiel calls such prophets "jackals among ruins" (Ezek. 13:4) since their influence is destructive rather than beneficial. With their false preaching, they have certainly not ventured into the breach and have never bothered to fortify the House of Israel, to hold fast in battle on the day of Yahweh (cf. Ezek. 13:5); they have not attempted to equip the people spiritually so they might survive in and overcome the crises which Yahweh is to bring down upon the nation on the day of Yahweh that is about to dawn.

They are, according to Yahweh, in reality no longer his ambassadors, since they do not carry his revealed message, even though they pose as such:

> I did not send these prophets, yet they have run with their message; I did not speak to them, yet they have prophesied. But if they had stood in my council, they would have proclaimed my words to my people and would have turned them from their evil ways and from their evil deeds. . . . I have heard what the prophets say who prophesy lies in my name. They say, "I had a dream! I had a dream!" How long will this continue in the hearts of these lying prophets, who prophesy the delusions of their own minds? They think the dreams they tell one another will make my people forget my name, just as their fathers forgot my name through Baal worship (Jer. 23:21–22, 25–27).

While they labor under the delusion that they are proclaiming God's revealed will for the contemporary situation, their message is nevertheless influenced and colored to such an extent by their own interests and by the people's desires that they are really no longer engaged in God's service. On the contrary, the people and their situation are being prepared for the divine judgment and resultant national ruin by their one-sided and false proclamation (Jer. 27:15)—all because their own hearts, and not God, are speaking.

Since they do not point out and condemn that which is wrong in the life of the people, but merely present a positive picture of the nation's future, they who were to be leaders have become false guides. Von Rad comments in this regard: "As far as we can see from the relevant texts, their colleagues' proclamation of salvation was particularly suspect in the eyes of the 'true' prophets ([1 Kings 22:11ff.; Mic. 3:5ff.; Jer. 6:14; 14:13; 23:9ff.; 28:5–9; Ezek. 13:16]). It is probable that the false prophets and their predictions of salvation coincided with the interests of the national cult."[4]

On account of this state of affairs, God, by means of the prophet, gives
the following instruction to his people:

> This is what the Lord Almighty says: "Do not listen to what the
> prophets are prophesying to you; they fill you with false hopes. They
> speak visions from their own minds, not from the mouth of the Lord.
> They keep saying to those who despise me, 'The Lord says: You will
> have peace.' And to all who follow the stubbornness of their hearts
> they say, 'No harm will come to you.' But which of them has stood in
> the council of the Lord to see or to hear his word? Who has listened
> and heard his word?" (Jer. 23:16–18).

Already a century earlier Isaiah had said: "Those who guide this people
mislead them, and those who are guided are led astray" (Isa. 9:16).

Sometimes, as in the case of Nehemiah's opponents, a false prophet
was hired to oppose the representative of God (cf. Neh. 6:10–13). In
such cases he could be very self-confident and even arrogant toward the
true prophet (cf. 1 Kings 22:24–25), especially when he enjoyed the
support and authority of the state. Such a situation came up in the life of
the prophet Amos when he, as a southerner, had to proclaim the divine
message of judgment to the northern state and people at the sanctuary of
Bethel. On this occasion Amaziah, the high priest precisely because he
was actually under the control and in the service of the northern state,
tried to silence and eliminate Amos by saying: "Get out, you seer! Go
back to the land of Judah. Earn your bread there and do your prophesying
there. Don't prophesy any more at Bethel, because this is the king's
sanctuary and the temple of the kingdom" (Amos 7:12–13). Caught in
this dilemma, however, Amos did not in the least allow himself to be
deterred or disheartened. He based his right to continue preaching solely
upon his divine call and mission as a prophet (Amos 7:14–16).

True as well as false prophets did not merely deal with so-called
spiritual and moral matters. Their preaching very definitely also involved
political issues and social consequences, precisely because the God of the
Bible made use of social, military, and political processes to save or
punish his own people and other nations. This is quite evident in a
number of Old Testament passages, among which the Jehu coup d'etat
(2 Kings 9–10) and the whole political issue of whether or not Judah
would submit to the Babylonian overlords in the time of Jeremiah (Jer.
27:1–15) are notable examples. In the latter case Jeremiah does not
hesitate to intervene, by means of the divine word directed at the king and
the people, in the national politics of his time and in opposition to the
ruling and popular political opinions:

> I gave the same message to Zedekiah king of Judah. I said, "Bow
> your neck under the yoke of the king of Babylon; serve him and his
> people and you will live. . . . Do not listen to the words of the
> prophets who say to you, 'You will never serve the king of Babylon,'

for they are prophesying lies to you. I have not sent them," declares the Lord. They are prophesying lies in my name. Therefore, I will banish you and you will perish, both you and the prophets who prophesy to you (Jer. 27:12, 14–15).

For Judah this meant a choice between rival theological interpretations, namely whether or not the divine covenant guaranteed the continued security and protection of Jerusalem, the city of God, and of his temple, and enabled them to resist the mighty Babylon. If the inhabitants should refuse to heed Jeremiah's call to repentance, obedience, and trusting faith in God in favor of following the false prophets and the popular political ideas of the times, God would have no alternative but to punish them for their folly and unrepentant attitude by causing the state to fall.

In the prophetic literature of the Old Testament where these spokesmen of Yahweh address either his people or the pagan nations, it is evident that Yahweh intervenes providentially and determinatively in the affairs and destiny of his people Israel and of other nations (cf. Amos 9:7). In both Old Testament prophecy and the Deuteronomistic theology there is very often an inseparable connection between obedience to God and his covenantal demands on the one hand and personal and national well-being on the other (cf. Deut. 28), between religion and politics, and between true theological insight, genuine proclamation of the divine message and future well-being (shalom) and happiness (cf. Jer. 25:4–11). Precisely for this reason a fine distinction and a decisive choice between the true message of God, as proclaimed by his servants, and the popular opinions of the people, between the holy will of Yahweh toward covenantal love, justice, righteousness, and peace in the land and willful self-indulgence and selfish desires at the expense of the well-being of one's neighbor, are as important for us as for ancient Israel.

A closer consideration of certain recurring characteristics of the false prophets reveals that their proclamation was very often heavily influenced by an extreme form of nationalism and a selfish concentration on their rewards in personal acceptability (1 Kings 22) and material gain (Mic. 2:11; 3:5–6, 11). This created a situation in which, although they had at their disposal the same historical and theological traditions as the true prophets, they, unlike the latter, ignored or concealed certain theological truths (for example, the threat of covenantal curses) and overemphasized and misconstrued others by wresting them from their proper context (for example, their misapplication of truths like the covenantal solidarity and promised protection of Yahweh with respect to his people Israel). Jeremiah states the following reasons for such misdemeanor: "The priests did not ask 'Where is the Lord?' Those who deal with the law did not know me; the leaders rebelled against me. The prophets prophesied by Baal, following worthless idols. . . . Among the prophets of Samaria I saw this repulsive thing: They prophesied by Baal and led my people Israel astray'' (Jer. 2:8; 23:13). Evidently these prophets proclaimed their message under the influence of and inspired by the spirit of the foreign Baal religion of the "Umwelt." They have not stood in the council, that is, in the presence, of the Lord and therefore did not receive his Word (Jer. 23:18). For, says God—and this is the ultimate touchstone—". . . if they had stood in my council, they would have proclaimed my words to my people and would have turned them from their evil ways and from their evil deeds'' (Jer. 23:22; cf. also Jer. 23:14). Hence ''the prophets are but wind and the word is not in them'' (Jer. 5:13).

The real tragedy was that the false prophets who had appeased the people by means of their soothing but false messages, proclaiming to them that which their corrupt hearts were eager to hear, had a disastrous influence upon the people and their future. According to the evaluation in the book of Lamentations, offered after the fall of the Judaean state, these false prophets let the people down by not pointing out their evil to them in time (in an effort to avert the danger of their own possible exile), but rather ''have seen for thee false oracles and causes of banishment'' (Lam. 2:14).[5] Ezekiel likewise emphasizes how the unrealistic and delusive evaluations and pronouncements of the pseudoprophets were injurious to and finally catastrophic for the nation. These prophets had covered up the wrong attitudes and damaging actions of the people, but such a cover-up is like flimsy whitewash which will surely be swept away when Yahweh's storms break loose upon the national wall (Ezek. 13:10–11, 15).[6] Worst of all, it is God himself who is being dishonored and defiled by such conduct (Ezek. 13:19). But, says Yahweh,

> Therefore tell those who cover it with whitewash that it is going to fall. Rain will come in torrents, and I will send hailstones hurtling down, and violent winds will burst forth. When the wall collapses, will people not ask you, ''Where is the whitewash you covered it with?'' . . . . When it falls, you will be destroyed in it; and you will know that I am the Lord. So I will spend my wrath against the wall and against those who covered it with whitewash. I will say to you, ''The wall is gone and so are those who whitewashed it, those prophets of Israel who prophesied to Jerusalem and saw visions of peace for her when there was no peace,'' declares the Sovereign Lord (Ezek. 13:11–12, 14–16).

Ezekiel comes very close to the essence of their wrongdoing when he says to the false female prophets:

> You have profaned me among my people for a few handfuls of barley and scraps of bread. By lying to my people, who listen to lies, you

have killed those who should not have died and have spared those who should not live. . . . You disheartened the righteous with your lies, when I had brought them no grief, and you encouraged the wicked not to turn from their evil ways and so save lives (Ezek. 13:19, 22).

And how terrible it is that when the people become guilty because they have pampered and venerated their own ideas as idols in their hearts and unrepentingly have refused to heed God's admonishing call from the lips of the true prophets, he subsequently would actually allow the false prophets, as a permanent measure of punishment, to mislead the people even further unto ultimate destruction. In the end, both the pseudo-prophet and the disobedient, stubborn hearer will perish under God's judgment (Ezek. 14:7–11).[7]

Since the holiness and honor of God's name, as the holy, just, and almighty God, have been desecrated by the conduct of the pseudo-prophets, quite a number of Old Testament texts announce and portray God's judgment and punishment on them (e.g. Deut. 18:20; Zech. 13:2,7; Jer. 29:15–17; 31–32). However, the terrible force of lies and falsehood becomes shockingly evident inasmuch as it was not the false prophets, but rather the true prophets of God who had to suffer under the adamant rejection and disdain of the people, even up to the point of death. The spokesmen of God in biblical times could do very little to protect themselves and could very often do nothing more but leave their case in the hands of Yahweh the righteous judge for defense and vindication (cf. Jer. 20:12).

The final result of false prophecy is tragic and far-reaching in its detrimental effects: it fills the hearts of the righteous person, the true believer, with grief, but strengthens the hands of the unrighteous so that he continues in an unrepentant and remorseless manner with his wrong attitude and conduct. Therefore, says God, will he rescue his people from the hands of the false prophets. Then they will know that it is he, Yahweh, who has acted: "You will no longer see false visions or practise divination. I will save my people from your hands. And then you will know that I am the Lord" (Ezek. 13:23).

Perhaps the most important factor in determining whether prophecy is true or false is the fact that prophecy is not determined merely by the content of the message, but especially by the inherent interaction between the prophet, his hearers, and the situation, between the truth and the specific moment in time. The Old Testament in particular illustrates clearly that the truth of God never appears in abstraction, but is always proclaimed with a specific focus, in a particular "kairotic" moment in time. If a prophet does not honestly and correctly understand the particular time and situation, then, regardless of whatever good intentions he may have, he could still turn out to be a false prophet. Perhaps in a somewhat simplistic but nevertheless basically correct manner A. S. van der Woude describes the matter as follows: "False prophecy did not intentionally distort the truth of God, but it did not understand the moment, the hour of the truth. By so asserting, we do not launch any implicit attack on the message itself, but rather on the separation between the message (or doctrine) and life."[8]

Passages such as Isaiah 37 and Jeremiah 7, 14, 23, 27, and 28 provide classic and revealing examples of how a certain revealed truth, when it is proclaimed offhand in an undefined, one-sided manner, without taking into account the particular circumstances, in a specific situation can actually turn into untruth, into a fallacy. In order to understand these scriptural passages we must remember that it is clear from texts like Deuteronomy 30:20 and Jeremiah 7:3 that Israel's privilege of continuing to live in the promised land which God had given them in terms of the patriarchal covenantal promises was subject to the condition that they would honor Yahweh's covenantal intentions in obedience to him. God had indeed established his throne in Zion and had made the temple his earthly abode. And Isaiah the prophet did actually once, in a specific historical moment and situation in time—during the siege of Jerusalem by the Assyrians in the time of Hezekiah—proclaim that Zion would not be invaded. That was a specific promise of God to strengthen the faith of the king and people in that particular situation (cf. Isa. 37). When, however, that particular truth is applied forthwith to any other time and situation and is misused as a basis for a permanent, unconditional security with respect to the future, that theological truth then turns into untruth and false proclamation. In like manner, when the inhabitants of Judah, in following the false prophets, conceal and leave out of account the *conditional* nature of God's promise for continual security and appeal to the presence of the temple as a guarantee for their future existence, the one-sided and uncritical application of an earlier revealed truth, without taking into account the changed circumstances, has changed truth into untruth (Jer. 7:1–10). Then God says that it is "deceitful words that cannot profit" in which the people try to trust.

It was indeed a revealed truth, a covenantal promise (cf. Deut 28:7, 13), and a recurring historical experience for the people of God that he had in the past actually led them to victory in battles and had protected them against their enemies. But this protection was always related to the condition that the people fulfill God's covenantal demands (cf. Deut. 28:1; 13–15). When (as the true prophet, Jeremiah, complains) the false prophets turn this revealed truth, which is conditionally determined and applies only in certain circumstances, into an ahistorical, constant fact, then it has become a lie, a fallacy which God himself rejects so vehemently that he even refuses to listen to intercessory prayers on behalf of a foolish people who allow themselves to be misled in such a manner (Jer. 14:11–16). We can therefore agree to a large extent with A. S. van der Woude when he says:

The falsity of false prophecy lies not in one particular theological idea nor even in a theological half-truth, but actually in the restriction of the truth of God to a nonhistorical, static, and impersonal ideology which is made to serve for any arbitrary lack. The truth of God has in pastoral work (which ultimately both the pseudo- as well as the true prophets wanted to perform) its own hour, its own particular time, its own kairotic moment.[9]

The Judahites accepted as automatic and inevitable the truth that God would normally protect his people against their enemies and listened eagerly to the false message of security and peace proclaimed by the false national prophets. They consequently counted upon their own diplomatic ties and military capabilities rather than upon a return in devotion to and a repentant and obedient trust in faith, in Yahweh their God. In this way, for example, the correct political interpretation and most expedient policy became a serious point of contention in the struggle between the true spokesman of God, Jeremiah, and the false prophet Hananiah. The true proclamation of the divine Word and the well-intended divine counsel was consequently conveniently dismissed by the false prophets and the people as being national treason and a threat to state security. Those who proceeded to fight against the enemy, Babylon, under such circumstances—without divine authority—in a self-willed and headstrong fashion, in that situation in that moment (contrary to the situation of the battle against Amalek and Jericho) in reality fought against God's punitive instrument Nebuchadnezzar and hence God himself (Jer. 27, 28). He who does not understand the hour and situation correctly inevitably also does not know how to discern the true message of God for that moment in time and consequently becomes, even unintentionally, an opponent of God and a liability and encumbrance to the coming of his kingdom.

A most important and decisive question arises at this point: What does God demand of his faithful servants in the historical moment that calls for thorough evaluation and conclusive decisions?

1) God's people should first of all keep in mind, when dubious opinions and a seemingly false message are being proclaimed in the name of God, that false prophecy is sometimes allowed by God to exist as a test of true and total love for him (Deut. 13:1–3) or as an affliction and punishment by God on an insensitive and disobedient people (cf. 1 Kings 22). In this way such a people are being made ready for the judgment of God through continued obduracy in the face of the true proclamation of God's Word or through continued deception under the influence of false prophecy.[10] In such a situation God's counsel and injunction to his faithful ones are: "You must not listen to the words of that prophet or dreamer. It is the Lord your God you must follow, and him you must revere. Keep his commands and obey him; serve him and hold fast to him. That prophet or

dreamer must be put to death, because he preached rebellion against the Lord your God. . . . He has tried to turn you from the way the Lord your God commanded you to follow. You must purge the evil from among you'' (Deut. 13:3–5).

2) The Old Testament indicates how true and false prophecy may be distinguished in practice, namely by evaluating any particular proclaimed message in conjunction with and in the light of the total revelation of God received already. In such a way, for example, certain elders of Judah evaluated and accepted Jeremiah's oracle of doom concerning the destruction of the temple and city as a true message from God on the basis of a similar Word from God which the prophet Micah had proclaimed a hundred years earlier. In our case it would mean that all theological and/or ecclesiastical pronouncements on the South African situation, its interhuman relations and way of life, constantly will have to be tested and evaluated in all honesty in the light of the biblical message as a whole. This includes matters concerning which the theological debate is being conducted at the present time, as for example the question of the relations between soteriology and the unity of God's people, between the fellowship of faith and the diversity of nations, and the biblical viewpoint(s) on matters like social justice, poverty, the distribution of wealth, and the value of personal freedom and of a continued national existence.

3) A fatal characteristic of the false prophets of ancient Israel was that their own ideas and emotions, their popularity among their people, and the benefits the prophets received from them, as well as the feigned political benefits to be gained from their own insights and decisions, dominated their minds and hearts to such an extent that they were not really free to listen to the Word and Spirit of God. H. E. Freeman rightly remarks:

> Whereas the false prophet calculated from the contemporary situation which result would most probably occur and would be most in harmony with the religious convictions of the sinful people, the true prophet proclaimed things completely contradictory to outward appearances and contrary to the popular religious convictions of the people. Inspired by Yahweh, the true prophet had a holy disregard for the acceptability of his message and a personal unconcern for the consequences, with respect to his own welfare.[11]

Holy Scripture demands of us *the intentional exclusion,* by means of a careful and obedient listening in faith to what God teaches us concerning his will for our situation, of any influence by external factors, of whatever nature, which could distort an honest exegetical interpretation and a courageous proclamation of God's Word. We must carefully exclude factors such as personal or national self-interests or one's own preconceived ideas or desires—such as personal/national advancement or personal/national survival as the highest priority or supreme ideal—in fact, any institution or any attempt directed at obtaining personal gain which could harm the credibility of the gospel of Jesus Christ and the interests and advancement of the kingdom of God in our country and in the world.

4) Another challenge which God presents to us by means of Holy Scripture is that the message of his Word should be understood and proclaimed contextually. The preacher should therefore:

a) make a thorough analysis, factually and in terms of an ethical evaluation, of the situation and the circumstances within which the Word is to be proclaimed; consequently,

b) the message of God has to be proclaimed in accordance with the actualities and demands of the particular situation, at that point in time, without, however, thereby distorting the fundamental truths of the gospel. When the truth of God is related and translated in such a meaningful manner to the practical everyday existence of individuals and communities in terms of their total existence as responsible people before God, then and then only does the proclamation of the Word achieve its real purpose.

5) Scriptural passages like Amos 7:10–17 (the clash between Amos and Amaziah, the high priest of Bethel), Jeremiah 20 (Jeremiah's stand against Pashhur, the high priest of Jerusalem), and Jeremiah 28 (the struggle between Jeremiah and the false prophet Hananiah) present in an exemplary fashion the inspiring message that the true prophet and witness remains obedient to God and committed to his message regardless of any opposition from theological, ecclesiastical, or political circles.

6) God calls upon his people and warns them to distinguish clearly between a true and false proclamation of the divine Word, not only with a view to their own well-being but also because false prophecy creates a distorted image of God's nature, attitude, and will, which causes them to remain unrepentantly in the delusion and grasp of their erroneous ideas:

I have heard what the prophets say who prophesy lies in my name. They say, "I had a dream! I had a dream!" How long will this continue in the hearts of these lying prophets, who prophesy the delusions of their own minds? They think the dreams they tell one another will make my people forget my name, just as their fathers forgot my name through Baal worship. Let the prophet who has a dream tell his dream, but let the one who has my word speak it faithfully. For what has straw to do with grain? declares the Lord (Jer. 23:25–28).

7) In the final analysis it remains a precarious matter to proclaim the message of God, since it is never to be taken for granted that the audience

would recognize and accept it as true prophecy and hence as the expression of God's will. All that can be done in the end is to present to society those convictions, created in us by the Word and Spirit of God, as a testimony, in the form of a confession of faith.

G. D. CLOETE

7

"Let Us Hold Fast Our Confession"

The traditional articles of faith characteristic of the history of the Church are often treated as if they were taken directly from the Bible. It is only when church members are confronted with a new article of faith, like the DR Mission Church's Belhar Confession of 1982, that questions arise, such as: What is a confession? How does it come about? What purpose does it serve?

It is normally accepted that a confession is the Church's response to the call of God in a concrete situation. This call of God is heard in the Bible, the Word in which God reveals himself. It seems logical to accept that the Bible itself, the New Testament in particular, does not contain any formal confessions. Research in this field has, however, proved this assumption wrong, and it is now generally accepted that the kerygmatic purpose of the Bible does not exclude historical realities and the religious experiences of the first believers of early Christianity.

Differently put, the diverse forms in which the biblical proclamation is presented also include the possibility of the expression of faith by means of confessions. The complex manner in which the biblical message is presented to us, namely as proclamation, as admonition, as instruction, and as catechism, makes it difficult to identify specific forms, like confessions.[1] A concrete New Testament example is provided by the document generally known as the letter to the Hebrews. It is in itself a puzzling piece of Scripture, not least because it contains various allusions, obviously clear and understandable to its recipients, that present the reader of today with challenging problems.

One of the significant traits of Hebrews is that it uses the concept *homologia,* or confession,[2] in such a way that it suggests that it was intended in a formal or definite sense. This possibility, including the resulting questions as to the nature and content of the supposed confession, has been the subject of thorough research.[3] In this chapter I will restate some of those arguments and comment on the possible ways in which this letter could have been understood by its readers. In order to do

93

this it seems first of all necessary to discuss those sections where the relevant concept is used.

The first example is Hebrews 3:1: "Therefore, holy brethren, who share in a heavenly call, consider Jesus, the apostle and high priest of our confession."

The words "our confession" enhances the idea that this is a formal confession.[4] The question is whether the content of this so-called confession is also expressed in verse 16 or perhaps even in verse 2. (Verse 1a will not be considered here, since it is only the mode of address.) The following can be noted:

The word "consider" is followed by the object which supposes the normal flow of the sentence. Verse 2 also confirms this continuity.

The words "the apostle and high priest" together with the name "Jesus" could form the confession. This is supported by the use of the definite article, which should be applied to both names. Although it is brief, this is not necessarily an objection, because the early Christian confessions are conspicuously concise (see 1 Cor. 12:3). There are, however, theological objections against arguing that these words form a confession, the primary one being that nowhere else in the New Testament is Jesus referred to as either apostle or high priest, much less as both. It also seems unlikely that this might be an excerpt from an existing confession. "Jesus" can be read both as subject and object, but this contributes little toward solving the problem.

Thus, the confession referred to in 3:1 probably refers to a confession in some other context, which could be inside or outside the letter. If one considers the content of the letter as a whole, the titles "apostle" and "high priest" used to refer to Jesus Christ in this text refer to other basic themes that are developed by the author.

The second occurrence of the word "confession" comes in Hebrews 4:14: "Since then we have a great high priest who has passed through the heavens, Jesus, the Son of God, let us hold fast our confession." Here again the impression is given that what is referred to is a confession in a formal sense. This is strengthened by the verb "hold fast," which here means to cling tightly to, to grip, and may refer to something with a dogmatic content. Once again, it is not clear whether the confession referred to is actually stated in this verse. The first part of the verse (4:14a) is meant to relate to 2:17 and 3:1. Another factor which casts doubt on the presence of the confession is the reference to Jesus' heavenly journey, since confessions in early Christianity tended to emphasize his earthly work of salvation.

Verse 14b, "Jesus, the Son of God," however, strongly lays a claim to be at least part of the confession. This expression is well-known from earlier tradition (Mark 1:1; Matt. 16:16; John 20:31). In addition, it is in a more complete form, "Son of God," instead of "Son" only, as in 1:2, 8 and 3:6. This is followed by the characteristic exhortation. In summary, we can state that 4:14 has very clear indications of containing a confession in the words "Jesus, the Son of God," but whether it can be regarded as the complete confession referred to in this letter is doubtful (see also Acts 8:37).

The third instance is found in Hebrews 10:23: "Let us hold fast the confession of our hope without wavering, for he who promised is faithful." Again, one is left with the impression that here we have a reference to a formal confession, although the content is not mentioned. This is supported by the verb "hold fast," which here has the meaning of anchorage[5] and is strengthened by the qualification "without wavering," to underline the idea of steadfastness. The cultic atmosphere of the context in which this exhortation appears also supports the idea of a fixed formula. There is an interesting relationship to the idea of "hope"; "hope" is here regarded as the object (and not the action) and is as such not unusual in the New Testament. Christ is also called "our hope" in 1 Timothy 1:1. The reference to a confession which focuses on Jesus gains an eschatological dimension with the addition of the concept of hope.

In addition to these three instances, the verb "confess" occurs two other times in Hebrews. Of these, only 13:15 is of any significance: "Through him then let us continually offer up a sacrifice of praise to God, that is, the fruit of lips that acknowledge ["confess"] his name." Here professing the name of Christ is likened to the bringing of a sacrifice of praise in the Old Testament (Lev. 7:12; Ps. 50:14,23).[6] The cultic context of the words is again very obvious (cf. also verse 16). Even so, the use here is not so much a matter of a formulated confession as it is a natural expression of the glorification of God. The author's choice of the verb "confess" is somewhat striking, since another, more logical choice could have been made, but his situation probably determined his choice.[7]

There seems to be a consensus that if Hebrews includes a confession at all, the opening verses 1:1–4 are the strongest candidates: "In many and various ways God spoke of old to our fathers by the prophets; but in these last days he has spoken to us by a Son, whom he appointed the heir of all things, through whom also he created the world. He reflects the glory of God and bears the very stamp of his nature, upholding the universe by his word of power. When he had made purification for sins, he sat down at the right hand of the Majesty on high, having become as much superior to angels as the name he has obtained is more excellent than theirs."

The position of this passage as the introduction to the letter (the rest of the letter being a kind of exposition), its clear poetic style and liturgical structure as well as the high concentration of theological truths it contains are all indications that it is ideally suited to be the confession alluded to later in the letter. Put another way, it is clear that this passage forms a carefully formulated and artfully constructed unit. Whether one should consider all four verses or only parts of them as belonging to the confession requires further investigation.[8]

The letter begins differently from other New Testament letters in that it does not start with a salutation. It instead has a peculiar, formal introduction, probably meant to introduce the most important themes which are developed in the rest of the epistle. From a grammatical viewpoint, it is clear that certain phrases resemble or at least reflect traditional forms. Verse 1 seems to be the author's own creation, although in structure it is reminiscent of the opening of the Gospel of Luke. The subject of the principal clause in verse 2 is God, and it has two subordinate clauses in verse 2, both based on forms from tradition. Verse 2b points to Christ as the heir and is supported by other New Testament references, such as Galatians 4:7 and Romans 8:17. That means that we actually have two subjects, God and Christ. Verse 2c in turn points to Christ as the mediator of creation, a familiar theme with Paul (1 Cor. 8:6; Col. 1:15ff.). It seems, therefore, that the author either purposefully set about creating this with particular linguistic skill and artistic ability or made use of an existing song or psalm which he adapted to form this pericope. Since these are themes that he later develops in greater detail (6:17–20 and 9:15 on the heirship and 11:3 on the creation), the evidence suggests that the author relied on his own creativity in composing the pericope. Verse 4 also shows some characteristics of a song which correspond to Philippians 2:5–11 (see also 1 Clem. 36). Again, however, in content as well as structure, the passage in verse 4 is immediately connected with what follows and does not stand alone as a single, cohesive unit.

Finally, attention should be paid to verse 3. The following is significant: the verse starts with *hos* (''who,'' or ''He'' [RSV]), generally accepted as a possible beginning to a song. The subject has now changed from ''God'' to ''the Son.'' The content can clearly compare with the christological hymns found in Colossians 1:15–20, Philippians 2:5–11, and 1 Timothy 3:16. It is, however, possible that this section underwent certain redactional adaptations, such as the inclusion of the words ''when he had made purification for sins,'' which the author integrated in a masterly way with the existing material. The indications are that it is possible that the confession referred to by the author is, although not totally, at least partially present in 1:3. This fragment of confession, like the others, contains such basic characteristics as references to the preexistence of the Son, the Son as the image of God, the Son as mediator and supporter of creation, his humiliation and exaltation, etc.

Our conclusion with regard to Hebrews 1:1–4 is that it contains enough stylistic and traditional features to support the supposition that this could be a section which functions, if not totally, then at least partially, as a confession with a liturgical purpose.[9]

In sum, the following points are significant:

1. The strong parenetical, catechetical (6:2), liturgical, and cultic character of the epistle creates an atmosphere and context in which a confession could fulfill a logical function.

2. The way in which the concept "homologia" is treated, namely as if it is a fixed formula, further supports this impression. This must also be seen in view of the late date of this letter.

3. The letter in general tends to refer to and depend on the traditions of the past, as demonstrated by its repeated references to the Old Testament.

4. On the question whether the confession mentioned by the author is itself contained in the letter, the following should be kept in mind:

No section can be identified explicitly as being this confession.
The strongest candidate as the confession is 1:1–4, with verse 3 of specific importance. This passage occurs at the beginning of the letter; it has a unique literary character and composition; and it has a high concentration of theological content. Another candidate, however, is 4:14, which corresponds with other texts in the New Testament.

Whether it is actually recorded in the letter or not, the central focus of this confession is Jesus Christ, the Son of God, which means that it has a very strong christological emphasis. In the rest of the epistle the author elaborates on it and attempts to apply it to the concrete situation of the congregation he is addressing.

Perhaps even more important than the question whether we can trace the form and structure of this confession is the question concerning its function. To answer this question we must examine the circumstances of the people to whom it is addressed. It seems that this congregation existed in the periods of early Christian persecution, probably during the reigns of Nero and Domitian.[10] The letter gives clear evidence of physical suffering (13:3). The intimidation to which the readers were subjected included arrests, followed by torture and the confiscation of property (10:32–34). The author does more than simply recount the vicissitudes of human existence in general; he describes the experiences of the believers in this specific situation. It seems logical to conclude that they recognized in the actions of some human being or other the work of the devil: with power over death (2:14); as a being who should be feared; whose tyranny caused them to resort to prayer and tearful pleas; who forced obedience on them (5:7–8) and subjected them to slavery, etc. It is clear that these were people who were living under extreme forms of oppression in which they showed all the emotional reactions that could be expected under such circumstances.

As is often the case in such instances, these external threats gave rise to problems within the congregation. These included weak leadership, that is, leaders who proclaimed the gospel but who were not prepared to face the consequences thereof themselves (13:17). Others tried to exploit the situation by proclaiming a false gospel like the worship of angels, thereby leaving the believers a theology of escapism (chapter 2). The delay of the parousia, which could have meant their deliverance from these oppressive circumstances, was a great disappointment to them. In addition to this, the people were probably not in an advanced state of religious development and growth (5:11; 6:8), which made the whole situation suitable for apostasy, unfaithfulness, and a deterioration of morals (13:3–4).

There is a reasonable consensus that Hebrews, according to its structure, should be seen as a homily, a sermon, or a compilation of sermons drawing from both the Old Testament and Christian tradition. The author used a method of integrating and interchanging doctrinal and exhortative material, closely linking dogma and ethics. This makes this document almost unique in the New Testament. He depended heavily on the traditional material concerning the suffering, death, and exaltation of Christ, referring frequently to his suffering and exaltation (2:10; 12:2–3), his obedience according to the Gethsemane tradition (5:8; 10:5–9), his victory over death (2:14; 13:20), his ascension (4:14; 9:24), and his seat on the right hand of God (1:3; 8:1; 12:2).

With this method of integrating and interchanging, the author attempted to illustrate the meaning of the confession in such a way that it could serve as an anchor of the soul (6:19) and an inspiration to bewildered people. To put it another way, the author actualized the confession and made it the living Word of God to the suffering people (4:12) who were to listen to it and unite it with faith (4:2)—that is, obey it. In this way the confession was to become a *kairos*-confession to them, the voice of God "today," to exhort and console them.

The problem expounded in this letter can be put in the form of a simple question: Is it worthwhile to be a Christian under such circumstances? Or, putting it differently: What is the sense of believing in Jesus Christ? The letter is an attempt to answer these questions with a word of exhortation, not in the sense of rebuke or admonition, but rather in the sense of consolation and encouragement.[11] The author compares their situation with that of the people of Israel wandering in the desert on their way to the promised land.[12] Like ancient Israel, repeatedly tempted to return to Egypt, so these people also show signs of a yearning after their previous lifestyle and religious experiences.

The author's *solution* to this problem, the one advanced so often in Israel's history, is to convince the people that to persist is in the end more advantageous. Persisting requires two elements: holding fast to the traditional Christian confession and being able to depend on and follow trustworthy leadership. He combines these two requirements and superbly relates them to Jesus Christ, the Son of God. By comparing his person, life, and work with different characters, functions, and cultic activities of the old covenant and Israel's past history, he wants on the one hand to maintain a continuity while on the other pointing out the discontinuity which has come into being with the coming of Christ. At the same time he is able to hold up some of these figures as examples of faith worth following (chapter 11), without failing to point out immediately the perfect example (12:1–4). He refers to the timelessness of Jesus Christ who is the same yesterday, today, and forever (13:8) and in this way makes Jesus applicable to the present context. He now calls Jesus by different names—mediator, pioneer, perfecter of our faith—all of them efforts to make him relevant to the wandering people of Hebrews. In this respect two names in particular are related to the confession: "apostle" and "high priest."

The use of the name "apostle" applied to Jesus is unique. The word is probably not meant here in its technical sense, but is used rather to emphasize the function of Jesus as the messenger of his Father, a popular theme also in the Gospel of John. In John, that theme indicates the authority with which Jesus reveals the will and the Word of God. In Hebrews the meaning is the same, as the comparison with Moses makes clear. The role of Moses is dealt with in a comprehensive way;[13] even in the Old Testament, it was clear that Moses' priestly leadership was subservient to his prophetic task. In Hebrews Moses is pictured as a messenger of God, who bears witness to God, who speaks to the people in the name of God. In this his loyalty to God and to his task becomes clear. The Logos theology of chapters 3 and 4 stresses the fact that God is the first subject of the letter (1:1).[14]

Moses and the embittered, disobedient people of old who hardened their hearts now serve as models for the present people and their leaders. Moses knew what the consequences for his people would be when they disobeyed God's word, and for this reason he offered himself as a sacrifice, something that probably could not be said of the present leadership. For this reason also some people died in the desert and did not enter into the "rest" (3:11). Jesus Christ, the Son, is the last messenger of God. God spoke through his Son and he fulfilled his mission even until his death on the cross. Since he is the last messenger or "apostle," speaking the final word, he is more than merely an example: he has become the initiator of our salvation. In this respect he even exceeds the other messengers of God, namely the angels, even though they were also able to speak words attesting to God.

To make the confession real for his readers, the author applies the title "high priest" to Jesus. This title dominates the content of the letter. He interprets the earthly life of Jesus as one great priestly ministry and pays special attention to the important moments of his incarnation, his death on the cross, and his ascension. True to his method of referring to the past, he now compares Jesus' work first with Aaron, the representative of the Levitical priestly office of the old covenant, and, surprisingly, also with Melchizedek, the priestly king. He brilliantly indicates the strong resemblance between the Son of God and this mysterious figure from Old Testament times. Both are kings of justice and peace, both are without an ordinary father and mother, without a genealogical table, without a beginning of day or an end of life. Both also represent a priesthood which is everlasting. According to the author of Hebrews, the Levitical priesthood became subservient to that of Melchizedek when this priestly king met Abraham, since Abraham had to give him a tithe.

Unlike the name "apostle" which emphasizes the faithful transmission of the Word of God, the emphasis in "high priest" is on the brotherhood of Christ as it comes to the fore in his incarnation. This implies, of course, his humiliation, since in becoming incarnate he became less than the angels. As man he furthermore experienced fully the existence of man, his weaknesses and temptations, in all respects other than sin. In a dramatic description the author sketches the lowest point of human existence, namely man's suffering. In this Christ also became equal to us, even unto his death on the cross. This is the culminating point in his solidarity with man.

The author elaborates on a number of people from Hebrew tradition who could be called heroes of faith. The dominating characteristics of their lives were those which enabled them to suffer with the oppressed. He again portrays Jesus as the perfect example, the pioneer, the perfecter of our faith who, despising the shame, endured the cross. Jesus' signs of solidarity with humankind show him to be a merciful and faithful high priest, reconciling the sins of the people to the throne of God. By way of comparison the author also indicates the shortcomings of the Aaronitic and Levitic priesthood: its repetition of sacrifices, the succession of high priests, the necessity of sacrifices for the priest's own sins, etc. He consequently shows that these cultic and ritual acts, the covenant in the old dispensation, and the law all lost their meaning in the light of the unique and perfect sacrifice of Christ on the cross.

Another characteristic of Hebrews' interpretation of the high priestly office is its continuation in heaven, where Christ now sits at the right hand of the throne of God. His compassion with his people who suffer is not only a unique but past event. He still shares in the suffering of those who are tortured and are martyrs and pleads for them with God. In this way he is the originator of eternal salvation.

Thus, by using the designations "apostle" and "high priest" the author attempts to make Jesus Christ, and thereby "the confession," relevant for the people in their oppressive situation. This is his way to summon them to hold fast to the confession. It is also clear to him that in this manner the confession can fulfill the function of an anchor for the soul, a symbol of hope. Combined with reliable and credible leaders, it can also serve as a force against inner weaknesses such as dejection, infidelity, and even bitterness; it can help to resist external threats, like heresy and prosecution; and it can strengthen the people spiritually and morally against adultery, covetousness, etc.

It is the author's purpose to maintain the unity within the congregation (10:25).[15] Nobody should lag behind or deteriorate in the grace of God (4:1). They should support each other and encourage one another through concrete deeds of benevolence and charity and in this way show their solidarity with one another.

The confession should also remind them of the ultimate foundation of their faith, which is the reconciling work of God in Christ, the high priest. It should result in their absolute assurance of faith. The mediatory work of Christ should not be made cheap by deliberate and willful sin after they have come to a knowledge of the truth (10:26), because this will lead to a terrible judgment in which the opponents of the truth will be destroyed.

Finally, this confession serves to assure justice for those who hold fast to it. The present experiences of castigation should be seen as discipline, and although such experiences now bring sadness rather than joy, they nevertheless will ultimately result in the peaceful reward of justice for those who experience them. By carrying abuse with him outside the camp, Christ enables the people of God to reaffirm for themselves that they will reach the future city and will enter into his "rest" (3:18). In this manner they also give account of the hope inside them. For this reason, the confession is also named "the confession of hope" (10:23).

Hebrews then is a letter written on the basis of a confession. Of this confession we know little, possibly only that the author used excerpts from it which he applied and interpreted in an attempt to make it relevant for a congregation living in a situation of crisis. His answer to them in their struggle is clear: it is certainly more than worthwhile to persevere in faith and to hold fast in word and deed to their confession.

The DR Mission Church has drafted a confession accompanied by an explanatory letter. It is not intended to replace any previous confession, but is in fact based on them. Indeed, the draft confession is intended to make these traditional confessions real in such a way that the oppressed people of this country, who may tend to go astray, are called back to faith, that those who tend to become weak may be encouraged, that those who tend to doubt may find new hope.

8

Concerning Confession
in the Local Church

In the DR Mission Church, the word "confession" has achieved sudden life and prominence since that day in October 1982 when synod adopted its draft confession.

All at once, fundamental questions came up in the local churches concerning the Church and its confession. It is of course a basic responsibility of every local church to reflect deeply upon itself and its confession in this world. And only by deliberately entering into this process of reflection and accounting which the draft confession has set in motion will local churches experience the resultant deepening and enriching of the life of the Church.

MANY CALLINGS

The congregation fully shares in the life in this world, where, as the Church of Jesus Christ, it has many callings manifested in several different ways.

—It is called to be a therapeutic community concerned with the healing and curing of injury and illness.

—It is called to be a body, a fellowship of believers in the Lord Jesus Christ where lonely people find neighbors in the family of God.

—It is called to be a diaconal service organization, taking the need of the world to heart and going out to relieve distress in an attempt to make the world a better place in which to live.

—It is called to display missionary and apostolic zeal, to go out into the world—including the world of the neighbor close at hand—and to make all people disciples of Jesus Christ.

—It is called, in this world, to be the place where salvation is found, the salvation which the man of Nazareth brings.

The congregation has many callings, which it fulfills not only in what it does but also in what it is. The local church, wherever it exists and wherever it works, is of necessity a confessing church.[1] It is called to confess. It does not *have* a confession in the way it has a church building, or a service set for communion, or even a minister. It *is* a confessing community or it is no true church. Its confession is at its heart and thus throbs through the whole body. It is not a thing which is taken out by the congregation on occasion, perhaps to amuse and entertain guests, or even to alarm and shock them. Nor is confession an emergency measure. It is the character of the Church's faith inscribed in its soul.

CALLED TO CONFESS

It is clear then that the congregation is called to confess the Lord (Matt. 10:32; Heb. 13:15). This is not merely a once-and-for-all word concerning him that the Church can get off its chest and be finished with. The Church never completes this responsibility. It goes on continually. If the congregation is truly alive, it always has a confession to make in this world.

This confession is expressed in words, in deeds, and in creeds. The believer and the congregation declare themselves before God, before their brothers and sisters—their fellow believers—and before the whole world. It is spoken and acted upon simply and directly, in an easily understood manner. It proclaims its faith: "I believe in God the Father almighty, maker of heaven and earth . . ." (The Apostles' Creed).

It witnesses to its only comfort in life and death: "That with body and soul, both in life and in death, I am not my own but belong unto my faithful Savior Jesus Christ" (Heidelberg Catechism, answer 1).

It states its convictions: "We believe that God by his lifegiving Word and Spirit has conquered the powers of sin and death, and therefore also of irreconciliation and hatred, bitterness and enmity; that God by his lifegiving Word and Spirit will enable his people to live in a new obedience which can open new possibilities of life for society and the world" (From paragraph 3 of the draft confession).

Thus from generation to generation we hear from the heart of the Church its confession.

CONFESSION AND CREED

The confession of faith demands from the Church a creed. These two necessarily go hand in hand: first the confession, then the creation of creeds.[2] Thus it becomes possible by means of confession *to unite believers separated from one another by the centuries*. The local church today confesses its faith in words used by the new converts when they were baptized in Jerusalem and Rome in the second century and in words used by Guido de Brés in his Belgic Confession of 1561 and by the Synod of Dordrecht in 1619. The congregation of today carries the ancient confession into the future from day to day and establishes it anew in the heart of the young generation. The congregation thus identifies with its history. But the creed not only unites believers over the centuries. The creed and the act of confessing *unite believers spread out over all the world.* Believers in Cape Town confess they are one in Spirit with the Church of Jesus Christ scattered in many places far apart: an underground church in Moscow; a scarcely visible minority in Tokyo; a revered cathedral in Europe; a pleasant gathering under the blue sky at an outpost somewhere in tribal Africa.

If the confession were not expressed in a creed it could hardly serve to span time and space for believers.

LITURGICAL FUNCTIONING

The congregation confesses its faith in this world. This is done through its members as they scatter throughout society in everyday life. And it is done when the congregation assembles for structured worship.

When the congregation confesses its faith in worship it rises and stands. It speaks or sings its confession, or the worship leader reads it aloud and the congregation agrees in its heart. But however it is done, it is always done solemnly and with great conviction, counting on the sincere participation of every member.

It is thus appropriate for the congregation to stand as it confesses its faith. The church which confesses is but a pilgrim on the way to the ultimate destination. The confession is the pilgrim song of the believing crowd, the marching song of the Church as the *militia Christi,* the warriors of Christ. The confession of faith is also a sign of contradiction and conflict. Those who pronounce this confession also express that they accept the consequences. They implicitly declare themselves willing if necessary to confirm the confession spoken by mouth with the confession spoken by their own blood.[3]

In a liturgical setting, the confession may be used in different places depending on the specific function or meaning to be highlighted. The confession of faith can *follow the confession of sin* and the assurance of pardon. Here, the confession of faith is an act of acceptance of the forgiveness of sins and the pardon that comes in and through Jesus Christ. It is the joyful confession of the heart which lives by grace, which knows itself to be delivered and wholly pledges itself anew to the one who has saved it.[4] Traditionally this is the way in which the confession functions in the liturgical order of the Dutch Reformed churches. The confession of faith can also *follow the lesson.* The purpose then is "to set forth the whole Gospel of which the Scripture lections have proclaimed a part. It epitomises the Christian revelation to which the Bible as a whole bears witness.''[5] Here the confession of faith becomes an act in which the congregation anchors itself anew in the whole Word of God and binds itself to a life rooted in this Word.

The confession of faith can also *follow the sermon and the prayer*. Then it functions as the short and concise reply of the congregation to the whole service, but especially to the preaching.[6] Following this the congregation is blessed and dismissed to go back into the world. Here the confession is a declaration of willingness to serve God and his kingdom in the world all through the ensuing week.[7] Or at this point in the liturgy but before the blessing and dismissal, the congregation can go to the communion table. Then the confession becomes, as it has been traditionally, the symbol of the separation between believers and nonbelievers. Only believers are allowed at the table of the Lord. Here the confession is the bond of unity within the fellowship of believers preparing to eat the bread and drink the wine, the body and blood of Jesus Christ. By expressing this unity they also separate themselves from the world. But wherever the confession may be used in the liturgy—and it is good to change the order occasionally—true confession is always ''a testimony of faith, a *martyrium*. It is a willingness to stand for Christ, by word and deed, by life and death. It is the attitude of the baptized congregation.''[8] With the confession we repeat and confirm anew our baptismal vows in every service.

The Church has always held that in the worship service only those confessions which are universally accepted by the Church of Jesus Christ are to be used. Therefore the ecumenical creeds are used in the liturgy. The Eastern Orthodox churches and the Roman Catholic Church primarily use the Nicene and the Protestant churches the Apostles' Creed. But churches cannot simply rest contented with the fundamental creed. In its own way, following the light given to it in its unique circumstances, every church must continually attend to its confession and if necessary spell out in greater detail the truth of its confession concerning a given article of faith. This is what accounts for, for example, the Belgic Confession and the Canons of Dort. But these elaborations do not function liturgically in a direct way. In the liturgy only the voice of the entire Church should be heard. Therefore the draft confession—even after it has been given final form by the synod—will not function in the liturgy directly, as the ecumenical creeds do.

This however does not indicate that nonecumenical confessions have no bearing on the liturgy. When the congregation rises, saying: ''I believe . . . ,'' then that brief confession is representative of the total confession of the congregation. In this liturgical act of confession the total faith of the congregation as it is expressed in all of its creeds is drawn into the worship service, into the liturgical event. In this way the draft confession also functions as part of the liturgical confession of faith in the worship services of the local DR Mission churches. The draft confession, among others, spells out in greater detail what the Church means when it professes to believe in a ''holy catholic Church.''

There is another significant aspect to be considered. If the total confession of the Church is to be drawn into the liturgical event, then it is accomplished in this act, placed within the framework of the total life of the Church represented in the complete worship service. Therefore every time the congregation professes its faith—including only a specific article of faith like the draft confession—it is an act which is rooted in the confession of sin and the reality of the forgiveness of sins in and through the Lord Jesus Christ. And it is an act in which the congregation again anchors itself in the entire Word of God and sets itself up against the world and against false belief. And it is a bond which binds it to the fellowship of believers, affirming the baptismal vows. And it is the presupposition of the communion at the table of the Lord. And finally it is a sign of readiness to stand for the Lord Jesus Christ in word and deed in life and death.

CREED AND SCRIPTURE

The creed carries great authority in the Dutch Reformed family of churches, which protect their confession by means of doctrinal discipline. But the confession does not have absolute authority; it stands under the authority of the Word of God. Scripture is above the creed. The life of the Church stems from the Word of God and not from the creed. The confession must be a servant of the life given by the Word: ''In the confession the church expresses that which she has extracted from Holy Scripture as the truth of God.''[9] The confession, then, is a short summary of the teaching of Holy Scripture regarding fundamental truths, and every detail of it must be grounded in the Word. It is a work of man always subject to the test of Scripture. Any article of the creed must fall away if it becomes evident that it is in conflict with the teaching of the Word.

However, we adhere to the confession *not to the extent that* but *because* we believe it is in harmony with the Word of God. But this ''because'' does not grant the creed an absolute finality in the life of the Church. Our insight falls short. Our hearts stray. Therefore the confession is ever subject to the discipline and correction of the Word. It is fixed only to the extent that it purely professes the Word of God. This requires of the congregation always to listen critically, especially when a new creed is being drafted, to ascertain anew: Do we truly hear the voice of the Word in the phrases of the Creed?

The Church needs continually to work on its confession, because it is never completed. This does not mean, for example, that the Apostles' Creed needs to be revised, but that the Church has to augment and elaborate its confession in terms of the needs and issues of the day. The reformers added to the confessional standards of the Church. They did so in order clearly to state their position on the burning issues in Protestantism's confrontation with the church of Rome. The Church in every age has this responsibility as it is ever confronted by new challenges. The Church is a living body in which the Holy Spirit dwells to lead it in all truth to enlighten it, to purify it and to equip it for the task to which it is called in this world. "To this task," H. Bouwman claims, "also belongs the fathoming of the truth, which came to its knowledge by divine revelation: the understanding and confessing of the truth (Eph. 3:9, 18; 2 Tim. 1:10). The congregation of God must, in its own circle, confess and teach in order to instruct the young, the ignorant, and the straying and in order to arm itself against opponents and the teachers of fallacy."[10]

A confession must carry the stamp of its own time. The congregation must be able to live with its confession in the contemporary world and be able in terms of the confession to testify in its world of the king and his kingdom which are and which are coming.

The draft confession clearly bears the imprint of the Republic of South Africa and the stamp of 1982. The congregation, in considering it for approval or not, must make sure that, above all, it carries the stamp of the Word of God and continues the pure tradition of creedal formation in the Church of the Lord Jesus Christ. The local church is deeply involved in this process. It is a work that cannot merely be completed by presbytery and synod. The local church must determine whether it is willing to accept the responsibilities the task entails.

MATURE IN CONFESSION

The congregation thus has to grow and become mature in its confession. Every believer must grow. There is a time that each one is a newborn babe in Christ and is fed on milk. But there comes a time when the individual has grown to be mature in Christ and can take solid food. Every believer grows in this way, and the fellowship of believers, the local church, must also grow to maturity, must come of age. In this ongoing process there is a constant interaction between the individual member and the congregation. Maturity in confession means for the individual—and for the church—that one is capable of speaking for oneself. Capable to express and to declare oneself—not to stand perplexed and embarrassed, bewildered and confused, with nothing to say as one faces the attack and the challenge of the world. Maturity indicates that I can indeed independently express myself, accepting with my whole being full responsibility for what I confess. I do not then merely repeat others, smoothly and easily echoing what they confess. Maturity in this context means that, to some degree, I confess in my own unique way in terms of my own discoveries and insights and responsibilities and my own situation and my own time.[11]

This applies to every church which grows up into its years of adulthood, into its own individuality, into its own personality and character. Together with the generations of the past, continuing the tradition from which it was born and raised, the DR Mission Church confesses: "I believe. . . ." But if this church is truly to be an independent church, with its own destiny and its own calling in a situation uniquely its own, it must of necessity also come to its own confession.

TEACHING THE CONFESSION

The congregation must teach its confession to its own younger generation as well as to those from outside the church who come into it. This must be done first of all within the family circle. And it must be done from the beginning in the teaching program of the church, from the time of baptism until confirmation. It must also be done in its adult educational programs. In short, the church must educate its members in its parish meetings, in its youth work, in its women's and children's programs, in its meetings and retreats.

Teaching the confession to the next generation is not accomplished by a simple technique. It is one of the great arts of life—to teach the young generation the fear of the Lord and to train them therein to the point of personal maturity in confession. This learning process also involves acquiring knowledge. Although confession, just as faith, is made up of more than deep, sure knowledge, it still includes knowledge as a major component. Confession always concerns a reality of which I know something, something I know with certainty. The congregation knows something with certainty concerning the reality of God . . . concerning the reality of the congregation . . . concerning the reality of man . . . concerning the reality of the world itself . . . and concerning the reality of the world in its relationship to God. The congregation confesses to know, to know with all its natural faculties, deep down in the heart; it confesses to know by the living Word of God through the Holy Spirit.

This surety and knowledge is not going to be awakened and nourished in a formal classroom situation where information concerning the confession is handed down. It does not happen so much by the transference of knowledge as an isolated event. It happens in the process of cultural transference. This is what Deuteronomy 6:5–9 teaches:

And you shall love the Lord your God with all your heart, and with all your soul, and with all your might. And these words which I command you this day shall be upon your heart; and you shall teach them diligently to your children, and shall talk of them when you sit in your house, and when you walk by the way, and when you lie down, and when you rise. And you shall bind them as a sign upon your hand, and they shall be as frontlets between your eyes. And you shall write them on the doorposts of your house and on your gates.

The communication process which transfers confession into the heart of the young generation should be characterized by certain basic traits similar to those prescribed for the Israelites. L. O. Richards explains it in this way:

First is that the faith be experienced as a life commitment by adult models. Second is the expression of that faith life in words. Third is communication of that faith life in both concrete and abstract form, through adult modeling and verbal teaching in the context of shared experience. The biblical faith has always been meant to be communicated as a culture, as a total way of life, in the context of personal relationships and shared experiences.[12]

The congregation must teach its confession to the young generation in the same way they teach them their mother tongue—not in the class but in everyday life. Of course the classroom is part of life—but it does not represent the only avenue of learning. There are many things that we teach and many things that we learn outside the formal instruction of the classroom. The classroom must be part of the life experience of the congregation, undergirding the search to understand and to fathom and, to the extent that it is possible, account for its faith on rational grounds. But the transference of confession occurs also on deeper, less formal levels. Confession is communicated as a culture, as a total way of life in the context of personal relationships and shared experiences. It happens from heart to heart, that heart which is the source of life.

A confession is not an odd piece of baggage which the congregation can arbitrarily give to or keep from its young generation on its spiritual pilgrimage. Confession arises out of the life of the Church and is passed on and taught by the living congregation in all its attitudes and sentiments and deeds as it lives on from day to day. It is for this reason that L. O. Richards asserts:

While the biblical faith has been talked at us, we have been involved in living life with others whose attitudes, values and behaviours are hardly Christian. While we've worked in churches to impress the mind with biblical truth, the personality has been shaped through relationships with those (both saved and unsaved) who hardly have God's word "in their hearts."[13]

Confession lives not only in the mind of the Church or in the politics of the Church or in the apologetics of the Church. It lives in the heart of the Church and represents the shape of its entire personality and character.

The confession that the Church really infuses into the heart of its young generation is not necessarily the confession it teaches them in the classrooms of its Sunday School. It is rather the confession which arises from its lifestyle and personality which quietly is made part of their lives, from day to day, by way of cultural transference. Thus the young generation must be taught to come to maturity in confession. The test whether they are actually learning it comes in the ordinary affairs of daily life. P. J. Roscam-Abbing underscores this by quoting Goethe: "A talent builds itself in solitude, but character develops in the tumult of the world." "But," adds Roscam-Abbing, "if what is at stake is not talent or character, but confession that must be learned, both a silent seeking of God and an active entering into the stream of the world are necessary."[14]

Silence before God—for both the Church and the individual believer. Those who do not know this silence can never truly toil and battle for God in this world. Neither can those who are not prepared to enter into the stream of the world.

SAYING AND DOING

All of this demands that the congregation both proclaim and act out its confession. This places a heavy responsibility on the local church. First, it assumes the responsibility to proclaim. The believer must not only talk *about* the confession; he must express the words, the ideas, the teaching of the confession itself in the world. The confession has no other voice in society than the voice of the believer. A confession which is stored away in prayer books and formularies, or which is at most referred to in a catechism, is not a living confession. The voice of the confession must be heard in the words of the members wherever they talk: in the quiet of the inner chamber and in the busyness of the marketplace; in the local church and at work.

Second, believers must talk and *live* their confession. Of course, to talk is already to do something important. To talk is already to take a stand, to move away from neutrality, to become polemically and apologetically involved, and to declare as a witness. Simply to talk can be deadly dangerous. But to *live* the confession requires performance and action, actual deeds and the conduct of life. The congregation and its members must be doers of the Word (James 1:22) in obedience to the gospel of Jesus Christ whom they profess (2 Cor. 9:13). They must not merely confess the truth but abide in the truth (2 John), avoiding the terrible but real possibility that they can confess him by mouth while denying him by deeds and works (Titus 1:16; Matt. 23:3; 1 John 1:6). The members of the congregation, for instance, act their confession when they help their neighbor in his distress and render service. 2 Cor. 9:13 reads: "And because of the proof which this service of yours brings, many will give glory to God for your loyalty to the Gospel of Christ, which you profess, and for your generosity in sharing with them and all others" (TEV).

The Belhar Confession is one which lends itself exceptionally well to a direct translation into deeds. It addresses realities which cry out to become visible in the congregation of the Lord and in the world. Those who take this confession on their lips thus engage themselves in something very dangerous, the consequences of which they will not escape. The confession demands that the congregation stand in the world where God stands, namely against injustice and with those who are wronged. It talks of a reality where irreconcilability and hatred, bitterness and enmity have been overcome and asserts that the congregation must be the living sign and token of this victory in the world. And the confession does not merely address the problem of certain structures in society. It is concerned also with the disposition of the heart and the quality of the life of the Church in this world. The draft confession is above all a confession begging to be lived. It will test the believers also in their works.

Thus it becomes essential that every local church and every member must examine themselves and their deeds thoroughly in the light of the confession to see where they stand.

LOCALLY MADE TRUE

The congregation must proclaim and live its confession and make it real and true in the local situation, where it swims in the stream of the world. The confession of the church is never the property of the leaders of the general assembly or the synod, nor is it something that any church meeting—whatever the status of the meeting—may deal with as it will. It is never a document with which to play church politics or to be used as a negotiating device at some high ecclesiastical level. Synod, as the assembly of local churches and as an expression of denominational unity, indeed has an important role to play in the drafting and preservation of the creed as a bond of unity. But unless the confession lives in the heart of the individual believer and in the heart of the local church where people live by it from day to day it is a dead letter and all in vain.

And if the congregation goes into the world with its confession and encounters others, either friend or foe, who profess differently, what must it then do? Regarding the draft confession, this is today a vital question for the congregations of the DR Mission Church. And the answer that the church finds for itself on this matter and the decisions that will stem from this answer will radically influence meaningful church relations in the family of the Dutch Reformed churches.

What P. J. Roscam-Abbing writes on unity within pluriformity of confession is clarifying. He maintains that three things are necessary under these circumstances:

1. *To listen honestly to each other*. The other position probably offers much that is valuable. Division impoverishes both sides. Each group must endeavor to break through its one-sidedness by listening to the other with care and understanding. Surely something can be learned from the criticism of another point of view. In an honest interchange one's own convictions are also on the table and one must be prepared, if necessary, to change one's view.

2. *To point out clearly, where necessary, the doubtfulness or error of the other's position*. To love one another does not mean that we may not criticize each other. The truth must be taken seriously. Therefore we not only *may* but *must* purposefully reject that which we discern as heresy in the position of others—on condition that our rejection is based on a sincere and thoroughly considered conviction.

3. *To wrestle together toward mutual light*. We are not allowed coldly and indifferently to live past each other. Nor are we to generously accommodate all people in their own choices and thus gloss over differences. Nor are we to polarize and enlarge our differences or caricature the other side and doggedly persevere in our own point of view. It is essential to see in each other the fellow Christian, to exercise brotherly love for one another, to remain involved one with the other and together to remain involved with the gospel. Searching together might lead us to understand the gospel more fully. And as long as we have not received identical points of view, we must tolerate each other and our differences.[15]

Considering the upheaval the draft confession created and the decisions that need to be taken concerning the relationships between churches at both the local and national level, Roscam-Abbing's principles provide good and necessary guidelines for the DR Mission Church and everybody concerned. Before churches break ties, of whatever nature, with each other, everyone must be very sure that these guidelines have been observed all along the way.

CONFESSION AND POLITICAL ORDER

When the local church goes into the world with its confession it does not encounter only other believers and other churches. It encounters the total community in all its varying lifestyles and structures. A confession does not only say something about God and his heaven, about the believer and his church, but also something about the world. It says something about God as he comes to meet the world in Jesus Christ the Lord; and about the Church as it lives in the world; and about the world as it exists before God.

It is a dangerous and sinful world in which the congregation—which also has its own struggle against sin—makes its way in the light of its confession. One threatening danger is that the forces of the world may manipulate the Church and its confession into a corner where the forces at work in the world can relegate the Church to the status of a political pressure group and the confession to a manifesto. When this happens, the Church is no longer the Church. It is no longer free; it has become a slave and a puppet.[16]

The congregation does not confess with only the salvation of the individual in mind. It is involved in society, as, of necessity, it must be. This involvement, however, must never be along political party lines but according to the character of the Church. J. B. Metz, the well-known Roman Catholic political theologian, writes:

> Political theology claims to be a basic element in the whole structure of critical theological thinking, motivated by a new notion of the relation between theory and practice, according to which all theology must be of itself "practical," orientated to action. Only when this fundamental notion of theology is ignored can it be mistaken for a theology dabbling in politics, i.e., in direct contact with socio-political public life, which would be wrong. It is in fact one of the aims of political theology and its society-directed thinking to prevent the Church and theology being saddled as it were unwittingly with this or that political ideology. . . . Christianity and its message cannot be simply identified with a given political institution (in the narrow sense). . . . No political party can take as its platform that which forms the horizon of the critical stipulation of Christianity: the totality of history as reserved eschatologically to God. . . . On the other hand, the "negative conscience," the critical attitude to society in which the public claim of the gospel makes itself heard, must not be underestimated. Its critical contestation of socio-political conditions is a "determinate negation." It flares up in criticism of very definite conditions. Being a critical attitude to society, it may well take the form under certain conditions of revolutionary protest.[17]

Though we differ with Metz regarding revolutionary conduct, his basic argument is clear and acceptable: however positively and aggressively the congregation may be involved in society, the Church and its confession in the final analysis are not of this world and do not stand in the service of any worldly kingdom but in the service of the triune God and his kingdom. No structure is without its injustice, no society without its poor and no civil order without evil. Whatever poverty and injustice and evil the Church may have already conquered it must never live under the impression that it is within its or within anyone else's power to create on earth a millennium devoid of these realities. If the congregation is to continue its critical witness against the powers that be, then it must not be subservient to any political or social order. It must jealously keep vigil over its independence. The congregation can never expect that because of its confession and its witness against apartheid it will be instrumental in establishing a perfect dispensation of justice, and ownership, and goodness with which the church can unreservedly identify itself. The congregation should never be totally at home in the world. In a sense the Church is always alien.

STICK OR STAFF?

The congregation should continually be on its guard that it does not misuse its confession nor allow it to be misused by others. The question of how the congregation sees itself in relation to its confession and how it actually uses the confession is of vital importance. In 1961 the General Assembly of the Nederlandse Hervormde Kerk in the Netherlands addressed its local churches in a pastoral letter entitled ''On the Confession of the Church and Its Maintenance.'' Referring to this pastoral letter, P. J. Roscam-Abbing asks whether the confession represents for the congregation a staff to walk with or a stick to hit with.[18] Clearly a confession is a staff with which the congregation is to walk its road through the world. But is it also a stick with which to hit either those who proclaim false doctrine, or heretics, or people who have hurt the Church deeply?

Around the confession, roads part.

But confession binds together and includes.

Discipline, concerning both doctrine and life, is a biblical reality.

Somewhere there is a limit upon walking together, even after all the necessary allowance has been made for pluriformity.

In the process of sorting out and dividing and drawing boundaries, in determining future relationships in the light of the confession, the church uses its confession wrongly as a stick with which to hit:

if, wittingly or unwittingly, it uses the confession as an instrument to cause those who deep down still belong together in Christ Jesus to separate and part from each other;

if, wittingly or unwittingly, it gives to those things which are of less importance in the Word a higher standing than they deserve and makes of them a shibboleth;

if, wittingly or unwittingly, it settles as closed to discussion that which in the Word is still open to discussion;

if, wittingly or unwittingly, it raises as an immutable value that which in the Word is considered changeable;

if, wittingly or unwittingly, it declares as the only way that which the Word describes as a possible way;

if, wittingly or unwittingly, it raises to the level of an article of faith that which in the Word is merely a practical matter;

if, wittingly or unwittingly, it uses its confession to serve frustration, or hatred, or political aims, or rejection, and uses it merely to hurt someone and put him in his place.

When a confession is used as a stick in this way, it drives people apart. It then damages and destroys and ruins.

But confession is not intended for this end. It *is* a stick to protect the congregation against false doctrine and heresies, but it is *especially* a staff for the congregation to walk with.

The confession is a staff for the Church:

when it continually functions in the congregation as an instrument for profound self-examination to help determine whether the church really lives by the faith it proclaims;

when the congregation, by the light of its confession, can always retreat with other believers beyond that which separates them into that which unites and binds them together in a world of unbelief, suffering, grief, and struggle, namely the confession that Jesus Christ is Lord;

when it helps the congregation to see its calling more clearly and to fulfill it with greater dedication in this world;

when it is not merely a formulation of an abstract truth, but indeed an instrument of love and hope.

The draft confession wants to be a staff to support the congregations of the DR Mission Church as they go into society in Southern Africa—to serve the true unity of the Church of the Lord Jesus Christ, to be an instrument of true reconciliation, and to collaborate in bringing greater justice, consoling those who are stricken and the humbled. The confession does all this only in and through Christ Jesus the Lord and his Holy Spirit.

Our confession wants to be a stick to protect the Church from everybody and everything that work to prevent it from striving toward that calling.

Our confession does not want to and never should be a stick to beat with—no matter who is pressing for it. Against this the Church must be on its watch and must trust God in his grace.

J. J. F. DURAND

9

Belhar—Crisis for the Dutch Reformed Churches

It has become something of a commonplace to point out that a significant political change of direction in South Africa will only become possible with the backing of the Dutch Reformed Church. The commonplace is true, however. As long as the DRC is the bastion in which the majority of white South Africans can take shelter in the knowledge that it gives the policy of separate development theological and moral sanction, the chances are slim that any government will be able to mobilize sufficient support among the white electorate to effect fundamental changes to the present political system in South Africa. Nobody need therefore be surprised that increasing pressure has been brought to bear on the DRC during the last few years to change its standpoint. In 1982 the pressure from church and theological quarters provisionally reached its peak, and the effect has not remotely worn off. Or, more accurately: it is still too early to assess the true effect of the events of 1982.

The pressure mentioned here came both from within and from without the DRC and varied from a mild caution not to delay or thwart the reformist initiatives of the Botha government to an uncompromising demand that the DRC openly declare the system of apartheid to be un-Christian and confess its own share of guilt in its creation. The latter demand came especially from the ranks of those convinced that the government's changes are only cosmetic while the system itself remains unaffected and that, by building greater flexibility into the system, the government is merely giving it greater viability.

Theological pressure, especially from outside, is of course nothing new to the DRC. And yet 1982 was different. For the first time the DRC found itself in a position where its official stand with regard to apartheid was declared heretical by the World Alliance of Reformed Churches in Ottawa. At the same time its membership in the WARC was suspended along with that of the Reformed Church in Africa. It is true that the Ottawa decisions were dismissed by leading figures inside the DRC as being merely sensational, without any true significance. Condemnation of standpoints and suspension of membership is after all not unfamiliar to South African organizations with international connections. And yet the events at Ottawa were much deeper than the DRC apologists would have us believe—much deeper even than the decisions themselves would suggest.

The fact is that the Ottawa decisions were to a very large extent the result of a carefully planned strategy in which groups from the black churches in the Dutch Reformed family of churches played a leading role. The Ottawa decisions were the first sign of, and prelude to, an imminent theological confrontation between the DRC and those churches which came into being largely through the DRC's mission work—mission work conducted on the basis of a missionary policy in terms of which separate church formations were established for different population groups. This is the irony of Ottawa. In front of the world forum of Reformed believers the DRC was condemned as the creator of an un-biblical and oppressive political apartheid by those who are both its product and its victims, those very churches that the DRC frequently cited as evidence of the effectiveness and success of its missionary policy!

Ottawa should not have come as a surprise. Resistance against the political system of apartheid with its repressive influence on the black population groups of South Africa and also against its interpretation by the church had been building up in the younger Dutch Reformed churches for many years. In the late sixties and early seventies the black Dutch Reformed Church in Africa in particular became more critical. In the second half of the past decade the DR Mission Church and the Reformed Church in Africa (RCA), in which the Indian members are congregated, took the lead in voicing the protest. The establishment of the Broeder-kring is of great importance here. It is an ecumenical body consisting of mostly black and some white ministers from the above three churches whose goals are the unification of the Dutch Reformed churches (without the DRC if necessary), open and uncompromising opposition to apart-heid in the church and the state, and realizing the black Dutch Reformed churches' financial independence from the white DRC. The Broeder-kring was outspoken in its stand and did not hesitate to oppose those in the DR Mission Church and the DR Church in Africa in particular who were suspected of still being loyal, in the last instance, to the DRC.

Although it was the Broederkring, with Dr. Allan Boesak in the lead, which performed an unmistakable role before Ottawa, the WARC delegates from the DR Mission Church had not only Broederkring decisions to call upon but also a resolution passed by the DR Mission Church synod itself in 1978.

This resolution described the policy of apartheid and/or separate development as being in conflict with the gospel, since the forced separation on the grounds of race and color is ultimately based on a conviction of the fundamental irreconcilability of the people so separated. The synod went still further and showed that the system which emerged out of such a policy would—and did—inevitably lead to an increasing polarization of people. In this way the synod evaluated the South African situation. The policy of apartheid does more than just keep people apart. It polarizes, and out of this polarization comes conflict. This conflict, in turn, becomes an alibi to maintain the separation at all costs. This draws everybody into a vicious circle which can be broken only by changing the original premise. The DR Mission Church synod's 1978 resolution itself had an even earlier precedent. As far back as September 1948, the Wynberg Circuit declared that they could find no grounds in Holy Scripture for "colour apartheid." Although this critical voice from Wynberg never received the sanction of a synod resolution, the protest that it embodied was never completely silenced, until it was explicitly uttered in the resolution at Belhar in 1978.

Ottawa could indeed not have come as a surprise to the DRC. And yet the DRC was caught unawares by the severity of the castigation and the uncompromising manner in which its membership in the WARC was suspended. At the same time there was the sobering realization that the WARC would not have gone quite so far without the insistence of the DR Mission Church and RCA delegations. Why sobering? Because the DRC, with a recklessness that bordered on the unbelievable, totally underestimated the intensity and emotion that gave birth to the critical voices over the years. Perhaps recklessness is not the right word. What might look like recklessness is possibly related to the fact that apartheid has structured the South African social pattern in such a way that population groups, and therefore also the churches, are wholly isolated from one another and end up living in totally different worlds. Consequently the DRC could not really hear or feel or understand what the members of the black churches had to go through under apartheid. In this inability the DRC became the victim of its own propaganda. The black Dutch Reformed churches are not entirely free of blame either. The way in which they communicated their criticism and anxiety sometimes made it too easy for the seriousness of the situation to escape people who were already—for the reasons mentioned—suffering from a lack of sensitivity.

The Ottawa shock was only a prelude to what was to follow. The synod of the DR Mission Church assembled at Belhar and, following the lead of the WARC, declared a *status confessionis:* in the concrete South African apartheid situation, the confession of the Church was now at stake. The difference between the standpoints of the DR Mission Church and the DRC was more than theological; it became a confessional difference in which the dissenting standpoint could be no less than heretical.

The DR Mission Church, consistent with this stand and "with the deepest regret," accused the DRC of theological heresy and idolatry. A *status confessionis* does not necessarily involve the forming of a new article of confession, but more usually the reformulation of existing confessions with a view to a particular situation. The DR Mission Church rounded off its declaration of a *status confessionis* by compiling a draft confession which was unanimously accepted by the synod. In this confession, based on the doctrines of the unity of the Church, reconciliation through Christ, and the righteousness of God, heresies relating to the philosophy of apartheid are rejected one after the other.

The Belhar Confession is not only the provisional culmination of the confrontation within the Dutch Reformed "family" but also a new dimension in the confrontation. As far as the DR Mission Church is concerned, on the level of a confession of faith it finally broke away from the idea of being an ethnic church for "coloreds." As a church it is open to anyone prepared to support its confessions of faith, including that of Belhar. The new confession presents a hitherto unknown challenge for the DRC which places its very being in the balance. Its ecclesiastical policy and practice in respect of racial and national relations is rejected confessionally as being in conflict with some of the central tenets of Christianity. If it were to persevere in its policy, the result could only be that the DR Mission Church severs its ecclesiastical ties with the DRC, if, that is, the DR Mission Church is true to the gospel and to itself. The original communications gap between the DRC and the DR Mission Church has become a confessional one.

The DRC's first reaction—from its general synod of October 1982 in Pretoria—gives the impression that a parting of the ways is inevitable. This reaction can be understood in more ways than one. On the face of it, the synod's reaction was an unmistakable attempt to render the urgent appeal of the DR Mission Church fruitless for all practical purposes by expressing the synod's "sadness and dismay" over the "unreasonable accusation of theological heresy and idolatry" without, however, addressing the theological merit of the accusation. The synod did declare itself willing "to consult the Gospel anew in equal dialogue with the DR Mission Church to look for the answers to the various dilemmas," but rejected a proposal that the DRC's official stand on personal relations be received in cooperation with the other Dutch Reformed churches. The DRC would act on its own, although it agreed to discuss the matter with the other churches "at the right time." In this last decision the second facet of the DRC's reaction is clearly exposed: delaying tactics. A report on the revision of the official policy statement of the DRC is expected before the next synod meeting in 1986. Attempts to convene an earlier synod meeting specially for this purpose failed. In the meantime the official stand of the DRC remains unchanged.

At first glance these decisions look like a repetition of the inability of the past to grasp the import of the moment. After everything that had happened such obtuseness would exceed all bounds, however. It would be a fair judgment to say that the DRC was not theologically strong enough to cope with the event. The sterility of the particular theology of creation orders with which the DRC equipped itself in the difficult area of race relations rendered it incapable of responding sensibly. The alternative—a radical theological conversion—was not even considered by the conservative majority of the synod. The only solution was therefore to postpone the decision in the hope that the traditional stand would, with the passage of time, recover some degree of theological respectability.

The debate and eventual decision on the Mixed Marriages Act and Section 16 of the Immorality Act is a confirmation of the theological inability referred to above. In contrast to the convincing biblical arguments raised at the synod against such legislation by the government, the synod accepted a majority report which declared without any substantial theological argument "that the Mixed Marriages Act can still be justified in the complicated S.A. society" and that Section 16 of the Immorality Act should therefore not be repealed either. The background to this debate reveals even more clearly that the deciding factors were political and not theological. It was known for some time, for instance, that the prime minister, P. W. Botha, was prepared to consider changes to these laws. He had been approached by the Church of the Province of South Africa, the Methodist Church, and the Congregational churches with a request that the measures be repealed. His suggestion to these churches was that they should liaise with all the major churches to see whether they could not submit a uniform proposal to the government. It was in this way that the issue ended up at the DRC synod, which was clearly suspicious of liberalization and the potential dismantling of apartheid by the Botha government. Hence their decision. It is a simple fact that the Bible and theology fell before a camouflaged political onslaught dominated by the sentiments of the Conservative party of Dr. A. P. Treurnicht.

Several commentators have pointed out the contradictions in the synod's decisions and compared the decision on the Mixed Marriages Act with an earlier decision defining racism as being unscriptural and sinful. And yet the deeper political consistency within the theological contradictions should be seen. Politically it was easy to declare racism sinful because, in the view of the majority of the synod delegates, apartheid had nothing, incredibly enough, to do with racism.

These resolutions were not unanimously accepted by the DRC synod, of course. A significant number of delegates pleaded convincingly for a change of course, with a prominent role played by the church's professors of theology from Stellenbosch and Pretoria. But the soundest theological arguments fell apart against the brick wall of political conservatism.

Since the 1982 session of the general synod, most of the regional synods of the DRC have had their 1983 session. There have been, with one exception, no significant departures from the general synod mainstream. But this one departure is of some importance for it involves a regional synod—the Western Cape synod—with the closest ties of all regional synods to the DR Mission Church. This synod's decision can in a certain sense be seen as expressing the minority opinion at the general synod and as the most direct reply to Belhar from the DRC side. Belhar and its confession obviously featured at the general synod, but at the Western Cape synod Belhar was the backdrop against which every decision on the issue was evaluated. The questions raised at the synod by congregations of the Western Cape would have been unthinkable without the shock effect of Belhar and of the disappointing reaction of the general synod.

The resolutions of the regional synod that attracted the most attention in public were those stating, in opposition to the general synod, that the Mixed Marriages Act and Section 16 of the Immorality Act were in conflict with the Bible. Less sensational, but equally important, were the resolutions in which faith in Jesus Christ was submitted as the only qualification for membership of the DRC and in which the synod distanced itself from any efforts, past or present, to claim apartheid or separate development as a biblical dictate. To the latter resolution was added a declaration that apartheid in racist guise was a sin. This resolution obviously related directly to the *status confessionis* and the draft confession of Belhar. Admittedly, the synod did not see its way clear to declare apartheid as such a sin and a heresy, but it did express its agreement with the major points—in fact the greater part—of the Belhar Confession.

Thus was the first step taken toward dialogue with the DR Mission Church on confessional matters. The road ahead will not be an easy one, however, especially because the Western Cape regional synod cannot act in isolation from the rest of the DRC. There is a tense struggle ahead: not only between the Western Cape regional synod and the DR Mission Church, but also within the walls of the DRC itself. It is an open question whether the Western Cape synod's initiatives toward reform will be readily accepted by the rest of the DRC.

It is of course not true that the new voice now being heard in the Western Cape is limited to that region. In fact, several months before the meeting of the WARC and of the general synod of the DRC, an open letter appeared which provoked widespread response. The letter, signed by 123 persons who had received the theological training of the

DRC and had been ordained by the DRC, called upon the DRC to manifest a visible unity with the black churches, confirmed that there could be only one membership of one church, and rejected the system of apartheid (in words similar to those of the DR Mission Church synod in 1978) as an ideology opposed to the doctrine of reconciliation of the Christian gospel. Particular items of legislation, such as the Mixed Marriages Act and the Group Areas Act, which the authors of the open letter knew had their origin in the church and would be up for discussion at the synod, were singled out as reprehensible and in conflict with the gospel.

Both within and without South Africa the appearance of the open letter caused much excitement, presumably for two reasons: in the first place it condemned not just the results of apartheid—as in the past—but its very ideological basis, and in doing so went much further than the Western Cape regional synod would go; in the second place this was the largest number of ministers and theologians ever to oppose the official view of the DRC in public. The leadership of the DRC provided further publicity by effectively keeping the letter off the agenda of the general synod.

In spite of the fact that the open letter created a stir and was even hailed by some as a "historical turning point" in the DRC—presumably because of the large number of signatories—a sober assessment of its meaning and effect is called for, first of all because the number of signatories is misleading, a fact which was smugly stressed by the *Kerkbode*, the official organ of the DRC. Of the 123, only 44 were active ministers of the DRC. The rest all held nonministering positions or had chosen to serve as members of one of the black churches.

A second sobering point is the fact that in some respects the letter merely repeated issues upheld for the past three decades by opponents of apartheid in the DRC. The impression was left that on several cardinal points little or no progress had been made. It is therefore not surprising that the list of signatories included members of the church who had come a long way in the struggle against apartheid and who were (for that very reason) peripheral figures in the church. The signatories included no one who had any real influence at the hub of the church's leadership. In this regard the position had even deteriorated. More than two decades earlier, those involved in the Cottesloe Conference's condemnation of apartheid included a number of influential leaders of the DRC. The effect (both negative and positive) of Cottesloe was therefore much greater than that which the open letter could ever achieve, which made it a simple matter for the church leaders to brush the open letter aside.

The open letter was decidedly no historic turning point. And yet it was not without significance. The standpoint represented in it differs so radically from the official standpoints of the DRC—on the cardinal point regarding apartheid it differs even from the Western Cape synod—that it would not be farfetched to speak of two separate churches under the one

DRC roof. Nonetheless, this should not suggest a large-scale rift in the DRC. In the first instance this second "church" is virtually faceless. It consists of a widespread group of theologians, ministers, and lay members among whom sporadic criticism is heard but who have, until now, given little indication of a clearly outlined reform action. The Western Cape regional synod has now for the first time begun to give the reform initiative an institutional outline, but it is still too early to evaluate its effect. In any event, we must remember in the second place that those members of this group who departed radically from the concept of apartheid at religious as well as social and political levels out of evangelical considerations are but a small minority even among the signatories. Most of the group can at best be described as people whose Christian conscience is deeply aggrieved by the sometimes blatant, sometimes refined racism that is seen in the church, but who do not seriously question the ruling political system on Christian evangelical grounds. The resolution of the Western Cape synod on apartheid is a clear indication of this. Politically speaking the group in question supports the National party, and one of their greatest frustrations is that the church is hampering the tentative initiatives of the Nationalist government in the reform actions at last being initiated in South Africa. This in any event does not provide sufficient dissenting grounds for a schism of any significance within the church.

Finally, the lack of theological leadership is a significant characteristic of the opposition to apartheid within the DRC. The few theologians who could have made a significant difference here are to a large extent isolated from church activities, while, at a local level, few ministers would have the courage to give any real guidance to "dissenting" members. The lack of theological guidance at the local level has therefore been felt all the more acutely by worried members, especially during the first four months that followed the meeting of the 1982 general synod. The reactions of these people to the synod decisions varied from disappointed expectation to shocked indignation. At the same time there was a feeling of helplessness due to the inability to give effective ecclesiastical expression to this protest. A few letters of protest were published by members, and one or two petitions were presented to church councils. But nobody harbors any illusions about the eventual effects of these protests—hence the fact that for a small group of people continued membership in the DRC has become a problem. The logical outcome of this deeply felt disquiet would be to join, for example, the DR Mission Church, although there are factors that may make this a difficult step to take. One of these factors is simply geographical. The Group Areas Act has separated the color groups in South Africa to such an extent that congregational mixing across the color line would create problems for many. Whether or not many members will venture such a move depends on the intensity of their conviction. At the present moment there is not yet much indication of such a break from the DRC. There are reports in the larger population centers, however, of study groups who have been meeting with the 1982 confession of the DR Mission Church as a common base and subject for discussion. Whether this will lead to any further action is an open question.

Even if the break referred to above were to take place, however, it would have no marked effect on the DRC. The effect would be primarily local, and apart from some initial publicity the church would not be subjected to undue pressure. The net effect of the events of 1982 on the DRC will be something other than an internal schism. It is not the loss of a few members that is important, but the loss of true relevance within the socio-political makeup of South Africa. The DRC has often been described as a factor to be taken into account at the socio-political level in that it has had the dubious honor of more than once taking the initiative in the formulation of the South African political and social pattern of apartheid. The opportunity to play the leading role once again in changing this pattern was lost at the general synod of 1982. The decisive moment came and went. It may therefore come about that the DRC's future actions in this regard will be regarded as no more than reaction to political developments within Afrikaner circles. It is already said of the Western Cape synod that the changed political climate surrounding the constitutional amendments played a decisive role in its resolutions. The fact that this is not an entirely fair judgment—there is ample evidence that many delegates had their minds changed by theological arguments at the synod itself—does not alter the cynicism with which many people regard signs of movement in the DRC.

The center of theological and socio-ethical thought and activity in Dutch Reformed circles has undoubtedly shifted from the DRC to the DR Mission Church; 1982 was the watershed. There are several reasons why the DR Mission Church is singled out instead of the Reformed Church in Africa or the DR Church in Africa. The former has progressed to the same point as the DR Mission Church in almost every respect, and even further in some, but numerically it is such a small church that the general leadership of the DR Mission Church is indispensable. In addition, these two churches have come a long way toward unification, the first step in the direction of their eventual goal: the visible structural unity of all the Dutch Reformed churches. The DR Church in Africa is in a different position. This church's initial opposition to apartheid supportive thoughts and actions reached its height at the Worcester synod in 1975. Since then, at the next two synods, a change of heart obviously took place; both synods went out of their way more than once to avoid embarrassing the DRC. The latest meeting of the DR Church in Africa's general synod at Barkley West (1983) particularly underscored this tendency, especially in that it clearly distanced itself from the Ottawa decisions. So intense and so widespread was the disappointment at this action of the DR Church in Africa that there was even talk of manipulation by the DRC. The DR Church in Africa's financial dependence on the DRC, it was said, would facilitate such manipulation. And yet two decisions were made which showed that the DR Church in Africa might have changed its tactical direction, but that it wanted to stay theologically in line with the basic direction that had been taken by the DR Mission Church. Apartheid was condemned and the visible unity of the church once again proclaimed to be the deepest desire of the church. With these statements the DR Church in Africa aligned itself theologically with the DR Mission Church and the Reformed Church in Africa. The initiative taken by the DR Mission Church on the confessional issue will, as a result, inevitably influence future developments in the DR Church in Africa and its relationship with the other Dutch Reformed churches. There is no doubt, then, that the theological initiative is—for the present, at least—in the hands of the DR Mission Church. The question remains whether the DR Mission Church will have the spiritual energy to keep up this initiative. To answer this question one will have to look at other equally important questions that go hand in hand with the DR Mission Church's very essence as a church in the coming years.

The fact that the DR Mission Church desires consciously to be a confessional church within the South African context in the first place raises questions that cannot all be answered at this stage. Is the DR Mission Church prepared to bear the consequences of its confession if it develops that the confessional gap between the two sides cannot be bridged? Is the DR Mission Church prepared to do so in spite of the financial dependence of so many of its local congregations upon the DRC, especially in the rural areas? Is the DR Mission Church prepared to accept the internal consequences of its confession as well? These and other questions will be asked with increasing urgency.

In the second place the Belhar Confession will have more than just ecclesiastical consequences, in the narrower sense of the word, for the DR Mission Church. The confession does not only reject the ethnic separation of people but also declares that the church will side with those who are wronged and oppressed. It declares openly that "We believe . . . that in a world full of injustice and enmity [God] is in a special way the God of the destitute, the poor, and the wronged; . . . that the Church as the possession of God must stand where he stands, namely against injustice and with the wronged; that in following Christ the Church must witness against all the powerful and privileged who selfishly seek their own interests and thus control and harm others." The important question is *how* the DR Mission Church will carry out this standpoint in its ongoing critical confrontation with the political powermongers of South Africa. The answer to this question is becoming increasingly urgent in the light of the fact that the Labour party has decided to cooperate on the new constitutional dispensation of the Botha government with a view—in the words of the party leaders—to use the proffered political power as a lever with which eventually to enlist all blacks in a political solution to the South African situation. Although they reject apartheid in principle, they believe that this is the best strategy to adopt. It would be naïve to believe that this development would leave the DR Mission Church untouched. At its 1982 synod the church was unanimous in its condemnation of the system of apartheid in South Africa, but there was a significant difference of opinion at the synod on the way to be followed by the church in its opposition to this system. The decision of the Labour party will undoubtedly intensify the tension around this issue. The question is therefore *how* the church will live out its confession without becoming a political football. The General Synodal Commission of the church has indeed rejected the government's proposed constitutional changes at its session after the synod meeting, but it would be presumptuous to suggest that this has settled the matter.

In a certain sense the family of Dutch Reformed churches is a microcosm of South African society, reflecting all the various group tensions: the fears of the whites and the anxieties of the blacks, the arrogance and embitterment, the mutual suspicion and mistrust, but also, somewhere inside, a hope for something better to follow, a deeper willingness to forgive and to respond to the signs of benevolence that are appearing. It is this last faintly flickering and sometimes sooty flame that must not die. It must keep on burning as never before, for the next few years may prove to be the turning point of the history of South Africa.

Appendix:
Review of the Biblical Literature,
pp. 58–59

1. For the vital role that the defense of the poor played in the laws of Israel, numerous Old Testament theologies and commentaries offer some insight. In addition to the regulations mentioned in the text, there are many other laws and regulations which were introduced to care for and help those who were socially wronged. The sabbath itself was on occasion described in this way. Much research has been done, especially in recent years, on the sabbatical year and the year of jubilee. Compare, in addition to the lexicon articles, R. North's *The Sociology of the Biblical Jubilee* (a much criticized dissertation); B. Maarsing, *Maatschappijkritiek in het Oude Testament—het Jubeljaar* (1976); J. H. Yoder, *The Politics of Jesus;* J. Simonse, *Maatschappelijke gelijkheid* (1980), especially 39ff.; C. van Leeuwen, *Sociaal Besef in Israel;* the *Theological Forum*, 5 (1977), of the Reformed Ecumenical Synod, including contributions by Woudstra, Nusselder, De Graaf, and Vos; as well as further studies on the way in which the jubilee year plays a part in Isaiah 61 and especially in Jesus' important synagogue sermon in Luke 4, e.g. R. B. Sloan, *The Favorable Year of the Lord: A Study of Jubilary Theology in the Gospel of Luke,* and U. Busse, *Das Nazareth-Manifest Jesu.*

Though there exists general agreement on the fact that the sabbatical and jubilee years contain one or another authoritative message for the Church, the ways in which that message is formulated and made concrete diverge widely. Obviously, economic and labor practices cannot simply be transferred from one cultural period and from one economic situation to another. Even in the Old Testament, labor and economic conditions differ radically from one period to another. In the nomadic period, for example, totally different regulations were in effect than those that applied after the occupation of the country or again after the return from the exile. According to some exegetes, the sabbatical and jubilee years in all probability never really functioned in Israel. However, this does not alter the fact that behind all these changing regulations in their different dispensations and situations the same religious principle, namely the defense of the poor by legal principles and action, can be observed. This is the point made by A. Deissler, "Armut und Reichtum: Biblische Grundlegung in Alten Testament," *Christlicher Glaube in moderner Gesellschaft,* 89, where he refers to the essence of Yahwism which is at stake in all these apparently changing dispensations:

"This tolerance of varying social and labor relations has a border which may not be violated: that at which people begin to dispose of other people as of things."

2. Though the saving actions of God throughout the Bible leave no doubt as to how the destiny of his people in distress concerns him, it is nevertheless remarkable how the exodus plays a very special role as a paradigm of liberation from slavery and oppression, especially in the theology of liberation. Biblical scholars repeatedly return to this theme, sometimes incidentally and by way of supposition, but sometimes also explicitly and with detailed argumentation. Several examples can be quoted, including J. P. Miranda, *Marx and the Bible,* especially 77–109, and J. S. Croatto, *Exodus: A Hermeneutics of Freedom.*

There are in fact a number of critical discussions of this motif of freedom in connection with exodus. Among the most well-known is J. A. Kirk, *Liberation Theology,* especially 95–105 and 143–153, and G. Sauter, " 'Exodus' and 'Liberation' as Theological Metaphors: A Critical Case Study of the Use of Allegory and Misunderstood Analogies in Ethics," *Scottish Journal of Theology,* 34, 481–507. Sauter opposes the reducing or formalizing of a traditional situation to a fixed "pattern of experience" and transferring it by analogy to similar situations today, which are then analyzed according to the same "pattern of experience." Usually the analogy, which is necessary initially to bring about this transfer, is casually expanded by way of allegorizing to admit all sorts of details from the traditional situation into our consideration of the present one. According to Sauter, this causes a hermeneutical short circuit; it makes an illegitimate transfer from one set of circumstances to another. He briefly refers to Moltmann, Gutierrez, and Bloch to show that the result of this is inevitably that "either an ethical directive is derived directly from the talk about God or instructions for the formation of reality are reflected . . . back into the concept of God." Both of these almost direct connections between the doctrine of God and ethics he considers an inadmissable "short-circuiting of knowledge and of argumentation." Especially in Lutheran ranks, the warning voices against making direct connections between the doctrine of God and ethics are very strong. From God's actions of liberation in the Bible, say these voices, we cannot make simple derivations about what is expected of people today. According to Sauter, biblical expressions like "liberation" and "exodus" deal only with the freedom and living space which is granted to man and not with patterns of conduct which are held up before him.

It is not possible to go further into this question here, but it is clear that the question raises a number of issues: the relation between the evangelical "freedom" which is received and the "freedom" which is obtained by "political liberation"; the traditionally Lutheran fear of ethics according to norms and principles; and the basis and logic of Christian ethics. There is, however, no doubt about the fact that the Belhar Confession, which does not even refer to the exodus, exults in the first place in a doxological way in God's deeds of salvation. This God, who revealed himself in this way, calls his people to follow him in this, to reflect, in a manner of speaking, something of his willingness to render aid and compassion. Not a single reference is made to any possibility that human, church action could in fact replace God's work or render it unnecessary. There can be no misunderstanding concerning the minimum that is confessed here.

3. "The fatherless, widows and foreigners . . . each have about forty verses that command justice for them. God wants to make it very clear that in a special way he is the protector of these weak ones," J. F. Alexander, "The Bible and the Other Side," *The Other Side*, 11(1975), 57, quoted by R. Sider, *Rich Christians in an Age of Hunger*, 70, 203.

4. These allusions are so prominent in the Psalms that any of several could be cited for study, including 10:14–18; 12:6; 37; 72 (especially 1–4 and 12–14); 82; 109 (especially 30–31); 116; and 140:13. The genre as well as the structure of every psalm, however, must be considered, as well as the meaning and place of the Book of Psalms in the piety of the people of the covenant. It is important to remember that these are songs which function in the fellowship of faith between individuals or between the people and Yahweh, the God of the covenant; therefore, they ought not to be used outside of the relationship with this God, as slogans or battle songs composed by anonymous and unidentified poets. At the same time, however, these believers, poets, and people of the covenant were expressing themselves on their God, on who he was and how he acted, on how they learned to know him and what they expected from him. In this sense the Book of Psalms does indeed deal with the image that the people of the covenant had of their God, and thereby it also deals with the image of God in the church of the New Testament, who in a very special way made this song-and-prayer book their own.

The confession refers specifically to Psalm 146. This is the first of the group of "hallelujah psalms" (146–150) with which the Book of Psalms closes. It is usually placed in the group of "individual hymns of thanksgiving" (Westermann, Kraus). It has a very simple structure (according to Kraus, it was probably intended to be memorized). Verses 1–2 form the characteristic introduction to an individual hymn of thanksgiving. The poet summons himself to praise the Lord and sing to his honor. The reason is provided in the remainder of the psalm. The power of the Lord to save from distress is contrasted with the inability of people to do the same. The negative is expressed in verses 3–4: "Put not your trust in princes, in a son of man, in whom there is no help." This "help" literally means that he "cannot save." " 'Save' is best understood as establishing the sort of order in which there is no injustice" (McKay, Cambridge commentary). The "princes," the "special people" (De Vaux: "les hommes 'excellents' "), are the "rich rulers" (Kraus). They do indeed radiate a tempting strength (Kraus) and are therefore a real temptation for the faithful, but the poet says that trust in them to do justice and deliver from distress is futile.

The positive is expressed in verses 5–10 where the Lord is praised as the one who can and wants to save. According to Lamparter these verses are not doctrinal, but pastoral. Kraus, however, is of the opinion that they are indeed doctrinal. It is especially meaningful that there is talk of the "God of Jacob," because in the Old Testament this title specifically referred to his "protecting and saving function" (Kraus). In a very special and moving way the protecting role of the Lord is then praised. "He not only *can* help, but *wants* to and *will* also help. And his help is wonderful. Whoever is oppressed and can find no justice and is therefore left to his own destiny, *finds without even asking* the God of Jacob *next to him*, and he supplies what people withhold: he grants them justice. Whoever is hungry and finds closed doors everywhere, because man prefers to receive rather

than give and is led by the spirit of Cain, suddenly sees bread for his body"
(Noordtzij). Of vital importance is the fact, as several commentators point out,
that it is a feature of God that is described and praised here; the passage thus
concerns an essential aspect of the Old Testament image of God. Calvin, for
example, writes: "All of [these instances] bear upon the point, that the help of
God will be ready and forthcoming to those who are in the lowest circumstances,
that accordingly our miseries will be no barrier in the way of his helping us; nay,
that such is his nature, that he is disposed to assist all in proportion to their
necessity." Weiser says: "The oppressed and bowed down, the prisoners, the
hungry, the sick and the defenceless, as well as the strangers, orphans, widows—
all these people find help and deliverance in God. This is a typical feature of Old
Testament religion, which has its origin in God's self-revelation and his nature
and will." Lamparter asserts that in these verses a vitally important insight, *which
permeates the entire Old Testament,* is expressed. This insight is beautifully
paraphrased by Noordtzij:

> In addition to this he follows "the Lord" by a verb, but in the form of a
> participle, so it thereby becomes clear that God does not do that once only, but
> always anew. As long as there are prisoners, he liberates them and delivers
> those without rights from their conquerors, who disposed of them at will. As
> long as there are blind—and there are so many in the East with its uncleanness
> and carelessness!—he performs for them the miracle of healing and he makes
> the eye reflect the light of heaven again. Whoever goes bowed down under the
> burden of life can trust that the moment will come in which the Lord will help
> him up also. Whoever is just and has the right on his side, but does not find any
> justice from people, can rest assured that the Lord will one day help him to find
> justice, because he loves the righteous. Whoever has to live in a country that is
> not his fatherland, and therefore has no rights but only obligations, whoever
> therefore suffers even more than others from the rulers over men is "pro-
> tected" by the Lord; a hand is held above his head by the Lord; he surrounds
> him with his fidelity and accompanies him with his mercy. The fatherless and
> widows who have lost their natural protector and who therefore lose so easily
> in the struggle for life he keeps standing; he keeps them on their feet, so that
> the attacks of others on them have no effect. He, however, who is "godless,"
> he who does not take God into consideration, but thinks himself lord of his
> own fate and therefore wants to plan his own destiny, will experience how
> fatal his mistake was: God bends his way, so that he loses his direction and
> moves along a totally different course than he suspected; he rushes to his
> destruction and death. Thus does the Lord! And he does that always, because
> he is forever king, his will is always law.

5. No complete ethical system can be derived from the wisdom literature.
P. J. Nel explains in *The Structure and Ethos of the Wisdom Admonitions in
Proverbs* that the "ethos of the wisdom" must not be classified around certain
themes in order to try to provide a comprehensive picture of the "moral system"
that the wisdom would teach on a certain issue or subject. No attempt should be
made to construct a doctrine of everything the wisdom would, for example, have
to say on "riches and poverty." In reality the ethos of wisdom is concerned with
the "fear of the Lord," which finds expression in an obedient acknowledgment of

the "created order" or "world order." Within this religious context the wisdom authors make almost casual ethical references, based on common knowledge and everyday experience. This also applies to conduct concerning riches and poverty. One well-known conviction, for example, is that poverty is often due to one's own guilt in which laziness usually plays a major role (Proverbs 13:25; 19:23; 13:18; 21:17; 23:21; 29:3). Frequently there are, however, flashes of something of the deep-rooted Israelite conviction that God is in a special way attached to the poor. Thus one reads: "He who is kind to the poor lends to the Lord, and he will repay him for his deed" (19:17), as well as: "He who oppresses a poor man insults his Maker, but he who is kind to the needy honors him (14:31).

Viewed as a whole the final conclusions in the dissertation of P. H. de V. Uys, "Reg en Geregtigheid aan die minder bevoorregtes in die boek Spreuke," are worthy of consideration:

> In the Old Testament Yahweh is described as the protector of the poor par excellence; different from anyone else, the only protector! The principle of the protection of the less privileged is seen in the ancient Near East as a special virtue of the king. Thus also in Israel. In later Israelite times this principle was obviously neglected by the kings, and therefore this subject became the theme of the moral preaching of the prophets. The kings failed. . . . The general idea in regard to the protection of the weak was furthermore expanded to the ordinary people. The vertical prohibition and/or command of God had to be fulfilled in horizontal relationships. Though our word "less privileged" has retained little—if any—of a principle of law, it became clear that the attitude toward the poor, the woman, the widow, the mute, the foreigner, etc. must be seen against a juridical background. *Those people indeed had very few rights. In order to restore the balance in society, they had to be protected.* Therefore it was necessary to sanction their protection by the direct command of God and to make it a special virtue of the king." (202–203)

6. Concerning the concepts related to "justice" in the Bible there exists an amount of literature too vast to be easily surveyed. It is indeed a complicated question, with numerous facets. Of special importance is the study of F. Crüsemann, "Jahwes Gerechtigkeit im Alten Testament," *Evangelische Theologie*, 36(1976), 427–450. He specifically goes into the question of the way in which the two concepts ṣädäq and ṣᵉdāqā are connected with Yahweh and his deeds, an aspect which is normally neglected because the research usually deals only in general with "justice." He mainly examines the texts in which Yahweh's ṣädäq or ṣᵉdāqā is directly mentioned (50 of the 139 cases where ṣᵉdāqā is used, but only 11 out of 117 occurrences of ṣädäq), as well as the texts in which it is clear that the ṣädäq/ṣᵉdāqā is also done or realized by Yahweh, but where "his" justice is not so explicitly mentioned (possibly a further 24 texts with regard to ṣᵉdāqā and possibly another 41 with regard to ṣädäq). He inquires specifically into the images, expectations, and experiences of Israel which were expressed by these references to the justice of Yahweh. In his opinion there is a clear development in the history of traditions to be discovered. He distinguishes (especially with reference to D. Michel) clearly between ṣädäq and ṣᵉdāqā. The former denotes an attribute or *quality*, and the latter—which is much more frequently used of Yahweh—denotes a *deed* or action. From that it already becomes clear

that there is much more talk of the "justice of Yahweh" as a deed or action than of his justice as a characteristic or attribute—although the instances of an absolute use of the terms can of course also sometimes be applied to him.

In the second place the distribution of the occurrences throughout the Old Testament is very interesting. In many large and important sections they do not occur at all. The parts in which they do occur can, according to Crüsemann, be divided into four groups or periods in the history of Israel:

1. two examples from the time before the foundation of the state, with some aftereffects in other parts of the Old Testament;
2. the application of these older insights and traditions in the Psalms (which he places in the period of the kings);
3. Deutero-Isaiah; and
4. Trito-Isaiah and other postexilic prophets.

Crüsemann detects an obvious development in the change of meaning of these expressions through these periods of history and regards the reasons for this development to be obvious. The two oldest references are Judges 5:11 (the song of Deborah) and Deuteronomy 33 (the blessings of Moses to the clans). From both it becomes clear that ṣidqōt Jhwh is used to describe the "helping deeds of Yahweh on behalf of Israel," or "victories over enemies, deliverance from situations of distress." This is the justice of Yahweh! Furthermore, the same deeds, says Crüsemann, can be described either as deeds of Yahweh or as deeds of Israel. The aftereffects of these beliefs he detects in Micah 6:5 and 1 Samuel 12:7. When Samuel in his valedictory address mentions the "righteous acts" (KJV) of Yahweh he refers to the *saving deeds* toward the people of Israel and their ancestors!

The second group of references he finds in the Book of Psalms, where more than half of the examples occur. He dates a few of the psalms in which these terms are used in other periods, some dating from after the exile, in the late wisdom, or as part of the songs of kings which are related to Deutero-Isaiah. In the remaining psalms, he finds a clear difference between the respective uses of ṣᵉdāqā and ṣādäq. The former, as a quality or an attribute, is used only a few times in connection with Yahweh and is almost always used in an absolute sense (see, for example, the very important Psalm 85:11–14: the almost "personified" justice here stands for "the victory over distress and the restoration of a normal and beneficial situation"). Much more important is the way in which ṣᵉdāqā is used in the psalms. In almost 80 percent of the occurrences in the psalms it is directly connected with Yahweh (27 out of 34). Of this number the vast majority (17) is found in a single genre, namely the so-called "lamentation of the individual." As an example, Crüsemann refers to Psalm 71, the "lamentation of an old man":

> In thy *righteousness* deliver me and *rescue* me;
> incline thy ear to me, and *save* me! (2)

> My mouth will tell of thy *righteous acts*,
> of thy deeds of *salvation* all the day,
> for their number is past my knowledge.
> With the *mighty deeds* of the Lord God I will come,
> I will praise thy *righteousness*, thine alone. (15–16)

[Thy power] and thy *righteousness,* O God, reach the high heavens.
Thou who *hast done great things,* O God, who is like thee? (19)

My lips will shout for joy, when I sing praises to thee;
my soul also, which thou hast *rescued.*
And my tongue will talk of thy *righteous help* all the day long,
for they have been put to shame and disgraced who sought
to do me hurt. (23–24)

From the *plea* in this type of lamentation as well as from the *thanksgiving* at the
end of the psalm for the salvation that is expected, it becomes very clear that
the "justice" of Yahweh is "nothing else, nothing less and nothing more" than
the *salvation* of the supplicant from his distress. That this "justice" is no technical term but rather a synonym for other concepts like trustworthiness, salvation,
and mercy is evident in several psalms, including 40:11.

Crüsemann refers to the "extremely complex question" concerning the relation between the justice of Yahweh (as his deed or act of salvation to the one in
distress) and the guilt or innocence of the supplicant who is rescued. He comes to
the conclusion that "the righteousness (saving deeds) of Yahweh is primarily
concerned with the distress as such and not with the problem of guilt or
innocence."

In the third group of examples, from Deutero-Isaiah, Crüsemann observes that
the hopeless situation of the exile adds a new element to the historical development of the meaning of the concept. Israel is at present "far from deliverance"
(46:12), but "I bring near my deliverance, it is not far off, and my *salvation* will
not tarry; I will put *salvation* in Zion, for Israel my glory" (46:13). The parallel
expressions as well as the context convince Crüsemann that here the justice of
Yahweh functions as "an indication of the repeated (described in the most varied
images and genres) proclamation by Deutero-Isaiah of a *new and eschatological
deed of salvation.*" The ṣedāqā of the Lord, or his deed of salvation, is now
expanded eschatologically and universally (45:20–25, especially verse 21: "a
righteous God and a Savior; there is none besides me." With him there is ṣedāqōt
wā'ōz, "righteousness and strength," "deeds of justice and power that establish
or create salvation" (24).

Crüsemann's fourth group of texts is to be found "in Trito-Isaiah and in a few
later additions to Deutero-Isaiah(!)." He points out 56:1 as an example: "Keep
justice, and do righteousness, for soon my salvation will come, and my deliverance be revealed." He sees the second part of the verse, which describes the
coming "justice or deed of salvation" of Yahweh, as being part of the "earlier"
tradition. A new element is, however, added here, namely that God's people are
now expected also to "keep justice and do righteousness." Besides, it goes even
further: if his people lack that kind of "justice," then his "justice," that is "his
coming salvation," "his coming eschatological and universal salvation," will
become a condemnation of his people in a lawsuit. His justice will then mean not
salvation, but separation and destruction, rejection and judgment. In Isaiah 59 it
becomes clear in a touching way:

Behold, the Lord's hand is not shortened, that it cannot save; or his ear dull,
that it cannot hear; but your iniquities have made a separation between you and

your God, and your sins have hid his face from you so that he does not hear. For your hands are defiled with blood and your fingers with iniquity; your lips have spoken lies, your tongue mutters wickedness. No one enters suit justly, no one goes to law honestly. . . . Therefore justice is far from us, and righteousness does not overtake us; we look for light, and behold, darkness, and for brightness, but we walk in gloom. We grope for the wall like the blind, . . . we look for justice, but there is none; for salvation, but it is far from us. For our transgressions are multiplied before thee, and our sins testify against us; for our transgressions are with us, and we know our iniquities: transgressing and denying the Lord, and turning away from following our God, speaking oppression and revolt, conceiving and uttering from the heart lying words. Justice is turned back, and righteousness stands afar off; for truth has fallen in the public squares, and uprightness cannot enter. Truth is lacking, and he who departs from evil makes himself a prey.

The Lord saw it, and it displeased him that there was no justice. He saw that there was no man and wondered that there was no one to intervene; then his own arm brought him victory, and his righteousness upheld him. He put on righteousness as a breastplate, and a helmet of salvation upon his head; he put on garments of vengeance for clothing, and wrapped himself in fury as a mantle.

In this respect Verhoef is totally correct when he writes in a detailed and clarifying article:

The "justice of God" also refers to the lifestyle of the chosen people themselves. . . . The "justice" of God is felt when injustice is done in the life of the people. We know that, for one group in society, things were not as they should have been; these were the so-called *personae miserae:* the widow and the fatherless, the foreigner, Levite, and day laborer. Their rights (mišpat) were taken from them, and their only hope was situated in him who exercises tsᵉdāqâ, and therefore manages their lawsuit. To restore the right of the wronged is par excellence the function of the king and especially also of the promised messiah. This *"prejudice" or specific alignment in favor of the poor and the wretched* in the meaning of the word tsᵉdāqâ, was the beginning of a development on account of which the word later achieved the meaning of "favor," "mercy," "charity," and even "the giving of alms". . . . *In the Old Testament we have the interesting situation that the "just" is not only someone who fulfills the norms and who satisfies the demands of society but that he also is someone whose rights have been taken from him within the society. In the latter situation "justice" takes the form of saving and delivering, as against punishment and condemnation.* ("Sol justitiae illustra nos," *Sol Justitiae,* 1–23)

Sider states the matter equally emphatically: ". . . the Israelites soon discovered that Yahweh's passion for justice was a two-edged sword. When they were oppressed, it led to their freedom. But when they became the oppressors, it led to their destruction" (55). When he somewhat later raises the question whether God "chooses sides," he refers to Deuteronomy 10:17–18, where it is said that God "is not partial." But far from the idea that this implies a sort of "neutrality," it is immediately added that he therefore "takes no bribe, but executes justice for the fatherless and the widow, and loves the sojourner, giving him food and clothing." Sider comments:

> God is not partial. He has the same loving concern for each person he has created. Precisely for that reason he cares as much for the weak and the disadvantaged as he does for the strong and fortunate, by contrast with the way you and I, as well as the comfortable and powerful of every age and society, always act toward the poor. But he is biased only in contrast with our sinful unconcern. . . . God, however, is not neutral. His freedom from bias does not mean that he maintains neutrality in the struggle for justice. God is on the side of the poor! The Bible clearly and repeatedly teaches that God is at work in history casting down the rich and exalting the poor, because frequently the rich are wealthy precisely because they have oppressed the poor or have neglected to aid the needy. . . . God also sides with the poor because he disapproves of extremes of wealth and poverty. The God of the Bible is on the side of the poor just because he is not biased, for he is a God of impartial justice. The rich neglect or oppose justice because justice demands that they end their oppression and share with the poor. Therefore God actively opposes the rich. But that does not in any way mean that he loves the rich less than the poor. He desires fulfilment, joy and happiness for all his creatures. But that does not contradict the fact that he is on the side of the poor. Genuine biblical repentance and conversion lead people to turn away from all sin—including economic oppression. Salvation for the rich will include liberation from their injustice. Thus God's desire for the salvation and fulfilment of the rich is in complete harmony with the scriptural teaching that God is on the side of the poor. . . . God's concern for the poor is astonishing and boundless. . . . Consequently, God's people—if they are indeed his people—follow in the footsteps of the God of the poor." (*Rich Christians in an Age of Hunger*, 76–77)

7. The criticism of the prophets on the occurrences and structures of injustice in society is well known. However, it is a mistake that in this regard reference is often made only to Amos. The special emphasis on social justice in Isaiah 1–10, for example, is undeniable, as it is also in the rest of Isaiah and in Jeremiah, Ezekiel, and Hosea. J. Miranda, *Marx and the Bible*, tries to demonstrate from Hosea and Jeremiah that the expressions "to know God" and "to do justice unto the destitute," are identical in content. For the references in the confession to Isaiah 1:16–17 and Amos 5, see respectively the exegesis of D. H. Odendaal, "Directions for the Preaching of Isaiah 1:18," *Woord teen die lig*, 2, 58–63 (soon to be published in English), though he works in the framework of Lent and more specifically concentrates on the transition to verse 18; and of M. L. Fouche, "Directions for the Preaching of Amos 5," *Woord teen die lig*, 6 (not published at the time of this writing).

8. There is no difference of opinion about the fact that the contrast between rich and poor plays an extremely important part in Luke. Time and again he deals with the contrast between rich and poor, between the so-called "haves" and the

"have nots," between the socially privileged and less privileged, between the rulers and the oppressed, the powerful and simple people. Even if one only looks at those sections of Luke which have no parallel with the other Gospels, it becomes abundantly clear how much interest he shows in this issue. Already in chapter 1:46–55 it occurs in the very important Magnificat of Mary. This song is a typical psalm of praise, with introduction, main section, and conclusion. Of special importance are the expressions "*the low estate* of his handmaiden" (48), "scattered the *proud* in the imagination of their hearts" (51), "he has put down the *mighty* from their thrones, and exalted *those of low degree;* he has filled the *hungry* with good things, and the *rich* he has sent empty away" (52–53).

Leivestad, "tapeinos-tapeinōfron," *Nov. Test.,* 8 (1966), 36–48, points out (in contrast to Grundmann's discussions of *tapeinos* and related words in *TDNT,* VIII, 1–27) that neither in the LXX nor in the late-Judaic and Christian idiom is this expression used to denote a positive moral attitude (like humility or meekness). The most that can be said is that it is sometimes used in an ethically neutral, if not totally scornful, manner. It consequently refers to the objective state of man, that is to his position or status and not to his attitude. Luther therefore translated the term in this context as "insignificance" ("low estate") instead of "humility," because the latter possibility could create the impression that the word connoted a virtue or meritorious attitude, which was not the case. The RSV translates verse 48 correctly as "the low estate," while the TEV uses "his lowly servant" and translates verse 52 as "the lowly." They are lifted up! The primary idea is undoubtedly the Old Testament conviction that God has mercy on those who are poor, simple, insignificant, and oppressed.

In the first place, the term describes the low estate (of Mary) in the world. Whether the aspect of her humble attitude toward God must be completely excluded is not so sure. These two aspects do not necessarily exclude one another; on the contrary, the first one leads to the second one. The *huperefanoi,* the *dunastas,* and the *ploutountas,* on the contrary, are those who in status as well as in attitude are the opposite of the humble and the lowly. Schoonheim, "Der ATe Boden des Vokabel *huperefanos,*" *Nov. Test.,* 8 (1966), 135ff., wrote that *huperefanos* indicated self-exaltation: "The arrogant is antagonistic toward God and therefore also toward people, because he himself is a god and he sees people only as objects of his tyranny." Brown, *The Birth of the Messiah,* 337, commented in a similar way: "The proud look down on others because they do not look up to God." This term is an indication of "arrogance" (Bertram, *TDNT,* VIII, 525–529).

The significance of all these accumulated parallel expressions in the Magnificat is clear. God is praised as the one who, with his mighty arm, overturns the worldly maladjustments of rich and poor, needy and self-sufficient, humble and mighty. These contrasts should be understood sociologically as well as religiously, says Hoyt, since they concern the tension between the really powerful and humble, as well as the often resulting tension between arrogance and humility. (For the Magnificat, see also D. J. Smit, "Directions for the Preaching of Luke 1:48–55," *Woord teen die lig,* 1, 65–75, to be translated soon.)

Luke maintains these themes throughout his Gospel, sometimes by means of smaller references or additions, sometimes with explicit examples and statements. In chapter 2 he draws a humble image of the birth of Jesus: no place in the inn; the shepherds are seen as social outcasts, often even as criminals; his parents bring the sacrifice of the poor, namely doves. In 3:10–14 John the Baptist's exhortations toward the three groups of people all have to do with this theme: the crowd must be generous, the publicans should not exploit, the soldiers (or rulers) should not misuse their power and desire greater riches. In chapter 4 a key pericope is found. In the synagogue in Nazareth Jesus quotes the section on the jubilee year from Isaiah 61 and defines his own coming and his task in terms of that. Exegetes generally acknowledge that Jesus' statement that the gospel is preached to the poor occupies the central position and receives all the emphasis. This is the nature and the mystery of his Messiahship, and it is even more wonderful than the miracles of healing that he does. Jeremias and others are of the opinion that it was precisely this emphasis on the poor that led to the rejection of Jesus in Nazareth, because it was offensive to those who heard him and who expected something different.

Still another remarkable and important section is Luke's version of the Beatitudes in 6:20–26, which reads: "Blessed are the poor (not "in spirit" like in Matthew); "Blessed are you that hunger now" (not "hunger and thirst for righteousness" like in Matthew). The impression that these statements concern real poverty and hunger is confirmed by the so-called "woe-expressions" which Luke includes: ". . . Woe to you that are rich, for you have received your consolation. Woe to you that are full now, for you shall hunger." In verses 32–38 the disciples are exhorted to lend without expecting something back, to do good, to show mercy, and to give generously.

In chapter 8 Luke tells of the women who served Jesus with their possessions as well as of the seed which was, among other things, suffocated by wealth—but these events and sayings are recorded elsewhere, as are the references in chapter 9 that the disciples were sent out without money, which is again referred to in chapter 11. In chapter 11 there is another call to mercifulness, which, again, also occurs elsewhere. In chapter 12:16–21 the parable of the rich fool appears, which only Luke relates and which ends with the warning: "So is he who lays up treasure for himself, and is not rich toward God." The immediate subsequent warning against the cares of life and a fruitless and sinful striving after food, drink, and possessions does have a parallel in Matthew, but not the concluding verses which once again summon the disciples to give alms. In this way a treasure in heaven is obtained. In 14:7–11 he relates the quite practical parable about the places at a marriage feast and concludes with the remark that he who humbles himself will be exalted, and he who exalts himself will be humbled. The following verses are powerful in their direct impact: "He said also to the man who had invited him, 'When you give a dinner or a banquet, do not invite your friends or your brothers or your kinsmen or rich neighbors, lest they also invite you in return, and you be repaid. But when you give a feast, invite the poor, the maimed, the lame, the blind, and you will be blessed, because they cannot repay you. You will be repaid at the resurrection of the just' " (14:12–14). This command to exercise concrete love of the neighbor toward the poor and the outcast was clearly a reprimand to the Pharisees and everybody else who excluded the ordinary "people of the land" from those toward whom one should practice love.

The eschatological aspect is very prominent in all these sections: just relations will be restored at the last day and charitableness and love toward the less privileged will be rewarded. The same theme comes to the fore in the parable of the great banquet which follows. Jesus explains that the joy of the kingdom will not be tasted by many of those invited, but most certainly by "the poor and maimed and blind and lame," even if they have to be "compelled" to enter. (The addition in Matthew about the guest without a wedding garment does not even occur in Luke.) Another parable in Luke without a parallel is the strange sermon on the unrighteous steward in 16:1–9. Obviously the point is that the disciples should view earthly possessions as opportunities to assure a place for themselves in the "eternal habitations" by making friends "by means of unrighteous mammon," in other words by charitableness. It is for this reason that the Pharisees, "who were lovers of money," scoffed at him (14), causing Jesus to reprimand them by saying that "what is exalted among men" is an abomination in the sight of God.

Equally clear is the touching parable of the rich man and Lazarus (whose name means "God helps") on the fact that the law and the prophets teach mercy and that he who does not attend to that will also not listen even if someone were to rise from the dead (16:19–31). Especially remarkable is the fact that Luke mentions no moral qualities of either the rich man or Lazarus but simply describes only the abundance of the one and the poverty of the other. (Although it is impossible in this overview to make any sort of a complete list of the relevant literature, the famous meditation of Noordmans cannot be omitted. It is the title meditation in his book *Zondaar en Bedelaar* and hinges upon a comparison between the parable of the Pharisee and the publican [or sinner] and this parable of Lazarus [or beggar]. It struggles in a fascinating way, in a way which may sound foreign to us, with the question whether God's grace does not include both forms of distress. It is also included in his *Verzamelde Werken*, 8, 15–25.) The episode with the rich ruler, who had to distribute all his possessions among the poor and who could not follow Jesus because he was very rich, is also recorded by Matthew with more minor alterations. The expression which Jesus uses just after that to show what discipleship implies, namely "to leave everything," occurs often in Luke; see 5:11, 28 and 14:33: "So, therefore, whoever of you does not renounce all that he has cannot be my disciple." Also, the conversion of Zaccheus, "a rich man" who finally gives away half his possessions to the poor and refunds fourfold that which he has extorted, occurs only in Luke.

This is not the proper place to examine these passages in more detail and to try to draw conclusions. From the abundant data, however, it becomes clear how central this question was to Luke. It is equally certain that these expressions should not be spiritualized, as if Luke talked only about spiritual or religious poverty and riches, about the distress of sin and the deeds of the soul. For the early Christian church these were words of immediate comfort. God has mercy on the "have nots," the destitutes and lowly of this world. A great deal of literature is available on this subject, much of it inexpensive and written in a popular style and therefore easy to use. In addition, there are of course a variety of detailed studies on the individual texts. Some of the most well-known general works on this theme are H.-J. Degenhardt, *Lukas: Evangelist der Armen;* R. Koch, "Die Wertung des Besitzes im Lukasevangelium," *Biblica,* 38, 151–169; L. T. Johnson: *The Literary Function of Possessions in Luke-Acts;* W. Schmithals, "Lukas: Evangelist der Armen," *Theologia Viatorum,* 12 (1973), 153ff.; R. J. Cassidy, *Jesus, Politics and Society;* C. H. Lindijer, *De armen en de rijken bij Lukas;* D. L.

Mealand, *Poverty and Expectation in the Gospels;* L. Schottroff and W. Stegemann, *Jesus von Nazareth—Hoffnung der Armen.*

9. See D. J. Smit, "The Preaching of the Miracles," *Woord teen die Lig,* II/1, planned for publication in 1984 (and for translation into English).

10. See P. J. Robinson, "Directions for the Preaching of Matthew 25:31–46," *Woord teen die Lig,* 6, for a detailed discussion of literature and interpretations.

11. The emphasis on the mutual showing of love, on communion, on the struggle for equality, and on the distribution of personal possessions in the early church is well known. Numerous theories on the organization of the lifestyle of the church, on the deaconship and its meaning and function, on the witnessing power of a sober and sharing lifestyle, and even on "economic systems" have been built on these facts. A very careful, balanced, and respected opinion is that of M. Hengel, *Property and Riches in the Early Church.* He tries to trace some lines of the social history of early Christianity on the assumption that it could be of "exemplary significance" for today's Christians. Although we should not expect a "ready-made program" or blueprint to emerge, the early church practice does provide the "basic impulses" for our own conduct and behavior. He investigates not only the information from Acts but also the entire image of early Christianity, including the Old Testament and Judaic traditions, the ancient philosophy of natural law and its influence on the church, the data from the Gospels concerning Jesus' attitude and conduct, the so-called "love communism" of the primitive community, various material from Paul, the apocalyptic traditions, Clement of Alexandria, Cyprian, and the popular philosophy and the basic cultural preconceptions of that time. Finally, he makes certain important conclusions as a "kind of bridge" between early Christianity and today. Some of these explain his point of view very clearly:

1. We cannot extract a well-defined "Christian doctrine of property" either from the New Testament or from the history of the early church. . . .

2. Primitive Christianity contains a radical criticism of riches, a demand for detachment from the goods of this world and a conquest of the barriers between rich and poor through the fellowship of agape. All this comes about under the shadow of the imminent coming of the Kingdom of God. It robs "unrighteous mammon" of its force. In the further course of the history of early Christianity this stimulus leads to a tense controversy over injustice and the limitations and relative necessity of property. [In his historical review on the role of wealth and poverty in church history, W. Kerber, "Armut und Reichtum," *Christlicher Glaube in moderner Gesellschaft,* 17, 102, says that some patriarchs emphasized so strongly the idea that possessions are meant for the benefit of all people and that consequently no one should dispose of it alone that historians judged that their viewpoints boiled down to a total rejection of private possessions. Kerber himself is of the opinion that this is a wrong conclusion, because the modern question concerning private possession was not in dispute at that time.]

3. Because they come from such a different situation, the various statements made in early Christianity can only be applied with many qualifications to our industrial society and the problems of possessions which oppress us today. [This is certainly true. The same conclusion can indeed be reached on other grounds, as, for example, the true nature and authority of the Bible, which is not a textbook on economics and does not seek to be one, or from the diversity of economic situations and directions which are present in the Bible itself. This is the reason the confession does not present clear-cut economic or political alternatives or make choices between alternative systems. At the same time it does not, of course, alter the great importance of the Biblical "dream," "vision," or "perspective," also on wealth and poverty, which surely stays valid and normative for the Church through the centuries.]

4. For the first Christians the problem of possessions was a problem of personal ethics or at most the problem of relatively small groups. . . . The possibility of better social legislation was no more within their scope than the limitation of the economic omnipotence of the state. [What applied to the slave trade naturally also applies here. In changed circumstances, when Christian values and principles have spread and have started to influence and stamp the society and even the cultural traditions, that which was formerly unimaginable and impracticable now became imperative. When groups and individuals begin to receive political and economic power and responsibility and at the same time profess to be Christians who wish to live Christian lives, the questions concerning the implications of the evangelical lifestyle toward wealth and poverty also become vitally important for national and even international economic relations and structures. Of course the state or society never becomes the Church, and of course solutions and practices remain relative and subject to that which is possible and sensible, often viewed in the long term and always in the light of the restricting role that reality plays. These factors, however, also apply to an individual Christian or the Church's relation toward possessions and toward the neighbor, which makes it clear that it cannot be used as an excuse for state and society not to seek for a Christian lifestyle!]

5. As a result, early Christian ethics cannot provide us with any system of generally binding norms for today's society, nor does it set out to do so. However, we can gain certain insights from it. . . . One example is the idea that in some circumstances property leads man astray and puts him in danger, and that it can even seduce him into the misuse of power. Further, that for this very reason the misuse of power must be prevented by public controls and that those who own it must be obliged to use it also for the well-being of their fellow-men, or that a man's status and value in no way depends on his capacity to accumulate means of wealth. Readiness to refuse to become a consumer and to renounce luxury in a world in which extravagance and poverty often stand side by side can also very well be motivated by Christian tradition. . . .

7. Here we can see a dilemma which we have already met in part, although in another form, in the discussion on early Christianity: the crisis of property also proves to be the crisis of man, his selfish desire to assert himself, his struggle for power and his mercilessness. Here we can see what the fathers called *original sin*. It may sound old-fashioned today, but it is very real. . . .

8. Knowledge of man's selfish heart prevents the Christian from having an uncritical and utopian faith in the possibility of an ultimately perfect society, an infallibly political orthopraxy, a realizable, ideal "kingdom of freedom" which in some circumstances would have to be introduced by an act of force and whose goal would be the equality of all individuals and the end of "man's rule over men." [In the confession too there is no mention of such an idealistic, man-made realization of a perfect dispensation; on the contrary, it is confessed explicitly that the Church believes in God who wants to bring justice and real peace. The Church is only God's disciple and witness. Nothing is consequently subtracted from the so-called "eschatological reservation."]

9. This knowledge of man's selfish heart should not just lead to a resigned attitude which simply confirms and fixes existing social conditions. Precisely because man is entangled in his "boundless" egotism both as an individual and as a group, we are called to constant reform, to progress toward the better. ["Better" is of course something totally different from "perfect." The problem with the continuous appeal on the "eschatological reservation" is exactly that people hide behind it in order to make permanent the present, the—for them beneficient—status quo. Thereby that appeal, which is in itself absolutely true and legitimate, becomes an excuse for the lack of a biblical dream and for the failure to obey the call to discipleship. What H. Thielicke, *Theological Ethics,* calls "political radicalism" is rejected for the sake of a "false conservatism," and in the meantime the demand for implementing the Christian ethos remains a theological football and a neglected responsibility.]

10. Finally, as an example of faith, we may remind ourselves of the attempt of the first Christian communities to resolve the tension which destroys fellowship between poor and rich, freemen and slaves, and to do away with the oppositions. This moves between the "love communism" of the early community—which to our eyes seems unrealistic—and the more effective—but still endangered—compromise of the communities of the later period. This equalization created a healthy detachment from external goods, and at the same time overcame the barriers of status and class. The church, even today, could again become the place where mistrust and old prejudices are overcome and new forms of life and community are created on the basis of faith, love and hope. Furthermore, it is our duty as Christians and citizens to be ready to make sacrifices of our own and by pressure for better legislation, break down social barriers, help minorities to achieve justice, and bring complexes of arbitrary power under better, democratic control. In this way we shall rob the "demonic" nature of property of its force. (84–88)

If, in addition, we take into consideration the fact that Hengel shares the widespread mistrust of drawing ethical directives from the Bible and does not even want to draw political implications out of, for example, the Sermon on the Mount, it is clear that his comments represent the absolute minimum that has to be said.

12. In the Epistles to the Corinthians there are several sections which function repeatedly in this regard and which are the subject of frequent comment in the relevant literature. Especially the appeal of 2 Corinthians 8 and 9 to abundant

generosity, motivated by a reference to "the grace of our Lord Jesus Christ, that though he was rich, yet for your sake he became poor, so that by his poverty you might become rich" (8:9), is often discussed. Less obvious but still vitally important are the exhortations in 1 Corinthians 11 arising from the abuses in the celebration of the Lord's Supper. The argument in verses 17–34 forms a firm unity. Certain improper practices had developed around the celebration, so that Paul felt himself obliged to say that their "coming together" is not for the better, but for the worse (17). Therefore he did not commend them (22). With an appeal to the institution of the meal, familiar to them, he exhorted them to abandon this unworthy and inappropriate conduct (23–28). Whoever did not judge himself in the light of this truth, ran the risk of judgment (27–32). Therefore he concluded the exhortation with practical directives meant as a possible solution to the abuses which had developed (33–34).

The main exegetical problem is to try to understand the exact nature of these abuses. In a certain sense consensus exists on this. It is universally accepted that the improper practices became visible in loveless mutual conduct (Ridderbos, Berkouwer, Bornkamm, Goppelt, Bohren, Groenewald, Conzelmann, Wendland, Marshall, etc.). A considerable number of exegetes try to go back even further. They ascribe this lack of communal sense to still more deeply hidden *theological* motives in the form of an erroneous view of the sacrament. This misconception regarding the sacrament is then regarded as the actual point of Paul's rejection. Lietzmann's well-known theories played an especially influential part in this connection for a very long time.

An extremely important new direction in the debate was shown by the contribution of G. Bornkamm, "Lord's Supper and Church in Paul," *Early Christian Experience,* 123–160, which was generally accepted. He demonstrated that the problem was not with those who underestimated and undervalued the sacraments, but on the contrary with so-called "sacramentalists" or people who in fact overestimated the meaning of the sacraments. They attached such an exaggerated value to the sacrament that they totally despised the regular common meal of love (agape) or the congregational meal during which the sacramental act took place. In their opinion it was sufficient if everyone only shared in the holy sacrament, so that it was not really necessary at the common meal to wait for everybody. In their eyes it was clearly not wrong to start the meal of love before everyone was present or even to finish eating without leaving something for everyone. Bornkamm argued that it was therefore much rather the common meal of fellowship that was despised and devaluated than the sacrament. The meal was profaned. The reason for Paul's exhortation was that, in his opinion, through their loveless conduct and their scandalous violation of brotherly duty, in spite of their high esteem for the sacrament the very essence of the sacrament was endangered!

According to Bornkamm, the correct and required distribution of goods was neglected. While some feasted, others starved and felt their own poverty in a painful and (for the congregation of Christ) humiliating way. Instead of the congregation displaying the image of real communion between brothers and sisters in their communal worship and celebration of the sacrament, they showed an impudent picture of social dissension. From the data in the chapter, it is clearly the ordinary people, especially the poor and the slaves whose time was not at their own disposal and who consequently arrived late, who starved and were put to shame. Nobody was excluded from the "high and holy" sacrament, said Bornkamm, but at the preceding meal everyone pleased himself and nobody had any scruples about slighting the poor and the latecomers. "Everyone can imagine the very understandable reasons which may have played a role there: the very human tendency to a sociability among one's own; antipathy for the embarrassment that comes when rich and poor, free and slave, sit bodily at one table—real table-fellowship is something quite different from charity at a distance; the worry that the 'atmosphere' for receiving the sacrament may be spoiled by such an embarrassing rubbing of elbows with the poor. All that had led to the 'taking beforehand' of the one meal."

Paul's reproach was that such conduct, however understandable it might have been, was in direct conflict with the heart of the sacrament and might have deadly serious consequences for them. When he wrote in verse 29 that their conduct boiled down to the fact that they did not discern "the body (of the Lord)," it did not exclusively concern the holy nature of the elements which they failed to appreciate (i.e., in a sacramental-christological sense) but also the fact that those gifts actually bound them all together in the one "body" of the Lord—which they profaned (i.e., in an ecclesiological sense). Conzelmann also accepted this interpretation in his commentary and said that Paul did not plead for greater respect for the elements, but that his criticism was directed against the fact that everyone used the Lord's Supper for his own pleasure and religious benefit without realizing sufficiently that it was intended to unite them in love and community. In a very interesting—although speculative—study G. Theissen, "Soziale Integration und sakramentales Handeln," *Nov. Test.*, 16 (1974), 179–206 (also in his *The Social Setting of Pauline Christianity*, 145–174), entered further into this matter. He studied the social conflict behind the abuses and developed the thesis that the source of the problem lay not in theological differences but in social or class differences. He pointed out that the early Christian hellenistic congregations differed radically from other organizations and religious groupings of that time which were mostly socially homogeneous, representing a certain occupation or class. Christian congregations, on the other hand, displayed a great social variety. In his opinion a society with such a heterogeneous social composition had from the start an extremely difficult task in attempting to accommodate the divergent expectations, interests, and systems of values it represented. For this reason it could be expected that theological differences could frequently be influenced by all sorts of nontheological and social factors.

According to this theory the abuses at the Lord's Supper were not the fault of individuals, but the result of the strangeness between two distinct groups or classes, namely those who were able to provide their own meals and the poor. For an exposition of his theory, as well as a more detailed discussion of the pericope, see D. J. Smit, "Directions for the Preaching of 1 Corinthians 11:17–30," *Woord teen die Lig*, 4, 142–157.

13. Concerning James it is again vitally important not to ignore the genre or intent of the book and to deal with the content and its ethical exhortations in an illegitimate way. On the origin as well as on the theological nature of James, the Church throughout its history, from the early church through the Reformation up to modern exegesis, has known more difference of opinion than on any other New

Testament epistle (L. Goppelt, *Theology of the New Testament*, vol. II, 119). For a long time James was considered as essentially a Jewish document (Spitta, Meyer, Windisch). The name "Jesus," for example, occurs only twice. With the advent of form criticism, which was used by Dibelius and others, this point of view was abandoned, and it was generally accepted that the work belongs to a very special genre, namely the "parenetic document of instruction." This insight is of great importance for the case in question, because it means that the ethical exhortations in James are loose proverbs, without a definite order or theme, frequently joined with a key word only as transition.

Consequently the real question concerns the tradition or theological position of intent from which these loose exhortations originate; in other words, how they are meant and how they are meant to be heard—even today. Some (e.g., Schlatter, Mussner) relate them to the doctrine of Jesus himself, like the Sermon on the Mount and the beatitudes, while others locate them in the early period when the expectation of the parousia was still strongly centered on the immediate future and ethical regulations were colored by that imminent anticipation in a way the Church of the following generations could not maintain. The "decisive theological question" (Goppelt) is whether the parenesis of James is eschatological in the sense that it goes beyond the immanent, realizable, and attainable possibilities in the world or whether it does indeed provide practicable and feasible ethical exhortations.

The literature on James deals mostly with the question of the relation between faith and works (which implies the relation with Paul and the rest of the New Testament and even puts at stake the canonicity of the book). In this discussion the role of the law or *nomos* is very important. While the rest of the New Testament frequently makes clear that the *nomos* has expired for the Christian in some way or another, James states no less than eight times that the *nomos* still retains validity for the congregation. His references to the law as the "law of liberty" (1:25; 2:12) provide an important key to understanding this. With this expression he highlights the fact that the "law" is nothing else than the imperative side of the same "word," which was "implanted in" and which brought forth the believers (1:18, 21).

That "word" liberates man by grace for new possibilities in life and for new relationships. The "law" or the "works" are consequently only the reverse side of the "word" or "grace." He does not preach salvation on the basis of the works of the law, but only emphasizes the "imperative side" (Goppelt) of the word of the gospel. Of great importance is the fact that he calls that law "perfect" and "royal." The law is not the Old Testament or the Ten Commandments or the love command or any specific aspects of the Ten Commandments, as is often thought, but the total claim of God on man in the gospel. Of this total claim the Old Testament laws, the Ten Commandments, the command to love as well as his own loose parenetical references are only "examples." It is precisely because the law claims man entirely for God, that it is called "perfect" (*teleios*). Whoever fails in one of the laws breaks them all, because he transgresses against the one God who stands with his total claim behind these separate, almost exemplary laws. The parenetic prescriptions of this book may therefore not be isolated from this perfect and royal law of liberty, from the one who stands with his total claim behind these examples, as if they were ordinances with a timeless validity to be used in legalistic or casuistic applications or systems. In such a way the genre and meaning of these writings would be violated and the ethical exhortations abused. At the same time, however, these exhortations are valid and permanent examples of the total claim of God on man, so that they may also not be ignored or underestimated. Exactly in their loose interrelatedness they remain legitimate directions to the demands of God for us also.

In this sense it is remarkable to see the role which wealth and poverty play in the book. Already in 1:9–11, where trials or temptations are mentioned, James says: "Let the lowly brother boast in his exaltation, and the rich in his humiliation, because like the flower of the grass he will pass away. . . . So will the rich man fade away in the midst of his pursuits." The congregation obviously was very much aware of this gulf. Verse 14 reads that people are tempted when they are lured and enticed by their own desire, and verses 17ff. note that every perfect gift is from the father, but without any direct reference to riches and poverty. In the important verses 19–27 the doing of the word is contrasted with hearers who do not do and therefore deceive themselves. What must the hearers of the word do? In verse 27 it is said almost by way of definition: "Religion that is pure and undefiled before God and the Father is this: to visit orphans and widows in their affliction, and to keep oneself unstained from the world."

Immediately after that, in 2:1–13, the relations within the congregation between rich and poor are examined in detail. He states that Christians should not be partial in that they treat people differently on account of their outward appearances ("people should not be treated in different ways" TEV). Verses 1–4 clearly deal with "evil thoughts" or wrongful considerations which played a part in the conduct of their services of worship. "A poor man in shabby clothing" is treated with less honor in the gathering, and James rejects that as "making distinction among yourselves" and adds that they have "become judges with evil thoughts." The point is clear as crystal. The so-called "normal" relations which dominate society are abolished within the Church. There people are thought of and judged differently than in society. Other norms are valid. No one is made to sit separately, "here" or "there," "at the feet" or in "a good place" or an inferior place, in a gallery or any other separate location on account of various irrelevant considerations. Even the sharp division between masters and slaves—which was a much stronger social stratification than anything we know—does not play a role in the organization of the congregation in such a way that there too the poor are maltreated. Why not? Verses 5ff. provide the answer: because God himself, who never treats people in different ways, has chosen the poor, elected them, that is, treated them in a very special way. "Never treating people in different ways" surely does not mean "neutrality" or "objectivity" as is thought and asserted frequently. On the contrary, "Never treating people in different ways" is the same as "not judging according to their outward appearance," and that means not to treat somebody according to whether he or she is rich or poor. Whenever this rule is ignored it leads to inadmissible divisions in the congregation! Not treating people in different ways because of their outward appearance means to choose the poor, to assist and aid, to sustain and deliver them, like God, and not to treat them with the (usual) "dishonor" (6). The congregation indeed boasts to God who has not treated them according to their "outward appearance" and has not done unto them as they deserved. He has shown mercy unto them, and therefore they must also have mercy. The passage concludes with the exhortation that the judgment should be full of mercy to one who has shown mercy and it will be without mercy to one who has shown no mercy.

With that the case is not closed. In the next passage James explains that faith becomes genuine only if it finds expression in works. The illustration he chooses is once again derived from the relations between rich and poor. If a brother or sister is ill-clad and lacks for daily food, it does not help at all to wish that person all of the best without doing something to change his or her situation. In this way, he says, faith without works is dead. Such a faith cannot save anyone, even if some will confess with their lips that they are believers.

The first twelve verses of chapter 3 are used as an exhortation against the abuse of the tongue. This "little member" of the body causes incalculable damage because it is used by believers to praise God in their confession and services of worship and at the same time to curse men "who are made in the likeness of God." "Curse" must surely be seen here, like everything else in the book of James, against the Old Testament–Judaic background. It means to plunge someone into misfortune by bringing misery over him. There are of course various ways in which this can happen. It is not far-fetched at least to consider also the way in which the tongue is used to talk about the poor. This incongruity in the tongue's uses, however, is impossible for the Christian, writes James. A brackish spring cannot possibly give fresh water! From verses 13–18 he warns among other things against "jealousy and selfish ambition" (14, 16) and pleads for an attitude of "openness to reason," "mercy" ("full of compassion," TEV), and one that is "free from prejudice" (TEV).

In the first part of chapter 4 some of these motives are repeated, as, for example, the warning against selfishness, avarice, and pride (1–10) and that against speaking evil against one another (11–12). In verse 13 the right attitude of dependent trust in God is taught, once again illustrated by a clear reference to the traders or the rich who "trade and get gain" (13) and in the process start to think that they dispose of their own lives.

Even this is not the end. Chapter 5 is as stinging a condemnation of the "rich" as one can find:

> Come now, you rich, weep and howl for the miseries that are coming upon you. Your riches have rotted and your garments are moth-eaten. Your gold and silver have rusted, and their rust will be evidence against you and will eat your flesh like fire. You have laid up treasure for the last days. Behold, the wages of the laborers who mowed your fields, which you kept back by fraud, cry out; and the cries of the harvesters have reached the ears of the Lord of hosts. You have lived on the earth in luxury and in pleasure; you have fattened your hearts in a day of slaughter. You have condemned, you have killed the righteous man; he does not resist you.

Once again motives from the Old Testament and the Gospels are reiterated in various complaints against the rich. By implication the most fundamental of these is that they do not take God into account, do not reckon with him, and do not obey his commandments. It finds expression, however, in the fact that they do not understand the seriousness of the hour, the *kairos* ("the day of slaughter!"), but even more, that they treat the poor laborers with injustice, hold back their wages and by doing so have "killed" ("murdered," TEV) them.

James's language here reminds one of the well-known history of Bartolomé de Las Casas, the priest who was radically converted in 1514 in the Caribbean while reading the passage from Ecclesiasticus—Ben Sirach—34:18–22: "The sacrifice of an offering unjustly acquired is a mockery. . . . Offering sacrifice from the property of the poor is as bad as slaughtering a son before his father's very eyes. A meagre diet is the very life of the poor, he who withholds it is a man of blood. A man murders his neighbor if he robs him of his livelihood, sheds blood if he withholds an employee's wages." On account of this Las Casas began his lifelong struggle against the economic and social injustice committed against the Indians, in which he himself had previously participated as a matter of course and totally unwittingly. He could celebrate no mass or eucharist any longer, because the bread, as a symbol of production through the labor of man, was the life of the poor, and the bread he would have to sacrifice in the mass had in his opinion been taken from the poor and was therefore "stained with blood." The same radical identification with the poor expressed in James is also found in the Catholic narrative according to which the sixteenth-century missionary Franciscus Solano, when he was invited to a meal by a group of military conquerors, took a piece of bread while pronouncing the benediction and pressed it in his hands until blood started to flow from it. With the words "This blood is the blood of the Indians," he went back to the monastery without eating. Later he reportedly said: "I cannot eat from a table where people eat bread kneaded with the blood of the humble and the oppressed." (Both these accounts are found in Dussel, "Het brood van de viering: gemeenschapsteken van gerechtigheid," *Conc.*, 1982/2, 65–74.) What is certainly no legend is the account that the author Upton Sinclair on occasion read James 5:1–5 to a group of ministers, but said that he had been written by a well-known anarchist agitator. The ministers were highly indignant and declared that the agitator should be deported at once (Sider, *Rich Christians in an Age of Hunger*, 118). Immediately after this condemnation of the rich, James follows with an exhortation to patience, perseverance, and trust in the Lord (7–11).

All these data clearly throw important light on the questions concerning riches and poverty which remained valid and normative for Christians throughout the centuries. An illustration of the way this information should *not* be used is provided by G. Maier in *Reichtum und Armut*. He writes as a self-confessed "pietist," and evidently his intention is to try to reject or minimize all possible consequences which can be drawn from these passages in James as they relate to current socio-ethical questions. He repeatedly emphasizes that the book of James only concerns individual conduct in the life and worship of the congregation and that all sorts of issues were not condemned or dealt with by James. Even though that may be a correct version of how James understood his prescriptions in his situation, still it represents the kind of argument with which the slave trade too was biblically justified and defended: the Bible does not explicitly reject it; in fact it does not even express an opinion on it and by implication is not interested in these kinds of questions, but simply accepts them as given realities. However true this may be, it is clear that the biblical message creates new possibilities under new circumstances; in the light of these challenges its message must be actualized ever again in new ways. *This* is therefore the correct and legitimate way in which the "parenetic instruction" of James should still be made concrete by Christians who live from the "word" and the "law of liberty"—also with regard to riches, poverty, and economic relations. The "fatherless and the widow" have different faces and other names, but they are still with us, and to "visit them in their affliction" still remains "pure and undefiled religion."

14. There can be no doubt about the central importance of the command in 1 John to show brotherly love. References recur repeatedly in central places (2:9; 3:9–18; 4:8–20); "indeed, the author puts such love on the same level of importance as correct belief in Jesus Christ" (R. Brown, with reference to 3:23). The central theme of the epistle can perhaps even be formulated as "the fellowship of believers with God and with one another" (Du Plessis). The polemic point in the epistle is an attempt to link together fellowship with God and with one another against the preachers of false doctrine (antichrists!—4:3). His use of "commandments" in several other places—commandments which are neglected by the false teachers—applies undoubtedly also to this brotherly love. The false preachers swerve from the truth in their viewpoints as well as in their conduct (Brown, 84). This is perfectly in line with the priority which brotherly love receives in the Gospel of John. Brown argues that the preachers of false doctrine theoretically would deny that they do not love the brothers—as they understood this command—in spite of the fact that they did not in fact do so. "I propose that it was perfectly possible for the secessionists to affirm, 'We love one another, as Jesus commands,' and still to earn the epistolary author's condemnation for not loving the brothers." This is undoubtedly true. Brown himself tries to solve this apparent paradox by the theoretical interpretation that the two groups defined "one another" or "the brothers" differently. The secessionists were no longer brothers. Therefore John could condemn them—in an apparently unbrotherly and unloving way—and could describe them as demonic antichrists and false prophets and as the embodiment of the eschatological evil (*anomia*). When he summons the (real) brothers to love one another, he immediately follows this by saying that they should not receive the secessionists into their houses nor give them any greeting: "for he who greets him shares his wicked work" (2 John 10–11). It is even possible that apostasy was the "mortal sin" (5:15–17), so that he forbids the brothers even to pray for the secessionists!

This is of course only a debatable exegetical theory. But something about which there is no doubt at all is the fact that John views brotherly love as very *practical*, concrete conduct. This love must be done, must be made visible in *deeds* of self-sacrifice and in aid to those who suffer want. Chapter 3:11–18 makes this crystal clear. Of great importance is the fact that John frequently writes: "By this we know love, that he laid down his life for us." This does not mean that we knew beforehand what love was and then recognized God's love for us in the death of Jesus. It rather means that we saw for the first time what love really is when Christ laid down his life for us. God in a way "defined" love in the death of Christ. This is an important insight whenever the word "love" is used in an inflationist way. Everyone likes "love"—his or her own idea of love. Everyone likes it when John writes: "God is love." This order, however, should not be reversed. Nobody is allowed to say: "Love is God" and then to elevate one concept of love (sentimental, sexual, selfish, sectional, etc.) to a divine norm. John underlines emphatically that we "have seen" love, it was "made manifest" among us (4:9), we have learned "to know and believe" that love (4:16). In *that* love we must abide and according to that love we must live in order to abide in God. The cross consequently forms the norm and standard of true love.

In addition to that it is necessary to emphasize that we have *to abide* in this love. 1 John 3:16 should be read together with the well-known John 3:16; the one should not be disconnected from the other. Without 1 John 3:16, John 3:16 would be "cheap grace," false gospel. Without John 3:16, 1 John 3:16 would, however, be law. The two together, the commandment grounded in grace, the imperative on the basis of the indicative, our love the fruit (and not the condition) of God's love—that is the gospel!

The real purport of the text is the conclusion that we also should love one another in the same way. In verse 16 John says: "We ought to lay down our lives for the brethren" (like Jesus). With that he does not so much want to call us to martyrdom, but rather wants to show the limits to which our love should be willing to go. Even if it was never asked of us, we ought to love our brothers to such an extent that we would be willing—if it might be necessary—to lay down our lives for them, like Jesus. This high ideal—to which one can easily profess one's willingness knowing that in all probability one might never be asked to do so—is immediately brought down to earth. Whoever said "yes" to verse 16 ought to be willing also to do what seems in comparison to be a mere "trifle"— like sharing one's "world's goods" with the brother in need! In this way the "trifles" become the true test for our "great love." Between verses 16 and 17 he also changes from the plural to the singular. It almost sounds as if he wants to talk more intimately, directly, personally. Now we should no longer hide in large crowds or behind beautiful slogans. Are we willing to verify our impressive professions in unsensational and commonplace showing of love? "Love is the willingness to surrender that which has value for our own life to enrich the life of another" (Dodd). "It is easier to be enthusiastic about Humanity with a capital H than it is to love individual men and women, especially those who are uninteresting, exasperating, depraved, or otherwise unattractive. Loving everybody in general may be an excuse for loving nobody in particular" (Lewis). "Love means saying 'no' to one's own life so that somebody else may live" (Marshall).

The expression "closes his heart" of verse 17 should also be understood in this way ("heart" is the translation for *splencha,* or entrails, in ancient times regarded as the seat of the emotions). "To close the heart" denotes the refusal to do these deeds of practical service and love. Psychologically this can happen in several ways: rationalizing ("I don't have so much either," "it is his own fault that he finds himself in such a sorry plight," "what can I do at all—it is such a vast problem!" etc.), straightforward refusal, and a deliberate lack of love, or so-called "unawareness." One can consciously ignore and avoid all signs and reports concerning the distress of brothers and sisters. This is, however, also a form of "closing the heart" and of lovelessness. Maurer justly comments: "Of the fate, need, distress of so many people—including our 'brothers' in a narrow Christian sense—near to us as well as far away from us, we often do not even know. . . . But this not-knowing is simultaneously always a not-wanting-to-know and therefore the most cold-blooded form of hatred!" Closing the heart or not wanting to share our "world's goods" is indeed what is meant by "hatred." "For we wish him to perish whom we hate" (Calvin); "Hatred is the wish that the other person was not there; it is the refusal to recognize his right as a person, the longing that he might be dead" (Marshall). According to this interpretation, "hatred" is nothing else than to wish someone away, out of our immediate life and vicinity, because his presence makes demands which irritate us and which we do not see our way clear to fulfill. Consequently it is possible that we "hate" without hating consciously or even thinking that we hate at all; in fact, we can still continue using all kinds of slogans to convince others—and ourselves—that we in fact love those brothers and sisters! It is exactly to this "slogan"-like love that John implies the example of Christ. In verse 18 he pleads that the love of Christians should not be "in words or speech" (obviously: idle talk, intentions, promises, slogans), but "in deed and in truth," that is, it must be genuine, concrete, and meaningful.

The issue is therefore evident and simple:

> At least in the present situation, it would be inappropriate for Christians to think that they had accomplished their Christian duty by being ready for an—unlikely—act of martyrdom. The need of the world is for food, clothing and jobs, for those who have these things to share with those who have not. . . . The tragedy is that we have not learned to take this seriously. The need of the world is not for heroic acts of martyrdom, but for heroic acts of material sacrifice. If I am a well-off Christian, while others are poor, I am not acting as a true Christian. (Marshall)

With this 1 John stands firmly within the totality of the biblical message: "In being specific about the need to show love by helping the poor, the author is not holding up a new moral demand; rather he is reaching into the heart of Christianity's Jewish heritage" (Brown, 474).

Notes

NOTES TO CHAPTER 1

1. In well-known works like *RGG, TRE, RE, EKL,* and the *Christelike Encyclopedie* the term is not listed as a separate item. G. C. Berkouwer, *The Church* (esp. 278–309), and K. Barth, *CD* (various places, e.g. I/2 on confession and III/4 on *status confessionis*), do deal with it.

2. It seems as if many observers are of the opinion that it is in fact nothing less than "the most severe form of protest" which is possible in the Church. Time and again one encounters expressions like "the most shrill alarm" (Lohse), "the most heavy artillery," "explosives," "dynamite," "sharpest artillery," "high explosives," or "conflict material" to describe the use of the term.

3. See especially E. Bethge, "Status confessionis—was ist das?" (paper at the Evangelische Akademie Arnoldsheim, April 1982, published as *epd-Dokumentation,* 46/82, 1–28); R. Frieling, "'Status confessionis': Konfessionskundliche Hinweise zur Diskussion über die Erklärung des Reformierten Bundes" (August 1982, published as *Schnelldienst 1/82* of the Konfessionskundliches Institut des Evangelischen Bundes, Bensheim, and later in *epd-Dokumentation* 45/82, 1–7); M. Schloemann, "Der besondere Bekenntnisfall: begriffsgeschichtliche und systematische Überlegungen zum casus confessionis nach Daressalam 1977" (also translated into English; published in *Politik als Glaubenssache? Beiträge zum status confessionis in südlichen Afrika und in anderen soziopolitischen Konfliktfeldern (Frieden),* July 1983, Martin Luther-Verlag, Erlangen). When this article was completed in July 1983, that publication was unfortunately not yet available, so that references to the articles and recommendations it contains must be made without page references. Praeses C. Brandt of the Lutheran Church in Cape Town, who took part in this specific conference, has meanwhile made the unpublished papers available.

4. Schloemann, *op. cit.,* points out that neither the exact origin of that formulation nor the connection between the *casus confessionis* and the *casu scandali* is clear. No mention was made at that time of a fixed expression or a technical term.

5. Frieling, *op. cit.,* 2.

6. The Formula Concordiae is a detailed document meant to bring unanimity concerning several theological conflicts inside Lutheranism after the death of Luther. After several preliminary steps, the final acceptance came on 15 June 1580.

7. F. Lau, "Adiaphora," *RGG³,* I, 95.

8. Schloemann, *op. cit.*

9. D. Bonhoeffer, "Die Kirche vor den Judenfrage," *GS,* II.

10. Bonhoeffer, *ibid.,* 48.

11. K. Barth, *Theologische Existenz heute!* 32.

12. A reference to Barth's sixth thesis (*ibid.*, 24–25): "The fellowship of those belonging to the Church is not determined by blood and consequently not by race, but only by the Holy Spirit and by baptism. If the German Evangelical Church would exclude the Jewish Christians or treat them as second-class Christians, she would also stop being a Christian church."

13. Bonhoeffer, *op. cit.*, 126.

14. Bonhoeffer, *ibid.*, 127–128.

15. E. Busch, *Karl Barths Lebenslauf*, 268 (also in English and Dutch).

16. Schloemann, *op. cit.*

17. M. E. Brinkman, "Karl Barth en de belijdende kerk," *KTh*, 30 (1979), 28ff.; Busch, *op. cit.*, 20–23.

18. Bethge, *op. cit.*, 20–23.

19. See *Herderlijk Schrijven*, 1952; *Het vraagstuk van de kernwapenen: Noodzakelijke aanvulling van het Herderlijke Schrijven van 3 Juli 1952 betreffende het vraagstuk van oorlog en vrede*, 1963; *Woord en Wederwoord: Voortzetting van het gesprek over het vraagstuk van de kernwapenen*, 1964; Brosjure *Wederwoord op Wederwoord: namens Kerk en Vrede*, 1964; *Kernbewapening: Handreiking van de generale synode van de Nederlandse Hervormde Kerk voor een nieuw gesprek over het vraagstuk van de kernwapenen*, 1979 (meant as material for group discussion in congregations, on which more than 700 written reactions were received, which were then summarized for the synod of 1980); *Pastorale Brief*, 1980.

20. Also available as *epd-Dokumentation*, 38a/82 (19 August 1982). The quotations in this article were not taken from an official translation.

21. Many of those are conveniently collected in "Um Frieden und Sicherheit: Reformierte 'Gegendenkschrift' löst Kontroverse um Bekenntnisfrage aus," *epd-Dokumentation*, 45/82 (27 September 1982), 1–65, and "Um Frieden und Sicherheit, Folge 2," *Epd-Dokumentation*, 50/82 (5 November 1982), 1–60. In numerous theological and church journals (e.g., *Evangelische Kommentare*), this debate still continues.

22. J. W. de Gruchy ("Towards a Confessing Church: The Implications of a Heresy," in *Apartheid Is a Heresy*, ed. J. W. de Gruchy and C. Villa-Vicencio, 91, n. 3) thinks that this question was raised for the first time by R. Bilheimer, an American secretary at the Cottesloe Conference. Later it was treated explicitly by Beyers Naudé: "Die tyd vir 'n 'Belydende Kerk' is daar," *Pro Veritate*, IV/3 (15 July 1965); "Nogeens die 'Belydende Kerk,'" *Pro Veritate*, IV/6 (15 November 1965); and "Nou juis die 'Belydende Kerk,'" *Pro Veritate*, IV/18 (15 December 1965).

23. E. Bethge, "Eine Bekennende Kirche in Süd-Afrika?" *Am gegebenen Ort;* also included as an appendix in English in Bethge, *Bonhoeffer: Exile and Martyr*.

24. In the German version (it is also available in English), *Daressalam 1977*, his lecture and the reactions to it appear on 106–135, the resolution of the assembly on 212–213, and excerpts from the debate on 249–257.

25. E. Bethge, "Status confessionis—was ist das?" 23.

26. Visser't Hooft, for example, characterizes it enthusiastically as a "much more radical" happening than the foundation of the Program to Combat Racism (U. Duchrow, *Conflict Over the Ecumenical Movement*, 269–270).

27. In the USA some Lutheran groups and churches decided that disinvestment is a direct consequence of the *status confessionis*.

28. See for example "Kampf um das Recht und Streit um die Wahrheit: ausgewählte Stellungnahmen zur LWB-Erklärung über *status confessionis* im

südlichen Afrika,'' *epd-Dokumentation* 26–27/83 (6 June 1983), 1–107, which is only an excerpt from numerous resolutions and official correspondence. From this discussion an LWF consultation was organized at Bossey, Switzerland, from 25 February to 1 March 1982, where seven experts prepared a joint document, which is now being published as *Politik als Glaubenssache?* In April 1983 a meeting of the committee for study went further into this matter at Sigtuna, Sweden. At the seventh full assembly of the LWF in Budapest, Hungary, in 1984, this matter will also be continued.

29. *Ecunews,* 27 February 1980.

30. WCC Central Committee Minutes, August 1980.

31. ABRECSA Conference Report, 19.

32. Included as an appendix in De Gruchy/Villa-Vicencio, *op. cit.,* 161ff.

33. A. Boesak, ''He Made Us All, But . . . ,'' in *ibid.,* 1–9.

34. Included as an appendix in the agenda of the DR Mission Church synod, Belhar, 1982, 717–720.

35. Agenda 602.

36. Agenda 604–606.

37. R. Frieling, *op. cit.,* 4 with reference to an article by W. Kunneth in *Kein anderes Evangelium,* ed. R. Bäumer.

38. Bethge, *op. cit.,* 1, 8, 25.

39. H. de Lange, WCC Central Committee Minutes, August 1980.

40. It is ''vague,'' ''controversial,'' ''distracts the attention from the actual questions,'' ''has negative associations,'' etc.

41. The application of this expression on a general ethical question like world poverty, which is hardly taught by any Christian or defended in terms of the gospel, as well as the debate on the (controversial) possession of nuclear weapons deprived the term of a great deal of its expressiveness.

42. The Lutheran study consultation at Bossey recommended it, on account of several papers which requested it, as well as a diversity of similar convictions published since 1977 (e.g. that of G. Krusche, chairman of the study committee of the LWF in 1980).

43. Barth, for example, initially saw it mainly as a personal resolution. In most cases, however, groups of Christians confess out of one or another commonly held conviction. Ecumenical bodies have already announced it a few times, but their authority in this regard has been queried from different sides. The Cape Lutheran Church, for example, reacted with the opinion that a *status confessionis* cannot be forced from outside, but should be left to the parties really concerned. When specific churches or denominations declare a *status confessionis* it is of course clear that they will be and should be able to draw other consequences than ecumenical bodies.

44. Barth, *CD,* III/4, 79: ''The *status confessionis* is not, then, a permanent position.''

45. Bethge, *op. cit.,* 23.

46. Bethge, *op. cit.,* 3.

47. See H. Hafenbrack, ''Protestanten zwischen Bekenntnis und Pragmatismus,'' *epd-Dokumentation,* 45/82, 45–46.

48. R. Wischnath, ''Vom Stand des Bekenntnisses,'' *Deutsches Allgemeines Sonntagsblatt,* 10 October 1982, published in *epd-Dokumentation,* 50–82, 21. He is the author of the RB's original report.

49. *epd-Dokumentation,* 45–82 (24 August 1982), 8.

50. Berkouwer, *The Church,* 299ff.

51. See the clarifying article by T. Rendtorff, ''Die Herausforderung des Verfälschung des Evangeliums: status confessionis,'' lecture at an LWF study

seminar in Sigtuna, Sweden, April 1983, published in *epd-Dokumentation*, 26–27/83, 107.

52. R. Bertram, "Confessing as Re-defining Authority," in *Politik als Glaubenssache?*, *op. cit.*

53. H. Berkhof, "Das politische Zeugnis der Kirche—Zwischen Prophetie und Weisheit," lecture at Schloss Reichenberg, 11–15 March 1982, published in *epd-Dokumentation*, 45/82, 20–27. According to him this is exactly the difference between the Nederlandse Hervormde Kerk and the EKD's points of view on nuclear disarmament. He concluded with the hope that the EKD's "calm, mediatory, and wise" document would be followed in the foreseeable future by a prophetic word to show a way ahead.

54. In this way A. Szekeres, "Barmer Thesen in 1968," 274, wrote that these theses might sound anachronistic in 1968 in the Netherlands, but that they should have been a very relevant confession in 1968 in Hungary!

55. See the article by P. J. J. S. Els in this volume. After the DRC has over the years pleaded and worked, sometimes in surprisingly vigorous language and with almost untiring zeal, for the implementation of the philosophy of apartheid in state and society, it is obviously no longer necessary to advocate it so actively and openly. The status quo which has been obtained can simply be maintained by sober-minded, balanced, essentially timeless observations like "in specific circumstances and under specific conditions the New Testament makes provision for the regulation on the basis of separate development of the co-existence of various peoples in one country" and "a political system based on the autogeneous or separate development of various population groups can be justified from the Bible" (*Human Relations and the South African Scene in the Light of Scripture*, DRC, 1974, respectively 32 and 71). It is as though these "principles" are seen as theoretical possibilities, severed from the concrete present and the actual form these possibilities take in South Africa. No direct reference at all is made to the specific situation. Even the "principles," clad in clearly political terminology and operating with definite presuppositions, are presented as derived from the Bible, without any connection with practical politics. All the qualifications which are then added to them (justice; demand to love the neighbor) also remain theoretical. The criteria presented are not held up as a mirror image before the reality of the South African situation. The prophetical sound is totally missing. It is quite understandable why some delegates to the general synod in Pretoria in 1982 once again pleaded that if *Ras, Volk en Nasie* were to be revised, it should stick only to the fundamental biblical directives and not get involved in practical realities.

56. *epd-Dokumentation*, 50/82, 57.

57. In this respect the difference becomes clear between the rejections of racism, which occur with ecumenical unanimity, and the possession of nuclear arms, about which there are strong differences of opinion. (That the case is even more complicated becomes evident when one realizes that all who reject racism, including the DRC's general synod of 1982, do not agree that apartheid is in fact racism, while all who defend the possession of nuclear arms will nevertheless agree that peace is a matter of confession!)

58. Schloemann, *op. cit.;* Rendtorff, *op. cit.*, 107; E. Lorenz, "Status confessionis—eine Problemanzeige," *Politik als Glaubenssache?*, *op. cit.*

59. A. D. R. Polman, "Belijdenisschrift," *Christelijke Encyclopedie*, I, 551.

60. Seim, quoted by Bethge, *op. cit.*, 27.

61. Barth, *CD*, III/4, 77, in connection with the fact that the confession has no other purpose than the glory of God.

62. Schloemann, *op. cit.*

63. Bonhoeffer, "Was soll der Student der Theologie heute tun?" *GS*, III, 247.

64. Berkouwer, *The Church*, 300.
65. M. Buthelezi, in *Politik als Glaubenssache?*, *op. cit.*
66. See the remark of Bethge, *op. cit.*, 23, that the *solus* of Barmen and the *unum* of Dar es Salaam were missing in the rejection of nuclear armament (in 1958).
67. E.g., Bonhoeffer, "Die Frage nach der Kirchengemeinschaft," *GS*, II, 226ff.
68. *Politik als Glaubenssache? op. cit.*
69. *Politische Verantwortung*, 2 (1958), 4; quoted by Bethge, *op. cit.*, 21.
70. "Das Bekenntnis . . . , Erläuterung zu These I," op. cit.
71. *GS*, VI, 350ff., quoted by A. Boesak in his speech.
72. Bonhoeffer, "Zur Frage nach der Kirchengemeinschaft," *GS*, II, 238.
73. According to E. M. Huenemann, "On the Church in South Africa" (lecture delivered in 1982 in Ottawa), 1.
74. Bertram, *op. cit.*
75. E.g., Bethge, *op. cit.*, 28, thesis 12; P. Frieling, "Status confessionis," a paper before the General Assembly of the Evangelical Alliance, 27 October 1982, published in *epd-Dokumentation*, 50/82, 48.
76. Declaration of the Reformierter Bund, explanation of second thesis.
77. *epd-Dokumentation*, 45/82, 8.
78. E. Wolf, "Die Einheit der Kirche in Glaube und Gehorsam," quoted by H. J. Kraus, "Bekenntnis in der Politik," *Evangelische Kommentar*, 15/12 (December 1982), 687.
79. *epd-Dokumentation*, 50/82, 5.
80. Barth, *Theologische Existenz heute!* 32.
81. Frieling, *op. cit.*, 2.
82. Explanation of first thesis.
83. K.-A. Odin, "Glaubensstreit über Frieden," *Frankfurter Allgemeine Zeitung*, 5 October 1982 (published in *epd-Dokumentation*, 50/82, 16); T. Rendtorff, "Die Friedensstreit bedeutet Gefahr für die Kirche," *Frankfurter Allgemeine Zeitung*, 25 October 1982 (*epd-Dokumentation*, 50/82, 43).
84. "Moderamen des Reformierten Bundes: Stellungnahme," *Frankfurter Allgemeine Zeitung*, 30 October 1982 (published in *epd-Dokumentation*, 50/82, 59).
85. Bonhoeffer, *GS*, II, 226ff.
86. G. Nordholt, published in *epd-Dokumentation*, 50/82, 11.
87. G. Kretschmar, "Tendenzen und Perspektiven in der weltweiten Lutherischen Gemeinschaft," paper before VELKD's full assembly, 25–28 October 1977, published in *epd-Dokumentation*, 26–27/83, 55.
88. Bethge, *op. cit.*, 27.
89. H. J. Kraus, *op. cit.*, 687.
90. Bethge, *op. cit.*, 5: "Under certain circumstances it is the only possible way of proclaiming the gospel, but then it still remains the proclamation of the gospel."
91. Bonhoeffer, *GS*, II, 238.
92. Bethge, *op. cit.*, 17.
93. Especially in *epd-Dokumentation*, 26–27/83 there are numerous examples.
94. Some of the criteria which were laid down were either very vague and difficult to use in a specific situation, or one could ask whether they really applied to South Africa (though this was of course not the starting point or aim of their discussions). It was said, for example: "1) When the gospel is no longer considered the sole necessity for salvation; 2) when the life-giving good news is perverted into demands that kill; . . . 3) when it is no longer possible for the gospel to be proclaimed." When it was added that an abnormal situation of confession

had developed in which the gospel was threatened with "force and coercion," it became even less clear.

95. See the numerous facts in *epd-Dokumentation*, 45/82 and 50/82 as examples. The council of the VELKD immediately reacted with the unfortunate—and much criticized—declaration that a *status confessionis*, according to their opinion, could not be declared on political matters. The EKU assumed a mediatory position and differed from this formulation by the VELKD, but did say that political aims, although not political strategies, can nevertheless be derived directly from the confession.

96. Several interpreters differ on the question whether the differences of opinion can be ascribed to the structural differences between Lutheran and Reformed theology (Huber and Odin, for example, deny this very strongly). It may be true that these traditional differences do not play the only or even the most important role, but that the respective traditions do make the diverging viewpoints easier and more obvious is also clear. See for an interesting exchange of opinions on these differences *Kirchengemeinschaft und politische Ethik* (J. Rogge and H. Zeddies) and the discussion between P. Potter and E. Wilkens on the prophetical function of the Church, published as *epd-Dokumentation, 29/81*, 1–37.

97. See W. D. Jonker, "Kritiese verwantskap? Opmerkings oor die verhouding van die pneumatologie van Calvyn tot die van die Anabaptisme," *Calvyn aktueel?* (ed. E. Brown), 72–89; W. Balke, *Calvin and the Anabaptist Radicals*.

98. Rendtorff, *op. cit.*, 43–44.

99. Cf. *ibid.*, 44, whose reaction is typical: "This evil and infamous, at the same time extremely irresponsible [thoughtless], type of talk will hopefully only open the eyes of those who participate in the struggle with responsibility to see where a resolution without dialogue, a confession without brotherliness and apparent clarity at the expense of community, might lead."

100. Already during the seventeenth and the eighteenth centuries this was raised, especially by Gottfried Arnold. During that time, "dogmatic" or doctrinal influences were criticized from pietistic ranks as well as from the Enlightenment (according to Barth these two were, of course, two sides of the same coin, two manifestations of the same feeling toward life), and much more emphasis was laid on a Christianity of deeds or experiences; see Schloemann, *op. cit.*

101. W. A. Visser't Hooft, "The Mandate of the Ecumenical Movement," *The Uppsala 68 Report,* 320.

102. Rendtorff, "Die Herausfordering der Verfälschung des Evangeliums . . . ," 107.

103. K. G. Steck, *Die christliche Wahrheit zwischen Häresie und Konfession,* 25–27.

104. E. Lohse, *epd-Dokumentation,* 45/82, 39.

105. R. Wischnath, *epd-Dokumentation,* 50/82, 22.

106. In an explanation of the pathos behind "black theology," C. E. Lincoln gives cutting commentary in "A Perspective on James H. Cone's Black Theology," *Union Seminary Quarterly Review,* 31 (1975), 19ff.: "The essential burden of black theology is an interpretation and articulation of the black experience. It is a message addressed to the white man, and it has to do with the new apperceptions the black man has of himself and of his proper place in the scheme of things. It is a way of looking at the white man and his world through the other end of the telescope, seeing him in an unaccustomed perspective. The old white perspective made the white man larger than life. . . . One of the classical strategies of racism is to deliberately organize social and personal perspective in such a way that the practical oblivion of the proscribed subject is consistently accom-

plished. One need not take into account what one does not see, and what one does not see, for all practical purposes, does not exist. Practical invisibility—*oblivion*—is the common experience of black people in a world dominated by whites. The practical invisibility of blacks sustains the profane illusion that the world as presently ordered is the best available, and encourages the self-elected shapers of human destiny to indulge in the euphoria of fantasy. They want *not* to see blacks who are hungry, blacks who need housing, who for want of a modicum of power are always pawns, never players in the game. Racism always wants to conjure up at will blacks who will dig the mines. . . . At all other times the common wish is for black people to go away. To get lost. To vamoose. To vanish. And the strategies for black disappearance, psychological and physical, constitute the principal agenda for the racist enterprise. . . . White western theology has contributed significantly to the involuntary invisibility of black people—to black oblivion, if you please. The agony of the black oppressed has not been heard. The travail of the black masses has been ignored. For generations the fledgling doctors of the American church have adorned their academic rites with the customary haji to the hallowed centers of theological learning on the Continent, returning after confirmation to carry on in the old tradition. If God has been at all concerned with the protracted rape of black people the 'old tradition' has scarcely let it be known. If God was not more concerned, no more aware than the white theologians who have been 'doing' theology on behalf of all Christendom, then who can marvel at the fact that blacks have decided that they had better 'do' theology for themselves? The wonder is that so inevitable a decision comes so late. . . . Black theology is saying to white Christianity: *'Look! Look at us! We exist! We are people! We exist! We are black but we exist! We are persons. We exist! God affirms our existence. God protects our existence. You must learn to accept it and make room for it!'* "

NOTES TO CHAPTER 3

1. Quoted by W. Günther, *Von Edinburgh nach Mexico City,* 154. See also the instructive editorial by J. A. MacKay in the June 1944 edition of *Theology Today:* "Let the Church live on the Frontier."

2. This insight was well-formulated in the motto of the WCC's Commission for World Mission and Evangelization at Mexico City, 1963, "Mission on Six Continents"; H.-W. Gensichen, *Glaube für die Welt,* 40–42, 218–41; J. Verkuyl, *Contemporary Missiology: An Introduction;* D. J. Bosch, *Witness to the World;* J. Schmitz, *Die Weltzuwendung Gottes,* 14–16.

3. W. D. Jonker, "The Credibility of the Church," in *Missionalia,* 7/3, 114–127; J. Comblin, *The Meaning of Mission,* 40–42; J. Wallis, *Agenda for a Biblical People,* 18–33; H. Ridderbos, *Paul;* L. Floor, *Die Koninkryk van God en die vernuwing van die Maatskappy,* 36–38.

4. K. Barth, *CD,* IV/3, 2; see also D. Bonhoeffer in E. Bethge, *Bonhoeffer: Exile and Martyr,* 75; J. T. Bakker and K. A. Schippers, *Gemeente: Vindplaats van heil,* 79.

5. W. J. van der Merwe, *The Witness of the Church in Zimbabwe,* 34–40; C. J. Botha, "Calvyn se siening oor die eenheid van die kerk," in P. Meiring and H. I. Lederle, *Die eenheid van die Kerk,* 32–43.

6. K. S. Moodley, "The Reformed Church in Africa (Indian)," in *Theologia Viatorum,* 4/1, 60–70; H. Boer, *Pentecost and Missions,* 203.

7. J. du Plessis, *Wie sal Gaan?* in his preface; W. J. van der Merwe, *Gesante om Christus Wil,* 44–46, 52–53.

8. For a fundamental critique see J. C. Hoekendijk, *Kerk en Volk in de Duitse Zendingswetenschap*.

9. Van der Merwe, *Gesante*, 48.

10. P. J. Robinson, *Die presensie van die gemeente in die wêreld in sendingperspektief*, 120.

11. Hoekendijk, *Kerk en Volk*, 237, 246; J. du Preez, *Die koms van die Koninkryk volgens die boek Openbaring*, chapter 4; D. J. Bosch, "The Church and the Liberation of Peoples?" in *Missionalia*, 5/2, 29–35.

12. J. H. Bavinck, *Inleiding in de Zendingswetenschap*, 64; Ridderbos, *Paul*.

13. Rubem Alves quoted in C. H. Koetzier, *Die de verdrukten recht verschaft*, 106.

14. See D. J. Bosch: "The Church as the 'Alternative Community,'" in *Journal of Theology for Southern Africa*, no. 13, 3–11; Robinson, *Die presensie van die gemeente*, 272.

15. Verkuyl, *Contemporary Missiology*.

16. W. Nicol, "Commentary on the Draft Confession of the DR Mission Church," in *RESA Newsletter*, no. 2 (Dec. 1982), 23.

17. D. J. Bosch, "In Search of Mission: Reflections on 'Melbourne' and 'Pattaya,'" in *Missionalia*, 9/1, 3–18.

18. W. F. Keucher, *An Exodus for the Church*, 44; Verkuyl, *Contemporary Missiology*.

NOTES TO CHAPTER 5

1. Cf. Church Order, art. 37.

2. Acts, DRC synod, 1880, 56.

3. C. J. Kriel, *Die Geskiedenis van die Nederduitse Gereformeerde Sendingkerk in Suid-Afrika (1881–1956)*, 67.

4. Acts, DRC synod, 1880, 57.

5. Dort Church Order, art. 85.

6. Kriel, *op. cit.*, 72.

7. C. J. A. Loff, Dogter of Verstoteling (1981), 43–50.

8. Acts, DR Mission Church synod, 1881, 4, 5.

9. *Ibid.*, 9, 10.

10. *Ibid.*, 10.

11. *Ibid.*

12. Kriel, *op. cit.*, 107.

13. *Ibid.*, 108.

14. A. J. C. Erwee, "Die Ontstaan van die Calvyn Protestantse Kerk in S.A.," unpublished M. Th. thesis, U.S., 1970.

15. Church Laws, DR Mission Church, 1950, 5.

16. J. W. Brooks, " 'n Teologiese-Missiologiese Beoordeling van die Aktes van Ooreenkoms tussen die Ned. Geref. Kerkverbande in Suid-Afrika," unpublished M. Th. thesis, U.S., 1982, 35.

17. W. D. Jonker, *Die Sendingbepalinge van die Ned. Gereformeerde Kerk in Transvaal*, in the series *Kerk en Wêreld* (Potchefstroom, 1962).

18. *Ibid.*, 14–18.

19. *Ibid.*, 15–16.

20. *Ibid.*, 20.

21. Acts, DRC synod, 1965, 118–119.

22. Acts, DR Mission Church synod, 1966, 354–362.

23. *Ibid.*, 289.
25. Acts, DR Mission Church synod, 1970, 271.
25. *Ibid.*, 397–399.
26. *Ibid.*, 397, 398.
27. *Ibid.*, 398.
28. Acts, DR Mission Church synod, 1974, 231.
29. *Ibid.*, 232.
30. *Ibid.*
31. *Ibid.*, 446–453.
32. *Ibid.*, 361.
33. *Ibid.*, 362.
34. *Ibid.*, 362, 363.
35. Acts, DR Mission Church synod, 1978, 333.
36. *Ibid.*, 438, 439.
37. *Ibid.*, 489.
38. *Ibid.*
39. Acts, DR Mission Church synod, 1982, 500.
40. *Ibid.*, 621.

NOTES TO CHAPTER 6

1. Gerhard von Rad correctly observes: "we can see Jeremiah searching deliberately for practical criteria to identify the false prophet. . . . The very fact that Jeremiah could not point to any criterion that might in principle answer the question—who was the false prophet and who the true—showed him the full difficulty of the problem; for there could be no such criterion in respect of form or content. Just because Yahweh was not 'a God at hand, but a God far off' (Jer. 23:23) there could be no standard method of any sort by which he granted revelation" (*Old Testament Theology*, vol. II [1965], 209).

2. A. S. van der Woude, "Ware en valse profetie in Israel," in G. C. Berkouwer and A. S. van der Woude, *Wat is Waarheid*, p. 70.

3. Von Rad, *op. cit.*, 210, n. 27.

4. *Ibid.*

5. "The visions your prophets had on your behalf were delusive, tinsel things, they never pointed out your sin, to ward off your exile. The visions they proffered you were false, fallacious, misleading" (Lam. 2:14).

6. "Since they have misled my people by saying: Peace! when there is no peace. Instead of my people rebuilding the wall, these men come and slap on plaster. Tell these plasterers: It will rain hard, it will hail, it will blow a gale, and down will come the wall. Will not people ask: 'Where is the plaster you slapped on it?' Well then, the Lord Yahweh says this: I am going to unleash a stormy wind in my anger, torrential rain in my wrath, hailstones in my destructive fury. I mean to shatter the wall you slapped with plaster, to throw it down and lay bare its foundations. It will fall and you will perish under it, and so you will learn that I am Yahweh. When I have exhausted my anger against the wall and those who plastered it, I shall say to you: The wall is gone, and so are those who slapped it over with plaster, these prophets of Israel who prophesy about Jerusalem and have visions of peace for her when there is no peace—it is the Lord Yahweh who speaks" (Ezek. 13:10–16).

7. "The Lord Yahweh says this: Come back, renounce your idols and give up your filthy practices; for if any member of the House of Israel—or even any foreigner living in Israel—deserts me to enshrine his own idols in his heart and,

clinging to the cause of his sins, then comes looking for the prophet to consult me, he will get his answer from me, Yahweh. I will turn against this man; I will make him an example and a byword; I will cut him off from my people; and you will learn that I am Yahweh. If the prophet is led astray and speaks, it is I, Yahweh, who have led that prophet astray; I will stretch out my hand against him and will wipe him out from my people Israel. They will bear the weight of their faults, and the fault of the prophet will be as grave as the fault of the man who consults him" (Ezek. 14:6–10).

8. Van der Woude, *op. cit.*, 18.
9. *Ibid.*
10. *Ibid.*, 19.
11. H. E. Freeman, *An Introduction to the Old Testament Prophets*, 109.

NOTES TO CHAPTER 7

1. Some of the oldest comprehensive works on this theme are: A. Seeberg, *Der Catechismus der Urchristenheit;* O. Cullmann, *The Earliest Christian Confessions* (ET). More recent is V. H. Neufeld, *The Earliest Christian Confessions*.
2. See Heb. 3:1, 4:14, and 10:23 concerning the noun and 11:13 and 13:15 concerning the verb. Neufeld, *op. cit.*, 140, points out that in most cases in the NT where the verb is used, it is intended to introduce a confession formula, while the noun refers to specific declarations from tradition and not so much to actions of confession.
3. On this special theme, cf. G. Grässer, "Hebräer 1:1–4," *Evangelisch-katholischer Kommentar zum Neuen Testament*, 3; G. Thiessen, *Untersuchungen zum Hebräerbrief, Apocrypha Novi Testamenti*, 2; E. Käsemann, *Das wandernde Gottesvolk*, Forschungen zur Religion und Literatur des Alten und Neuen Testaments, NF 37; G. Bornkamm, "Das Bekenntniss im Hebräerbrief," *Aufsätze*, 2; H. Zimmermann, *Das Bekenntnis der Hoffnung;* F. Laub, *Bekenntnis und Auslegung*.
4. F. F. Bruce, *The Epistle to the Hebrews*, 55, gives preference to this, as does F. W. Grosheide, *Commentaar op het N.T.*, 96. P. Andriessen and A. Lenglet, *De Brief aan de Hebreër*, 66, differ from this.
5. Neufeld, *op. cit.*, 136, points out the close connection of the two words with "homologia."
6. Especially J. Thuren, *Das Lobopfer der Hebräer*. He is of the opinion that the congregation viewed themselves as the extension of Judaism, the true Judaism.
7. Grosheide, *op. cit.*, 316.
8. Grässer, *op. cit.*, makes an excellent analysis of this section. He comes to the conclusion that it here concerns a "hymnischen Christusbekenntniss" (67). Thus also Bornkamm, *op. cit.*, 195–198.
9. Grässer, *op. cit.*, 69, refers to places where the issues of baptism (4:14; 6:4; 10:23), the eucharist (13:10–16), and the worship service (10:25) are raised.
10. Chapter 2:3 advocates the later origin of the so-called second generation Christians. It thus comes closer to the period of Domitian. The emphasis on the sacrifice gives the impression that the temple (though actually here it is called tabernacle) was still standing, and that indicates a situation before 70 A.D., in other words nearer to the time of Nero. See also the reference to Italy (13:24).
11. Andriessen, *op. cit.*, 15.
12. Following Käsemann, *op. cit.;* also N. Dahl, "A New and Living Way," *Interpretation* (1951).

13. The use of the article does not completely allow that only "apostle" is connected with Moses.

14. Käsemann, *op. cit.*, 11ff., emphasizes the Word.

15. H. N. Ridderbos and A. A. Spÿkerboer, *Eén belÿdende Kerk,* 62, points out the significance of the confession for unity.

NOTES TO CHAPTER 8

1. A. J. Bronkhorst and H. Ridderbos, "Belijdende Kerk," in *Christelijke Encyclopedie,* vol. I (1956), 549–551; K. Dijk, *De Dienst der Kerk,* 16–26.

2. For the motivation behind the formation of creeds, see H. Volten, *Rondom het Belijden der Kerk,* 181–227, and O. Cullmann, *Die ersten Christlichen Glaubensbekenntnisse.*

3. A. C. Barnard, *Die Erediens,* 573.

4. A. Kuyper, *Onze Eredienst,* 257–258.

5. R. Abba, *Principles of Christian Worship,* 53.

6. Barnard, *op. cit.,* 573.

7. G. van der Leeuw, *Liturgiek,* 175.

8. *Ibid.,* 173.

9. H. Bouwman, *Gereformeerd Kerkrecht,* 1, 325.

10. *Ibid.*

11. P. J. Roscam-Abbing, *Komen als geroepen,* 57.

12. L. O. Richards, *Youth Ministry,* 45.

13. *Ibid.,* 61.

14. Roscam-Abbing, *op. cit.,* 60

15. *Ibid.,* 61.

16. See also K. Barth, *CD,* III/4, 73–86.

17. J. B. Metz in *Sacramentum Mundi: An Encyclopedia of Theology,* ed. K. Rahner et al., vol. V, 35–37.

18. See also A. A. van Ruler, "Plaats en Functie der Belijdenis in de Kerk," *Visie en Vaart,* 50–127.